Québe

D0469216

Off the Beaten path™

Help Us Keep This Guide Up to Date

Every effort has been made by the authors and editors to make this guide as accurate and useful as possible. However, many things can change after a guide is published—establishments close, phone numbers change, facilities come under new management, etc.

We would love to hear from you concerning your experiences with this guide and how you feel it could be made better and be kept up to date. While we may not be able to respond to all comments and suggestions, we'll take them to heart and we'll also make certain to share them with the authors. Please send your comments and suggestions to the following address:

The Globe Pequot Press
Reader Response/Editorial Department
P.O. Box 833
Old Saybrook, CT 06475

Or you may e-mail us at:
editorial@globe-pequot.com

Thanks for your input, and happy travels!

OFF THE BEATEN PATH™ SERIES

Québec

by Katharine
and Eric Fletcher

The
Globe
Pequot
Press

Old Saybrook, Connecticut

Cover and text design by Laura Augustine
Maps created by Equator Graphics © The Globe Pequot Press
Cover photo by Images © PhotoDisc, Inc.
Illustrations by Carole Drong

Library of Congress Cataloging-in-Publication Data
Fletcher, Katharine.
      Quebec : off the beaten path / by Katharine and Eric Fletcher. —
1st ed.
      p. cm. —(Off the beaten path series)
      Includes indexes.
      ISBN 0-7627-0276-1
      1. Québec (Province)—Guidebooks. I. Fletcher, Eric. II. Title. III. Series.
F1052.7.F58   1999
917.1'4044—dc21   99-10640
                                              CIP

Manufactured in the United States of America
First Edition/First Printing

*To our dear parents, who encouraged us both,
from our earliest years, to explore the paths least trodden,
to celebrate the differences among all Earth's peoples,
and to wonder at our natural world.*

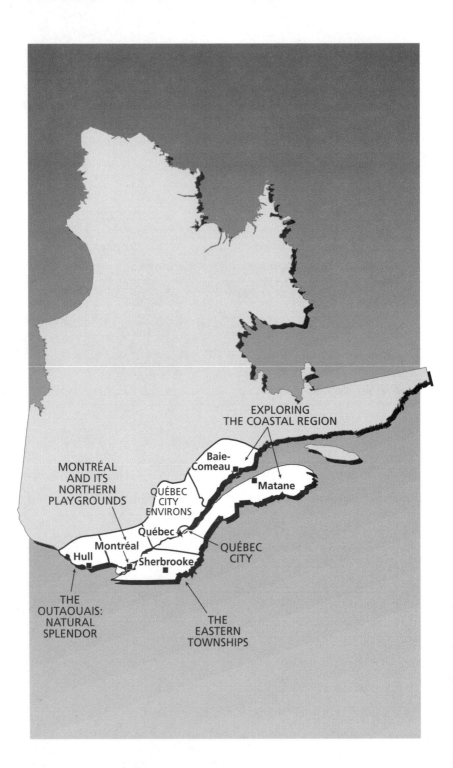

EXPLORING
THE COASTAL REGION

MONTRÉAL
AND ITS
NORTHERN
PLAYGROUNDS

QUÉBEC
CITY
ENVIRONS

Baie-
Comeau

Matane

Québec

Montréal

QUÉBEC
CITY

Hull

Sherbrooke

THE
OUTAOUAIS:
NATURAL
SPLENDOR

THE
EASTERN
TOWNSHIPS

Contents

Acknowledgments

First and foremost, thanks to the residents of Québec, who welcomed both of us warmly into their homes, businesses, and hearts. You shared your pride of place and your deep knowledge of Québec with us. *Merci à tous!*

We want to applaud the tremendously helpful Tourism Québec staff. We cannot begin to name you all, so please accept our heartfelt thanks for providing insights, making recommendations, and answering interminable questions as we traveled the province. We salute you all!

We also want to thank the residents of the Pontiac, that part of Québec's Outaouais region in which we so delight to live. Since we moved here north of Quyon in May 1989, we've been accepted—as well as welcomed by you. Some say that newcomers like us are always regarded as "from away" and are never accepted. Well, that's hardly true here in the Pontiac where people have shared so much with us.

A special thanks to neighbors Amber Walpole and Chuck Lalonde, who have been so good about looking after our cats, Chico and Tigger, while we're off on our travels. And to Maureen Tessier for her advice about French idioms. Katharine wants especially to thank her writing buddies, Yvonne Jeffery Hope and Laura Byrne Paquet, who offer tips and support and thus make this writing life a continually exciting challenge. Thanks, both!

And where would we be without our readers? A huge vote of thanks to George Toller, who calls with Pontiac insights so frequently. You give such incredible feedback, George.

Finally, thanks to our editor Gail Gavert and our Globe Pequot team for making *Québec: Off the Beaten Path* a reality.

To our readers: We hope you enjoy exploring our Québec. Have fun!

—Katharine and Eric Fletcher

Welcome to Québec

We live in *la belle province* (the beautiful province) and—well, that says it all, in our opinion. We moved here a decade ago and now live in the Outaouais (it's pronounced *OOO-tah-ways*) region of West Québec. Our farmhouse is a mere 45 minutes north and west of Ottawa, the capital of Canada, which is in the neighboring province of Ontario. The border between the provinces is the Ottawa River, known in French as *la Rivière de l'Outaouais*.

In fact, if you look at a map of the province, water defines it, both inside and out. The Ottawa is a tributary of the St. Lawrence—or *Saint-Laurent en français*—which in turn flows into the Atlantic Ocean. Québec's Gaspé Peninsula—or *Gaspésie* in French—juts into the Gulf of St. Lawrence. And farther north, Québec touches on Hudson and James Bays.

And wait until you check out the interior watersheds. Where we live in spectacular Pontiac County, we are fortunate to have what's known as Québec's triple play of rivers: the *Noire* (Black), Dumoine and Coulonge. For whitewater canoeing, they are unrivaled. Northeast of the province's capital, Québec City, there's the mighty Saguenay River, forming a true glacial fjord. There is world renowned whale watching here, notably at the Saguenay's confluence with the St. Lawrence. Meanwhile, down in the Gaspé we'll discover the Restigouche, Matapédia, and Cascapédia, celebrated salmon rivers. Finally, coursing north from the New England states is the Richelieu River and Lake Champlain, a historic trading route between the Thirteen Colonies, now the United States of America, and Canada.

Which brings us rather neatly to politics. Ever since the fateful conquest of Québec City, on the Plains of Abraham in 1759, and the ensuing fall of New France *(Nouvelle France)* via the Treaty of Paris in 1760, Québecers have gnawed at the bone of independence. There was the famous uprising against British rule, known as the Rebellion of Lower Canada, in 1837–38, led by a hero of Québec, Louis-Joseph Papineau. To bring us into this century, in 1967 the president of France, General Charles de Gaulle, stood on the balcony

Meaning of Québec

"Québec" is an Algonquin native word meaning "place where the river narrows" and was first used in 1601 on a map depicting the present site of Québec City. By 1763 it was used to describe the province.

of Montréal's City Hall to shout the unforgettable rallying call *Vive le Québec Libre!* ("Long live a free Québec!") to thousands of Québecers on June 24—the special holiday of Saint-Jean-Baptiste Day in this still predominantly Catholic province. His words annoyed Canada's then-prime minister Lester B. Pearson and terrified federalists throughout Canada. Even today the words are a rallying call for separatists who want the province to secede from Canada.

Past injustices, real and perceived, and the deep conviction that the Québecois are "a people" have kept the desire for separation—or for the perplexing "sovereignty association"—a life-sustaining force in the hearts of some residents. Throughout the sixties and ensuing decades, Québecers have rallied to yet another call, to be *maîtres chez nous* (masters of our own house), eschewing the official bilingualism policy introduced by former prime minister Pierre Elliot Trudeau in the 1970s.

Current Québec premier Lucien Bouchard—whose title, quixotically, is *prime ministre* in French—called a referendum on October 16, 1995, on the question of whether Québecers wanted to remain in Canada. The mandate of his party, the Parti Québecois, is to separate from Canada. Fortunately, from our point of view—we are federalists—that referendum was defeated, but only by a wish and a prayer, with 51 percent voting no. Bouchard hopes for yet another referendum (we call these votes "neverendums").

Amid all of the political navel-gazing, life jogs along relatively happily among ordinary people, whether they speak English, French, or whatever. Oh sure, there are such provincial government institutions as the "language police," who wander the cities and countryside threatening shop owners with stiff fines if English or other non-French languages figure on their signs. But here in Québec there's contagious *joie de vivre*. There are vivid native legends, born from long winter nights when the wind howled in the bush. There are the morality tales, arising from the French and Irish Catholic spirit of sin and repentance. And there's the revelry in March associated with the sugar shacks (where maple sugar is rendered from sap), where old-time music is played while folks lap up pancakes covered in maple syrup and tap their feet to the rhythm. There's the sophisticated, internationally recognized *Le Cirque du Soleil,* with its incredibly intricate circus acts, and the red-toqued snowman *Bonhomme,* the mascot of Québec City's Winter Festival.

What are we doing here, you might ask? Eric was born in British Columbia and moved to Ottawa in 1966. Katharine was born in England and moved to Toronto, Ontario, in 1958, then to Ottawa in 1974. We moved together to Québec in 1989. We love Canada passionately and our Canada includes Québec. In the *Outaouais,* or West Québec, where we live, residents voted over 93 percent *against* separation and *for* a unified Canada during the 1995 referendum. Where we live, people came here from Germany, Ireland, Scotland, England, Lithuania, and Poland. The Outaouais, you see, really symbolizes Canada: a microcosm of our nation within the bosom of Québec. A model for how we can all get along, if you ask us.

Québec. *La belle province.* It's a complex place that inspires passionate love. Come and visit. Often. Don't shy away from using the French language. Experience the diversity. Revel in our beautiful farmland, our spectacular rivers and woods, our vibrant cities. Explore her ways and you, too, will love beautiful, enchanting Québec.

Keys to Québec

We thought we'd start by giving some insiders' tips on how best to travel in Québec. Let's address this business of French language right off the top.

Language

American, Australian, British, and other tourists to Québec are astounded at how much French language they see and hear. "It's as if we were in France," they murmur. Some find it intriguing and exhilarating. But sometimes it can be intimidating.

If you don't speak or read French at all, the best way to get around in Québec is to have a completely open mind and to be flexible. Have a smile on your face. Try to master just a few pleasantries such as the lovely greeting *"Bonjour,"* which means "Good day."

At the back of this book is a small glossary of French words and phrases. Pronunciation can be mystifying: If you are up for it, buy a French language cassette tape such as those offered by Berlitz to listen to and give yourself a feel for this beautiful language's rhythms and inflections.

During our travels while researching this book, Americans we met were uniformly cheerful. They were enjoying Québec. Some traveled in recreational vehicles complete with beds and kitchens so they didn't have to deal with the nuances of ordering food in restaurants or of arranging accommodations.

You don't have to take that route if you don't care to. Many people in Québec speak a little English, and if they don't, often someone nearby will. If all seems hopeless (sometimes you're exhausted by the end of the day), smile and see if our French glossary at the back of the book helps. Point to a phrase, smile, and we feel you'll be well looked after. And if you want to start in a region of Québec that eases you into the province, come to us here in the Outaouais, where almost everyone is bilingual to some degree. (We're not biased: The Outaouais simply is one of the loveliest introductions to Québec you'll ever get.)

Tip: Ask for English Translations

If you don't read French, you can ask for English translations at such places as museums or restaurants. To ask if they have translations of informational material, such as guidebooks or menus, the all-purpose phrase is, "Avez vous une guide en anglais s'il-vous-plâit?" To pronounce the phrase, simply say "Avayvoo une gid en englay seal voo play?"

We were delighted to find that some provincial and local museums had binders available with English translations of major exhibit information panels. But note: The binders are often not displayed, nor are they automatically offered. You must ask for them. Most museums, however, do not have translations.

Federally operated museums, historic sites, and services offer bilingual services. Why? Because the government of Canada is officially bilingual and all staff are supposedly fluent in French and English. (The only Canadian province that is officially bilingual is New Brunswick.) Places you can usually rely on for bilingual services include post offices, ferry docks, and tourist information centers. Federally operated locations usually display the Canadian flag or have the flag printed on their signage.

Tourist Information

Follow the distinctive "?" symbol for help at one of Québec's tourist information centers. In fact, we suggest that the first stop you make— no matter which entry point into Québec you use—is at one of these centers. Whether at a provincial or local center, we've found staff to be friendly and helpful, even if they are not bilingual. Best of all, you can pick up excellent local or regional maps that show even the smallest roads. Information centers at or near the U.S. border have brochures explaining road signage, how to claim reimbursement for sales tax you are charged while visiting Canada, and other details you might find useful.

You'll also find informative tourist guides prepared in English for each of Québec's nineteen tourism regions. They are informative and useful, but be aware that they list only the attractions and locations of tourism association members. Many of the places we include in this book are also listed in the guides, but we've also found many others that are either new or have chosen not to be members of the associations.

The maps in this book are intended as general guides only, so do plan to use more detailed maps as you travel. You'll find them at the tourist information centers and you can also contact the provincial government for maps. Getting maps before the trip can save you a lot of frustration later.

Do you have access to the Internet? If so, visit the Tourisme Québec website at www.tourisme.gouv.qc.ca/anglais/home_a.html (e-mail: info@tourisme.gouv.qc.ca), where you will find links to each of the tourism regions in Québec.

Tourisme Québec can be reached by regular mail at C.P. 979, Montréal H3C 2W3, or by calling (800) 363-7777 (toll-free from Canada and the United States), or consult your travel agent.

For information on handicapped access in Québec, contact KEROUL at 4545 avenue Pierre-de-Coubertin, C.P. 1000 succursale M, Montréal H1V 3R2; (514) 252-3104; fax (514) 252-0766.

For snowmobile trail maps and information, contact Federation des clubs de motoneigistes du Québec at 4545 avenue Pierre-de-Coubertin, C.P. 1000, succursale M, Montréal, H1V 3R2; (514) 252-3076; fax (514) 254-2066.

Entering Canada and Québec

U.S. citizens do not need a passport to enter Canada, but you should have photo identification. Contact Canada Customs at (800) 461-9999 for current information. Ordinarily, crossing our peaceful borders is not a problem. Long may that last.

Handguns are not welcome in Canada. They will be confiscated at the border or you will be refused entry. If you plan to bring in a gun for hunting, check with Canada Customs for restrictions before you leave.

The American Consulate General is at Place Félix-Martin, 1155 rue Saint-Alexandre, Montréal; (514) 398-9695; fax (514) 398-9748. The mailing address is CP 65, Station Desjardins, Montréal H5B 1G1.

Money

The Canadian monetary system has 100 cents to the dollar. Common denominations of paper currency, in various colors, are $5, $10, $20 and, less commonly, $50 and $100.

Coinage starts with the penny, or one cent, followed by the nickel, or five cents; dime, or ten cents; quarter, or twenty-five cents, and, less commonly, the fifty-cent piece (if you find one, keep it as they're quite rare). Then we come to what Canadians affectionately call the "loonie"—the one-dollar coin with the picture of a loon on one side. And then, just so the loonie wouldn't be lonesome, the Royal Canadian Mint produced the "twonie," or $2 coin, adorned with a polar bear and the Queen.

For U.S. visitors, Québec can be a bargain: As we prepared this book, the Canadian dollar was worth less than 66 cents U.S. and was slipping lower. Many places will gladly take U.S. dollars, but you will usually get a better exchange rate at banks. You probably don't need to change a lot of dollars, however: Québec is well-equipped with automatic teller machines (ATMs), and many establishments accept debit cards for payment.

Holidays in Québec

January 1 and 2; Good Friday; Easter Monday; Victoria Day (third Monday in May); St-Jean-Baptiste Day (June 24); Canada Day (July 1); Labour Day (first Monday in September); Thanksgiving (second Monday in October); Remembrance Day (November 11); Christmas Day (December 25); and Boxing Day (December 26).

Road Signs and Rules

If you don't speak or read French, signage—especially on highways—can be brutal. To help you get oriented, we've included some of the more common terms in the glossary at the back of the book.

If you're stuck, ask a police officer for directions. Many are bilingual.

Québec, as in all of Canada, uses the metric system. Distances are given in kilometers on road signs, and speed limits are posted in kilometers per hour: 50 kilometers is about 30 miles; 100 kph is about 60 mph. You'll find drivers tend to push the limits on the major highways, but the posted speed is safest on secondary roads. Radar detectors are illegal in Québec, and police can confiscate them.

Fuel is sold in metric volume: A liter is roughly equivalent to a quart, with approximately 4 four liters to a gallon. Yes, gas is more expensive than in the United States, but, hey, the taxes embedded in the price pay for our great roads!

Signs that include references to a time of day usually use the 24-hour system or a variant. Instead of 4:15 P.M., for instance, the sign can indicate 16:15 or 16h15. Watch for it especially on parking signs.

One Québec traffic rule differs from other jurisdictions we've traveled in: *It is illegal to turn right on a red light.*

Getting Around

Québec is big: almost three times the size of France and more than ten times the area of Maine, New Hampshire, Vermont, and Massachusetts combined! Most of its 6.5 million people live within 100 miles of the U.S. border, with only a few small pockets of industrial sites and native villages in the vast territory to the north.

While Québec's roads and highways are generally excellent in the south, there are still plenty of challenging back roads to explore. A glance at a map will show you that very few roads extend north. The few that do exist have long stretches with no services, may have rough pavement or graveled sections, and often are traveled by lots of big trucks. We've driven all the main routes described here in our sedan without any problems. We've also included a few route suggestions for the more adventurous or for those of you itching to put your sport-utility vehicle to the test. Some really off-the-beaten-path attractions are accessible only by gravel roads, but we'll warn you about that in the text. And because we don't like to backtrack, we've tried to find routes where you won't need to retrace your path.

That being said, there are some well-known "nightmares," and we'll try to steer you clear of them. First of all, road signage can be perplexing, a fact exacerbated by language. Montréal's road tunnels can be claustrophobic to some: Just take a deep breath and relax. And you haven't really driven until you've experienced Montréal's raised auto-routes. The main tip is, try to avoid stressful situations such as rush hours, typically 6:30–9:00 A.M. and 4:00–6:30 P.M.

Hitch a Ride on the Moose

*D*on't have a vehicle? Want to explore the back roads? Contact the Moose Travel Company! This service transports Canadian visitors around a figure-eight loop through both Ontario and Québec in a comfortable van. It's a simple, efficient concept that follows the international demand for JOJO—jump on, jump off—tourism. Owner Neil Crawford told us that people jump on at, say, Québec City, and travel to a destination such as Baie-Saint-Paul, spend a day or so exploring, then jump back on and head to Tadoussac. There are three package loops you can buy, all tax-included. The Moose Trail is a 3,000-km loop through Ontario and Québec; the 1,500-km Beaver loop covers Ontario but also links to Montréal and Wakefield; the Loony Trail is exclusively in Québec. Information: Moose Travel Company, 6070 Highway 7 East, Second Floor, Markham ON L3P 3A9; 888–816–6673; fax 905–471–0404; Web site: www.moosetravelco. com; e-mail: moosetc@sprint.ca.

WELCOME TO QUÉBEC

Québecers love to travel. We were told that throughout Québec (with the exception of the Outaouais), about 95 percent of tourists are French-speaking and upwards of 85 percent are Québecers. The park-like hinterlands of Montréal and the city of Québec can draw astonishing crowds. In summer and on winter weekends, rush hours can be just as vexing as during the normal work week as people escape from and reluctantly return to their jobs. Québecers also love cycling. Everywhere, bicycle paths are springing up, along old rail beds, highways, and byways. Come winter, rural regions are criss-crossed by snowmobile trails that, on occasion, cross roads. Bikers and snowmobilers are usually respectful of traffic, but as you drive your car, remember you are handling a potentially lethal weapon and drive defensively, always.

Montréal boasts a subway system called *Le Métro* (the Metro). It's inexpensive and efficient, and it offers another slice of Montréal culture. Here you'll find an underground city, full of shops and delis, along walkways that protect you from inclement weather. Along the way, you may be entertained by musicians in this underground world. Safe. Convenient. Inexpensive. Try it!

Staying in Touch

It currently costs the same to send a postcard, a letter, or a greeting card to the United States from Canada: 49 cents, including the pernicious GST (Goods and Services) tax. The overseas rate is 53 cents.

Similar to American zip codes, the postal codes you'll see in Canadian addresses help route mail efficiently; please include them.

You'll find telephones everywhere in Québec, and most phone booths accept credit cards and calling-cards. Calls are generally less expensive from 6:00 P.M. to 8:00 A.M. Many tourist information centers are equipped with phones so you can more easily call hotels or other lodgings for reservations.

As you'll see from the contact information we provide, many of the attractions and accommodations include Internet addresses. You'll find "cyber-cafés," providing computers and modem hookups for public use, in the most unexpected places. And you can use a modem from most accommodations. But ask first: Some people may want to be assured you will not ring up a big charge, and some hotels may have incompatible central switchboards.

Stores in major centers often carry the English-language *Montréal Gazette* as well as a selection of other Canadian and foreign newspapers. Check out a French-language newspaper: It'll give you another opportunity to brush up on your French as you follow stock prices or the weather forecast.

Ditto with television. Québec has some very good English-language television productions that never make it beyond the borders. More's the pity, in our opinion.

Hospitals and Doctors

We all aim to stay healthy, especially on vacation. So pack your usual medications, and don't forget any special ones you might require. If you do require medical help, Québec offers excellent health services and all cities and most towns have at least one hospital.

Québec has what are called *Centre Local de Services Communautaire* (CLSCs) to provide health and social services. You'll see signs on roads pointing to them. If you are in a small town, a CLSC should serve your needs for routine health problems. In areas with hospitals, you will see the international sign, an **H** on a blue background, directing you to the facility.

Weather

Québec enjoys four seasons, with refreshing springs, hot summers, crisp autumns—and cold winters. But don't let the cold scare you. Québec is a wonderful place to visit in the winter. With the right clothes, you don't have to feel the cold, and there is so much to do: skiing, snowshoeing, skating, snowmobiling. In our opinion, January and February are among the best times of year to visit Québec. And come summer, those frozen lakes you might ski over in February are just the place to cool off on a hot day. Major newspapers in either language carry daily weather forecasts.

Food

Fresh local produce plus regional recipes equals delicious, memorable meals. Delectable *tarte au sucre* (sugar pie) is made from maple sugar, while *la tortière* is the famous meat pie. There's Matane salmon, fresh from the river. Crisp *pommes* (apples) and throat-warming *cidre de pomme* (apple cider)—hard or soft. Tasty microbrewery *bière* (beer). Tangy *chèvre* (goat cheese). Sweet *pain d'or* (French toast). Divine cassis (black currant liqueur). Moose, lobster, wild boar, caribou. Blueberries, strawberries, raspberries, and August's golden corn. You name it. *La belle province* serves it up with flare and a flourish.

And, of course, there's the province's real specialty, *poutine,* served up at innumerable roadside casse-croûtes, or snack bars. What the heck is "poo-teen" anyway? French fries with gobs of cheese curd sauce, covered in gravy. "You can't leave without trying it," some say. (Get the drift? We're not keen on the stuff, but millions love it.)

Restaurants

The word "restaurant," thank heavens, is bilingual and café and bistro are also common English words. But what of the ubiquitous Québecois *casse-croûte?* Perched beside the highway, it's a fast-food joint, really, where you can buy *poutine* and *le hot dog* and *le hamburger.* At the opposite end of the spectrum is the *relais gastronomique,* a fancy gourmet restaurant that usually denotes expensive and memorably delicious cuisine in a wonderful ambiance.

The words *Apportez votre bouteille du vin* posted at an eating place means you can bring your own wine. This is a really Québecois thing to do in restaurants that don't have a liquor license.

Économusées

As you travel throughout Québec, you will discover *économusées* (economuseums): small commercial operations, specifically designed to demonstrate and showcase both the tools and skills of artisans or specialty tradespeople as well as their final output. You can watch the labors of blacksmiths at their forges, weavers at their looms, apiarists extracting honey from their bee hives, and so on. Each *économusée* is owned and operated by the workers themselves, and financed by the sale of their products on site. You may find that only French is spoken, but usually you'll find someone who can help translate. Don't miss these fascinating places. For more information, contact Foundation des Économusées du Québec at (418) 694–4466.

Alcohol and Tobacco

In general, Québec has a more cosmopolitan attitude about alcohol than most other Canadian provinces. Consumption of alcohol is illegal in parks. That means don't brandish it about on your picnics or in the campgrounds.

Which brings us to the subject of our beer. It's stronger than yours. Beer is usually over 6 percent alcohol. Wine, hard cider *(cidre),* or the French apple liquor called Calvados is very alcoholic. Beer and wine is widely available at stores but spirits are sold through the government liquor outlets called Société des alcools du Québec (SAQ). Take care; be sensible and thoroughly enjoy yourself.

Drinking and driving is a punishable offense and is not taken lightly. There are road checks. If you are caught driving while impaired, you may lose your license and have your vehicle impounded. Don't drink and drive: have a designated driver and ensure that individual does not drink.

Although it is increasingly prohibited, smoking is still permitted in many places, and more Québecers die of lung disease and related tobacco-induced diseases than anywhere else in Canada. If you use tobacco, be aware that some people are allergic to the smoke and that in many restaurants it is not permitted.

Accommodations

Quick: What's the difference between a *gîte* (jeet) and an *auberge?* A gîte is a B&B operated by a family, at which breakfast is the only meal available. (Some, occasionally, will serve dinner if pre-arranged, but this is rare and mostly only in remote locations.) An auberge usually has a restaurant attached and is a bigger operation.

Gîte du campagne is a country B&B. *Ferme vacances* signifies a farm vacation. You'll see these along the byways.

Hotels and motels are widely available, ranging in price and style from the grandly opulent to the neat and affordable. Our favorites are mentioned in the appropriate chapters.

Forfait is a Québec expression for "package deal." Many auberges and gîtes offer such deals, and include anything from a B&B accommodation with a massage, or a whale-watching expedition, or even a tai chi lesson. Watch for this word because, just as in English, "package deals" are usually your best buy.

Parks

Some parks are federal and thus will be bilingually interpreted, with brochures and signs in French and English. Other parks are provincially operated and are unilingual French only. Sometimes services and guides are available in English as well as in Japanese and German. Ask.

It is illegal to hunt or fish without licenses and, in some cases (notably salmon fishing) you must register, too. Along some rivers, such as the

Cascapédia and Matapédia in the Gaspé region, fishermen are assigned to a specific pool. Rivers are protected rigorously and wardens actively patrol them. For an English-language booklet on fishing regulations, call Tourisme Québec toll-free at (800) 363–7777. Throughout the back roads, you'll find signs declaring that the territory is a ZEC *(Zone d'exploitation contrôlée)*, meaning it's a controlled hunting and fishing zone.

The prices and rates listed in this guidebook were confirmed at press time. We recommend, however, that you call establishments before traveling to obtain current information.

Québec City

The words *"C'est magnifique!"* will tumble from your lips as you begin to discover this truly magnificent city, the only walled city in North America. Thanks to extensive restoration projects in the old quarter—the Lower Town sector—with a little imagination, you can capture the ambiance of the city as it must have appeared in the 1700s.

Québec City holds a very special place in our hearts. We explored its cobbled streets and enjoyed many a candlelit dinner during those wonderful, heady days when we were first dating. The capital city of the province of Québec represents Old World charm, history, the birth of our nation—and romance. We spent countless hours wandering the city's streets, hand in hand, personally discovering some of its many restaurants. It's a place we've never tired of, for its many bistros, cafés, museums, parks, antique alleys, and artists' creations continue to intrigue us.

The most famous landmark of Québec City is the magnificent Château Frontenac, a definite must-see hotel. It towers atop cliffs whose sheer walls formed the strategic defense of the city, which troops led by the canny British officer General Montcalm scaled during his siege of the capital in 1759.

Largest Province
Three times the size of France, Québec is the largest of Canada's ten provinces, representing 15.5 percent of the country.

Stand on the boardwalk called the Terrasse Dufferin Terrace, which extends around the hotel, and from it look eastward, down the mighty St. Lawrence River beneath you. Drink in the spectacular views of the river; of a pastoral island, Ile d'Orléans, to the east; and of the rugged Laurentian Mountains to the northeast.

The history of the river and the land you survey can be traced back thousands of years. The St. Lawrence River was used as a trade route by Amerindians for upwards of 40,000 years. Of course, in our Eurocentric way, "discovery" of what is now Québec City is attributed first to Jacques Cartier in 1535.

In fact, the Celts were probably the first "Europeans" to land here, before 1000 A.D., and during that millennium, the Vikings were also

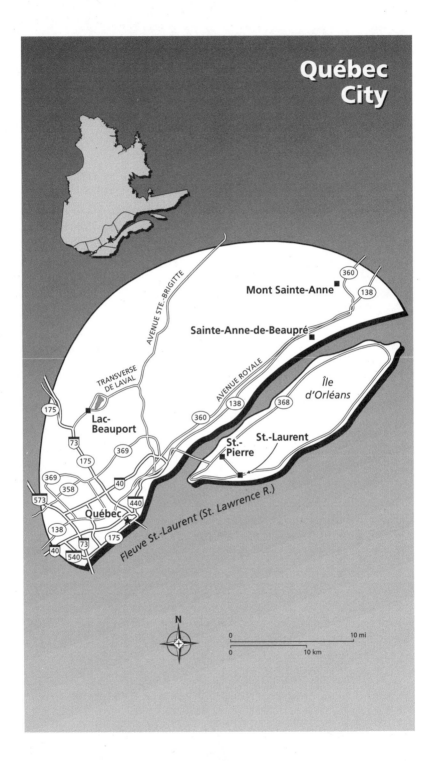

Québec City

Mont Sainte-Anne

Sainte-Anne-de-Beaupré

AVENUE STE.-BRIGITTE

TRANSVERSE DE LAVAL

AVENUE ROYALE

Île d'Orléans

Lac-Beauport

St.-Pierre   St.-Laurent

Québec

Fleuve St.-Laurent (St. Lawrence R.)

N

0   10 mi
0   10 km

thought to have claimed all the land along the Atlantic Coast. By 1500, Newfoundland had been claimed by Portugal.

The next major French explorer of the region was Samuel de Champlain, the "father of New France." In 1608 he had the first fortified habitation built, Place Royale, in what became Québec City's Lower Town, a site that can still be visited.

Predictably, Old World conflicts resulted in New World land grabs. In 1629, Britain's Sir David Kirk led an attack on Québec City and Champlain surrendered. So began the French-English conflict over the city. Four years later, France won it back and reinstated Champlain as governor.

The most famous conflict, however, became known as the Battle of the Plains of Abraham in 1759. British Major General James Wolfe led an ambush on the city by having 3,000 men scale the cliffs. On the windswept plains, Wolfe defeated French General Marquis Louis-Joseph de Montcalm—but both leaders lost their lives in this decisive encounter that lasted less than an hour.

The defeat also sounded the death knell for the aspirations of New France. By 1763, Britain and France signed the Treaty of Paris, transferring the French lands to the British and enfolding them into British America. Shortly thereafter, American General Robert Montgomery seized Montréal in 1775 and cast covetous eyes on Québec City. Since the British had cannily permitted those of French extraction to retain their language and religion, the two groups worked together to roust the upstart intruders. Québec City remained with the devil it knew, which evolved into the Canada of today.

That's what happened so long ago. Now let's begin our modern-day exploration of this fabulous, romantic city and its rugged hinterland. As our starting point, we'll use the city's principal landmark, the **Château Frontenac** (1 rue des Carrières, Québec G1R 4P5; (418) 692–3861 or (800) 441–1414; fax (418) 692–1751). It's hardly an off-the-beaten-path spot, but it simply cannot be missed. It was built in 1893 in the Châteauesque style, which noted architect Harold Kalman says is possibly the only truly Canadian architectural style. Note its sheer baronial castle walls and steeply-pitched copper roofline with dormer windows. Whimsical turrets and a stately bearing on the exterior complement the rich opulence of the wood-paneled interior. Château Frontenac resembles a fairy-tale castle of old, furthering the romantic mood of Québec City.

If you book a room here, it'll be pricey—but you expected that, didn't you? After all, such notables as Elizabeth Taylor and Alfred Hitchcock, Queen Elizabeth and President Franklin Roosevelt, and even the Harlem Globetrotters have all stayed here.

The site is situated on an incomparable location, on the very foundations of the former Château Saint-Louis, which was razed in 1834. The building itself has been home to French and English governors. Because of its prominence, the Château Frontenac provides a superb link between Québec City's Upper and Lower Towns.

Downstairs, the beautiful airy dining room serves incredible buffets. We've had breakfasts here that have really set us up for the day. Whether it's yogurt and fruit, muesli, bacon and eggs, or pancakes and muffins, you'll find exactly the breakfast you desire. Lunch is similarly scrumptious. Just make sure you bring a hearty appetite.

And what better way to work up an appetite than by a brisk walk outside? Head outside onto the **Terrasse Dufferin** in front of the hotel where you'll find a statue honoring **Samuel de Champlain.** Founder of Québec City, the explorer built Château Saint-Louis here in 1620. When he was forty, he wed twelve-year-old Hélène Boullé. His marriage contract stated that he had to wait two years before living with her, as she hadn't gained sexual maturity. She came to New France also in 1620 but hated it. So the young bride returned to France in

Château Frontenac as seen from the Citadel

1624, never to return. When Champlain died in Québec City in December 1635, she became a nun at the Ursuline convent in Paris.

Next to the statue find the plaque commemorating Québec City's designation as a **World Heritage site** by UNESCO in 1985, in recognition of it being the only walled city on the continent. Gaily colored, horse-drawn *calèches* can be found here. A 45-minute ride for up to four people costs about $58. Call Calèches du Vieux-Québec at (418) 683–9222.

Walk along the Terrasse Dufferin, looking south to Laval, and east toward L'Île d'Orléans. It was here that Montcalm planned his strategy for the defense of the city at the time of the conquest of 1759.

Continue along the terrace, which extends along the cliff's edge, to enjoy wonderful (and free) views of the St. Lawrence and the cliffs. Soon the walkway becomes the **Promenade des Gouverneurs** and starts climbing several sets of stairs. In winter, behind the château, you'll find a toboggan run that sends screaming kids down a safe, broad chute. During either summer's fabulous **Festival d'Été** or the famous **Winter Carnival**, there's lots of life and activity to enjoy here *en plein air*—in the fresh air.

You'll find the entire walk from the Château Frontenac to the Citadel via this series of boardwalks remarkably uncrowded. There are lots of benches along the way so you can catch your breath. We've always felt safe, even quite late at night, for this is a welcoming city that is used to visitors.

At the top of the final rise of stairs you suddenly emerge at a *belvédère* (lookout) just west of the star-shaped fortifications known as the **Citadel,** built by the British to defend the city against American attack, between 1820–1831. In the old 1750 powderhouse, the **Royal 22nd Regiment Museum** has an excellent collection of military artifacts. This regiment, located here since 1920, is part of the chain of command that makes this fortification the longest-standing military presence in North America. These days the regiment puts on such shows as the **Changing of the Guard** and **Beating of Retreat** during the summer. (Côte de la Citadelle, Québec G1R 4V7; (418) 694–2815; fax (418) 694–2853; daily 55-minute guided tours; $5.00 adults, $4.00 seniors, $2.50 for ages 7–17, handicapped and age 6 and under free, $12.50 family rate.)

Horses on the Plains

I adore horses and you can imagine my delight when the Plains of Abraham Battlefields Park was home to the Canadian Grand Prix jumping competition during the summer of 1997. We sat on a hillside looking down on the extraordinary sight of horses and riders from all nations negotiating the tough course of jumps for this world-class qualifying event. In the brilliant sunshine, with the wind whipping the horses' manes and tails, the event was a glorious, unexpected thrill.
—Katharine

West of the Citadel is a beautiful stretch of grassy parkland. This is the *Parc-des-Champs-de-Bataille (Plains of Abraham Battlefields Park).*

The Plains of Abraham take their name from a ship pilot and farmer named Abraham Martin, who owned land northeast of the Plains in 1646. It was near here that Generals Wolfe and Montcalm lost their lives in the Conquest of 1759. The battle actually took place near what is now the *Musée de Québec,* at the western edge of the Plains of Abraham. To find the museum, walk westwards, with the Citadel at your back, along Avenue Ontario, which becomes Avenue George VI. Follow the latter as it curves to the right and you'll see the museum beside the old prison. The Musée de Québec is one of the city's proudest gems, where you can view the history of the province depicted in prints, sculptures, paintings, and religious articles. (Parc des Champs-de-Bataille, Québec G1R 5H3; (418) 643–2150; fax (418) 646–3330; June 1 through September 7 daily, 10:00 A.M. to 5:45 P.M., Wednesday until 9:45 P.M.; September 8 through May 31: Tuesday through Sunday, 11:00 A.M. to 5:45 P.M., Wednesday until 8:45 P.M., closed Monday. $5.75 adults, $4.75 seniors, $2.75 students, ages 15 and under free.)

In front of the museum is British General *James Wolfe Monument,* which was erected in 1790, supposedly on the very spot where the great general died. Before expiring, he asked for water and his men retrieved some from a well, *Wolfe's Well,* situated just east of the monument.

Many monuments are located on the Plains. Surprisingly, Montcalm is not commemorated here, although a statue, donated by France in 1911, stands in a park bearing his name on Rue Laurier. But here on the 250-acre plains you can happily wander around, viewing such statues as that of *Jeanne d'Arc* (Joan of Arc) sitting astride her charger.

It's hard to leave the Plains of Abraham. We delight in it and evidently so do Québec City residents, who jog, walk their dogs, bike ride and, in winter, cross-country ski, toboggan, and snowshoe here. We think it's one of the very best spots in the city to learn about the history of Canada while taking in the fresh air and welcome breeze.

But leave we inevitably must. We suggest you walk down Avenue George VI to Rue Grand Allée Est and turn right. This marvelous street is lined with trendy restaurants and shops—and art galleries like the one we particularly enjoyed, *L'Héritage Contemporain* (634 Grande-Allée est; (418) 523–7337). It's a charming spot, with contemporary regional artists' works for sale, tastefully exhibited on the interior red brick walls. Gallery owner Mare-Klaudia Dubé wants to make people feel at home here. Enter this quiet oasis and we feel sure you'll be as delighted as we were.

Continue on down Grande-Allée est, which is home to some outstanding Victorian and Second Empire (with their Mansard roof) homes, now converted to businesses. During the **Winter Carnival** (late January through mid-February), this street is closed—for a **dog sled race.** Yes, come festival time the road is thronged with people—and to our infinite amusement, other dogs—who cheer on the canines as they speed past hauling their sleds and human mushers and careen full speed toward the Château Frontenac. We laughed with the doggy spectators who honestly seemed just as transfixed as their owners. Many wore jaunty bandanas, and several smaller doggies wore boots.

Looming on your left you'll soon see the baroque **Hôtel du Parlement (Québec National Assembly)** on your left, surrounded by statues of such notables as Samuel de Champlain and Georges Étienne Cartier, one of the fathers of Confederation. There are free tours of Québec's parliament buildings, and there's a good restaurant inside. *Assemblée nationale,* 835 boul. René-Levesque, (418) 643–7239.

Find your way to Rue Saint-Jean, a fun part of town, full of life, bustling cafés and, inevitably, of more history. Check out the **St. Matthew Cemetery** and **Church**—the latter is a heritage site and now houses the public library (418–691–6492; open Tuesday, Wednesday, Friday noon to 5:00 P.M., Thursday noon to 8:30 P.M., Saturday and Sunday 1:00 to 5:00 P.M.; closed Monday). It's all too easy to forget that Québec City was home to nationalities other than the French. Many years ago it was over 80 percent English-speaking. The cemetery opened in 1771 and is said to be Québec's oldest burial ground.

With parliament behind you and to the left, at the corner of Avenue Honoré Mercier, Grande-Allée becomes Rue Saint-Louis. Watch for a **cannon ball** lodged in the base of a tree between 59 and 55½ rue St. Louis. Look down this street: In front of you is **Porte Saint-Louis,** one of the six gates to the old Upper Town. Continue straight down until you

January/February:
Québec Winter Carnival; *two weeks, end of January to mid-February. Meet Bonhomme, the beloved snowman character of Québec City who sports his jaunty red toque (woolen hat) and typical French-Canadian hand-woven ceinture fléchée (sash) of many colors. Activities include ice carving, dog-sled races through the streets of the old city, and the extravagant Mardi Gras Ball, which you can attend in rented costumes, dine on sumptuous fare, and dance the night away.* **Carnaval de Québec** *(290 rue Joly, Québec G1L 1N8; (418) 626–3716; fax (418) 626–7252; www.carnaval.qc.ca; e-mail: comm@carnaval.qc.ca).*

July: *For more than 30 years, the* **Festival d'Été Québec Summer Festival** *has transformed Québec City into a wonderful, outrageous international festival of music and street theater during the first two weeks of July. Find out times and who'll be there by calling (888) 992–5200 or (418) 692–5200.*

Oldest grocery store in North America

While you're outside the walls of the old city, you could take a diversion to **Épicerie Moisan,** *which professes to be the oldest grocery store in North America, dating back to 1871 (699 rue Saint-Jean, Québec G1R 1P7; 418–522–8268; open daily 9:00 A.M. to 10:00 P.M.). Its old wooden shelves, curved glass display cabinets, and well-stocked shelves harken back to earlier times.*

find Rue des Parloir on your left. Stroll up here to the **Ursuline Convent,** a famous pilgrimage site, and on the next street, the **Ursuline Museum** (12 rue Donnacona; 418–694–0694; open February through November, Tuesday through Saturday, 9:30 A.M. to noon and 1:00 to 4:30 P.M., Sunday 12:30 to 5:00 P.M.; free).

The Ursulines came to the city in 1639 and, under the leadership of Reverend Mother Marie de L'Incarnation, the sisters taught and housed the *filles de roi* (daughters of the king), who were girls sent to New France to become wives to the mostly male colonists. General Montcalm's body was brought here after his death on the Plains of Abraham. Ironically he was first interred in a crater gouged beneath the altar by a British cannon ball.

As an intriguing aside, Donnacona Street commemorates the native **Chief Donnacona,** who accompanied Jacques Cartier back to France in 1536. One can only speculate as to what on earth the chief must have thought of the Atlantic crossing and of Europe. How we wish he'd kept a journal.

The twisty-turny streets here are something else. Along the way, look for the **Anglican Cathedral of the Holy Trinity** (31 rue des Jardins; 418–692–2193). It's important to recognize that Québec City was home to Protestants and Anglicans as well as to Irish and French-speaking Catholics. The famous Saint-Martin's-in-the-Field Church in London was the architectural inspiration for this cathedral. King George III donated many artifacts here, including a seat in the royal box. Benches are made of oak from Britain's Royal Windsor Forest—a wee bit o' Britain for you, in the heart of la belle province.

Return to the corner of Rue des Jardins and Saint-Louis. Look for two important Québecois houses here. The first is now home to **Aux anciens Canadiens** restaurant, which we heartily recommend you try (34 rue Saint-Louis, Québec G1R 4P3; 418–692–1627). The building boasts the typical French Canadian style of architecture: plain white front wall with an inset doorway, and a steeply pitched, bright red tin roof punctuated by three dormers. Its exterior charm is matched by its pleasing interior and simply superb regional cuisine served by costumed servers.

Nearby, watch for **25 rue Saint-Louis,** the oldest house in the city (1648–1650), where the Duke of Kent lived with his mistress,

Madame de Saint-Laurent. The lovebirds lived here for three years, after which time the duke returned to England to marry and to eventually father Queen Victoria. This house is important for another reason, though: In it, in 1759, the capitulation of Québec was signed.

Now descend Rue Saint-Louis and pass the **Place d'Armes** where troops used to practice their military maneuvers. On your right you'll see Château Frontenac but, for now, past the château, descend well-named **Escalier-Casse-cou (Break-neck Stairs)** to the old **Lower Town,** whose rooftops so delighted you from Terrasse Dufferin.

Immediately on your right find **Maison Louis Jolliet,** a house named after the explorer who, in 1673, paddled down the Mississippi. The house was built for him ten years later. A plaque identifies Jolliet as the discoverer of this river that used to belong to New France. Intriguing, isn't it, to contemplate that until the 1803 Louisiana Purchase, Québec City ruled that part of what is now the United States?

Now you're in the oldest part of the city. Wander around and absorb the flavor of the old port that's home to some of North America's oldest houses, all built of stone. It's charming, despite being jam-packed with tourists. Lots of restaurants, souvenir shops, and art galleries vie for your attention along the **Rue Petit Champlain** extending directly ahead at the base of Break-neck Stairs. If you head left on Rue Sous-le-Fort and then left again, you'll find historic **Place Royale** of **Notre-Dame-des-Victoires (Our Lady of Victory)** church. Built around 1688, it's the oldest church in Québec. Step inside (it's free) and look up to see a model of a sailing ship built in 1665–66—*Le Brézé*—suspended from the ceiling.

Outside and directly in front of the church is a bust of Champlain and the site of his 1608 settlement. Stand and look around you. All the buildings are of cut stone built in the old Norman style. Note the very low doorways and the small-paned windows. Each pane of glass was small because all

Aux anciens Canadiens Restaurant

crossed the Atlantic inside kegs. After successive devastating fires, houses began to be made of stone with raised gable-end roofs, a fire-retardant feature that was enforced by the mid-1700s. Fire was a major problem and this city, along with others like Montréal, suffered from conflagrations in which many lives were lost and businesses destroyed.

Fire regulations also decreed that all roofs had to be constructed of metal, and all had to have ladders affixed to them. Accordingly, in this reconstructed part of the city, you'll find ladders permanently mounted on the roofs. As well, many of these merchants' houses had ground-floor vaults used for storage of their goods.

Until the mid-1960s, Lower Town had become rundown. Then, with federal and provincial funding, the city looked to its past, examined old engravings that showed the architectural detailing of this part of the city, and restored its former glory. We're glad public funds were put to such superb use, as this is really the heart of our Canadian history.

Walk up Rue Saint-Pierre, passing the *Auberge St. Pierre Hotel* (79 rue Saint-Pierre, Québec G1K 4A3; 888–268–1017 or 418–694–7981; fax 418–694–0406). This old hotel offers lots of *forfaits* such as ski, cultural, romantic, and adventure packages. They're a good deal. We enjoyed our stay here as it was deep in the heart of the old Lower Town.

Directly opposite the hotel is the *Musée de la Civilisation* (85 rue Dalhousie, Québec G1K 7A6; 418–643–2158; fax 418–646–9705; Web site: www.mcq.org/english/index.html). There's lots to do and see here,

Québec City Ironies

*T*he song that became the Canadian national anthem was first sung on June 24, 1880, to celebrate St.-Jean-Baptiste Day, an annual holiday that Québec nationalists—or separatists—have adopted as their own. The national anthem, or "chant national," was not sung in "English Canada" until 20 years later.

On the other hand, you too can partake, for $5.00 and a reservation, of an **English Tea Ceremony** at the **Artillery Park National Historic Site**. Sit down with costumed guides and help reenact a nineteenth-century tea ceremony, which is ended with a joyous "God Save the King!" This all takes place in what's called the Dauphine Redoubt Officers' Mess, built in the 1600s. The entire complex, complete with museum, makes an intriguing spot to visit (2 d'Auteuil Street, P.O Box 2474, Main Post Office, Québec, Québec G1K 7R3; 418–648–4205, fax 418–648–4825).

including viewing a longboat found on this very site when the museum was being constructed. Plan to linger for at least a couple of hours.

Nearby, the arty **Hotel Priori** (15 rue Sault-au-Matelot, Québec G1K 3Y7; 418–692–3992; fax 418–692–0883) dates from the mid-1800s. The street name means "sailor's jump," referring to how sailors could jump from the street—the natural shore of the St. Lawrence at that time—into their boats. Today's hotel has been completely renovated, with art deco furnishings by the Martin family. Wander around Lower Town, exploring the enchanting antiques stores that crowd the streets. Many restaurants in this section of town are frequented by fewer tourists and more local residents.

Continue north along Rue Saint-Pierre, then left onto Rue Saint-Paul to find more antiques shops and, a bit farther along, the **Old Port** area, where you'll also see the train station. We greatly enjoyed **Pub Thomas Dunn** (369 rue Saint-Paul; 418–692–4693), which offers an outstanding selection of single malt scotch as well as Québec microbrewery beers. It's a fun spot and, at various price levels, you can sample small quantities of a number of scotches from ten to twenty-five years old. It's a lively pub where you can sit back and relax, taking in the atmosphere. Try the special meal of the day while you're at it.

> ## WORTH SEEING NEAR QUÉBEC CITY
>
> **Grosse Île Parc** is where thousands of immigrants were quarantined between 1832 and WWI. There's a guided tour and the western part of the site is explored on foot whereas the east and central parts of the island are served by a special tourist train. Fees vary from $30 to $50 depending upon where you get the boat and the duration of your stay (allow about four hours). The island is in the St. Lawrence about 50 kilometers east of Québec City on highway 20. Grosse Île and the Irish Memorial Historic Site, 2 rue d'Auteuil, CP 2474, Québec City, G1K 7R3; (418) 563–4009; fax (418) 241–5530 during the season or (418) 835–5443 off season; open daily May 1 through October 31; the fee charged by boat operators includes entry to site; bilingual.

While in the Old Port area you might want to check out rides on such boats as the **Marie Clarisse,** a beautifully restored schooner that is in the same class as the *Bluenose*—the craft on the Canadian dime. (800–463–5250 or 418–827–8836; fax 418–827–8206; Web site: www.familledufour.com. Departs pier 19 at 10:00 A.M., 1:00, 4:00, and 8:00 P.M. From May 15 to October 15, rates are $25 adults, $14.00 children under 12, under 2 free. Closed the rest of the year.) Originally a cargo ship used for hauling salted cod, the *Marie Clarisse* was shipwrecked off the coast of Nova Scotia in 1944. In 1946 it was refurbished but in 1974 it sank to the bottom of the marina. The Dufour family bought it and refurbished it again. On its regular tours, *Marie Clarisse* plies the St. Lawrence east almost as far as Île d'Orléans. Special cruises are also offered to Tadoussac and up Saguenay Fjord.

This schooner offers a wonderful way to explore the St. Lawrence and to relive the advance of Wolfe and his troops upon the city in 1759. While you're aboard, think of this: A cannon ball shot from the river reached Rue Saint-Louis, where you've just strolled. You can see it's no wonder that during the British siege in 1759, cannons more or less destroyed Lower Town.

PLACES TO STAY IN QUEBEC CITY

Québec Hilton,
1100 boulevard René Levesque Est,
CP 37120,
Québec G1R 5P5;
(418) 647–2411;
fax (418) 647–6488.

L'Hôtel du Capitole,
972 rue Saint-Jean,
Québec G1R 1R5;
(800) 363–4040 or
(418) 694–4040;
fax (418) 694–1916.

Château Laurier,
695 Grande Allée Est,
Québec G1R 2K4;
(800) 463–4453 or
(418) 522–8108;
fax (418) 524–8768;
e-mail: laurier@vieux-quebec.com;
Web site: www.old-quebec.com/laurier

PLACES TO EAT IN QUEBEC CITY

Café de la Paix,
44 rue de la Paix,
Québec;
(418) 692–1430.
Superb French cuisine served in the heart of Upper Town's Old Québec. Intimate, romantic, full of locals.

Restaurant Le Zenith,
17 rue Sault au-Matelot,
Québec G1K 3Y7;
(418) 692–2962;
fax (418) 692–0883.

Jules et Jim,
1060 avenue Cartier,
Québec G1R 2S5;
(418) 524–8570.
Well-known for its single malt scotch, enjoyed to the smokey voices of Edith Piaf and Charles Aznavour.

Café de la Terrasse,
Château Frontenac,
1 des Carrières,
Québec G1R 5J5;
(800) 441–1414 or
(418) 692–3861.

Québec City Environs

ying just beyond the limits of the old-world charm and romance of Québec City are wonderful treasures to explore in every season. Follow the circuit presented and give yourselves as much time as possible to savor these areas, for there is much to see and do.

Your general route is to leave Québec City heading east on Route 138 Est. Go north briefly on Highway 73 to Lac Beauport, then return to Route 135 and continue east. Wander through Île d'Orleans, then to Sainte-Anne-de-Beaupré (via chemin Royal—"the King's Road"), and veer north to Mont Sainte-Anne. Rejoin Route 138 Est, and at Baie-Saint-Paul go north again to the rugged Parc Grands Jardins on Route 381, then return to Baie-Saint-Paul and continue east past Malbaie to Saint-Siméon. Here you travel north on Route 170 toward Chicoutimi, exploring the fabulous Saguenay Fjord. Then you'll veer north and southeast to visit a wonderful bed-and-breakfast at Saint-Fulgence before returning via Lac Saint-Jean to the east. We suggest staying overnight at the ghost town of Val-Jalbert before heading south on Route 175 back to Québec City.

Some of these places—such as Mont Sainte-Anne, Lac Beauport, and Sainte-Anne-de-Beaupré—can be easy day trips from Québec City.

Lac Beauport

ead north on Highway 73 and turn right at Sortie 157 (exit 157) onto Boulevard du Lac toward Lac Beauport. This drive of perhaps twenty minutes is part of Québec City's backyard playground, offering summer cottage rentals, golf, water-skiing, swimming in summertime and during winter, fabulous snowmobiling, cross-country and downhill skiing. In fact, you'll be following in the footsteps of holidaymakers who, by the late 1800s, were riding north to Beauport and St.

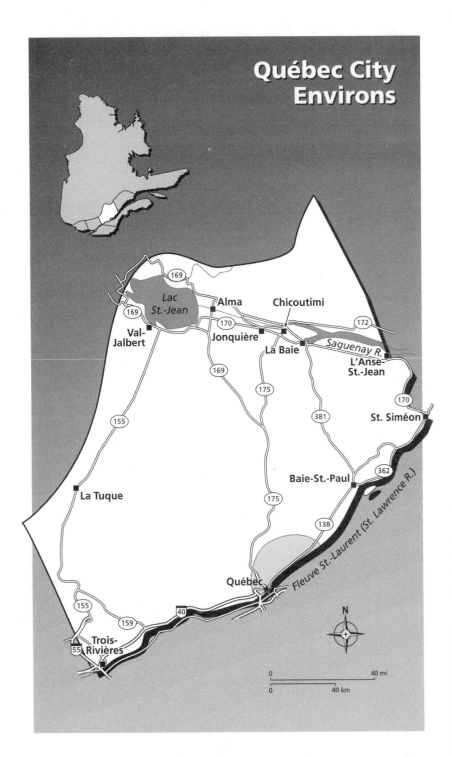

Québec City Environs

Lac St.-Jean

Alma

Chicoutimi

Val-Jalbert

Jonquière

La Baie

Saguenay R.

L'Anse-St.-Jean

St. Siméon

La Tuque

Baie-St.-Paul

Fleuve St.-Laurent (St. Lawrence R.)

Québec

Trois-Rivières

N

0   40 mi

0   40 km

QUÉBEC CITY ENVIRONS

Charles Lakes on horseback and carriage to take in the country air. Even then, this was a day trip.

Lac Beauport was settled in 1825 by Peter Simons, whose descendant Archibald became known as the "seigneur of Lac Beauport." In fact, the largely English-speaking community clustered around the lake in the 1820s was known as the Waterloo Settlement.

Come winter, there are miles and miles of cross-country ski, snowmobile, and snowshoe trails to explore. Eric had never driven a snowmobile before, so you can well imagine the thrill we had coursing over hill and dale. And on Lac Beauport itself, he really let loose and zipped across the completely safe, flat, and frozen surface. Québec has some of the most extensive snowmobile trails in the world.

AUTHORS' TOP PICKS FOR
QUÉBEC CITY ENVIRONS

Lac Beauport

L'Île d'Orléans

Montmorency Falls Park

*Avenue Royale
(the King's Road)*

Baie-Saint-Paul

Parc des Grand Jardins

Saguenay Fjord

*Kingdom of L'Anse
Saint-Jean*

*La Maraîchère du
Saguenay B&B*

Val Jalbert Heritage Village

We rented the snowmobile from **Moto-RAP—Randonées Arrière Pays,** which operates out of Mont Tourbillon, a golf course in summertime (Moto RAP; CP 800, Lac Beauport, PQ G0A 2C1; phone and fax: 418–841–3876). Rent for anywhere from one to seven days or more, but do note that there are many conditions, such as a minimum age of 21. Find out details first, so you won't be disappointed. Snowmobiling is fun to try, and don't worry if you don't have the gear. Moto-RAP rents everything you require, from helmets to boots and everything in between.

Me? On a Snowmobile?

I admit it. I've been a bit negative about snowmobiles in the past: They seemed noisy, polluting, hard to control. But I've had a change of heart. When we went out for what we thought would be a spin around a local trail with the good folks from Moto-RAP, I was surprised to find that the machine was quiet enough that I could still talk with Katharine. And the machine was comfortable, responsive—and fun.

In fact, by the end of the day we had covered almost 100 kilometers and I could have done more. The trails— winter highways, actually—are well-groomed and have lanes and signage just like roadways. I still prefer cross-country skiing, but I can now certainly understand the appeal of snowmobiling. And there probably isn't a better way to see the vast territory of Québec in the winter.—Eric

During our day of snowmobiling, we ate at **Manoir Saint-Castin,** a hotel and restaurant overlooking the lake (99 chemin Tour du Lac, Lac Beauport, Québec G0A 2C0; 800–561–4764; fax 418–841–2495). We watched skaters ply the snow-swept rink and dined on excellent fare. You can rent snowmobiles here, too, and there's downhill skiing nearby, plus snow rafting, snowshoeing, and many other activities. The Saint-Castin makes a good base for exploring, and the atmosphere is welcoming. English is spoken.

The hotel is named after the Baron de Saint-Castin, a man who arrived in New France in 1670 and, four years later, inherited the title of baron. A swashbuckling swordsman, Saint-Castin was a distant cousin to Aramis, one of the inseparable three musketeers made famous by author Alexandre Dumas. Apparently Saint-Castin had a fiery temper and actively fought the English when Admiral Phipps attacked in 1690.

Return to Québec City via Route 73 Sud, or to get past the city traffic, continue along the south shore of Lac Beauport on Chemin Tour du Lac to Traverse de Laval. Turn right and, after about 5 kilometers, turn south on Avenue Sainte-Brigette. As you enter the urban area, this road becomes Boulevard Raymond and connects with Route 40 Est. Follow Route 40 to the river, where it becomes Route 440, and you'll see the bridge to L'Île d'Orléans.

L'Île d'Orléans

This pretty island has borne several names. Algonquins dubbed it *Minigo,* meaning "bewitched place." When Jacques Cartier landed here in 1535, there was such an abundance of wild grape vines that he dubbed it Bacchus Island after the Roman god of wine and merriment. Perhaps sadly, he renamed it only one year later, giving it its current appellation, but for many years residents were dubbed "island sorcerers." This island is a haven for bird watchers (although the September hunting season can be a bit daunting, so we're told.) It's best to come for the spring migration, or to visit later, perhaps during October.

It's only since 1935 that there's been a bridge linking the island to the mainland. Be forewarned: In autumn's harvest time, the bridge can be really backed up because of all the urbanites coming in to pick their own fruit.

First you might like to drop into the Tourist Information Center to pick up maps and postcards and to orient yourself further. Follow the ? sign that immediately appears after you cross the bridge. After you visit there, proceed west on Route 368 to *Sainte-Pétronille,* which was first settled by the French in 1648. A Huron mission was built later, and during the 1759 siege of Québec, it was a British encampment. In the late 1800s it was a popular summer retreat, and today its architecture reflects both its humble beginnings as well as this early recreational period of cottage construction.

As you drive around the island, you'll see lots of woodlands. Many of trees are sugar maples, and there are a number of wonderful maple sugar "cabins" where you can sample this truly Canadian treat. Early spring is the sugar season, but many of the cabins are open year-round; check with the information booth near the bridge. In early February, we enjoyed a filling baked bean dinner with lively Québecois folk singers followed by delicious "tire-sur-neige" (snow-hardened) maple taffy at *Cabane à sucre l'En-Tailleur* (1447 chemin Royal, Saint-Pierre G0A 4E0; 418–828–3189; daily 11:00 A.M. to 3:00 P.M. and 6:00 to 9:00 P.M.).

TOP ANNUAL EVENTS IN QUÉBEC CITY ENVIRONS

February

La Classique is Québec's largest dogsled race held on Île-aux-Coudres with participants from across North America; (418) 438–2505

June

La Malbrest, a transatlantic sailing race between Malbaie and Brest, France; first two weeks of June; (418) 665–7733

Mountain Biking World Cup; end of June at Mont-Saint-Anne; (418) 827–1122

August

Le Festival du bluet (Blueberry Festival) in Mistassini; beginning of August; (418) 276–1241

Do you like chocolate? If you like it as much as we do, you won't be able to resist pausing at the pretty *La Choclaterie de l'Île d'Orléans* (196 chemin Royal, Sainte-Pétronille; 418–828–2252). We can vouch for the splendor of the dark chocolates filled with the island's very own maple sugar. It makes our mouths water just thinking about it.

Continue on Route 368, locally known as the *Chemin Royal.* Past the chocolaterie, watch out for the 1855 wharf and find *Anse au Fort (Fort Cove),* also known as Anse au Iroquois (Iroquois Cove), nearby, where the mission used to be home to more than 300 Huron Indians. They sought refuge from the Iroquois here and were sheltered for years by the Jesuit priests until, in 1656, an Iroquois raid destroyed their haven. It was only after the peace treaty of 1701 that colonists were safe from attack.

After leaving Sainte-Pétronille you approach Saint-Laurent and *Le Parc Maritime du Saint-Laurent (St. Lawrence Maritime Park)* (120 chemin de la Chalouperie, Saint-Laurent; 418–828–9672; fax 828–2170). The interpretation center here has displays depicting the region's shipbuilding era. The name of this street, Chalouperie, is derived from the wooden boats of the same name that the early settlers used to build.

In 1908 Ovide Filion founded the Saint-Laurent shipyard, and during World War II, naval warships were built here. Between 1908 and 1920 three shipyards existed in Saint-Laurent.

Return to Chemin Royal. On the left-hand side of the road, find the not-to-be-missed *Économusée de la Forge Pique-Assaut (Pique-Assaut Forge Museum)* (2200 Chemin Royal, Saint-Laurent; 418–828–9300). As with almost all of the économusées in the province, all the signs are in French. However, this won't prevent you from trying your hand at hammering a red-hot nail on the anvil. Many artifacts are on display, and the place has a shop.

Also in Saint-Laurent is the restful inn and restaurant *Auberge Le Canard Huppé (The Wood Duck Inn)* (2198 chemin Royal, Saint-Laurent; 800–838–2292 or 418–828–2292; fax 418–828–0966; Web site: www.canard-huppe.qc.ca; e-mail: canard@mediom.qc.ca). It serves splendid food prepared whenever possible from local produce. We thoroughly enjoyed our lunch of game terrine and smoked trout, finished off with an assortment of pastries presented with a flamboyant swirl of confectionery sugar. Nearby is a wonderful beach. The inn's helpful bilingual proprietor, Gaëtan Sirois, says there's great bird-watching, beach strolling, picnicking—and, come wintertime, cross-country skiing—at the water's edge.

This island is perfect for bicycling. We suggest booking one of the eight rooms at Le Canard Huppé, filling your day pack with water, binoculars, and a camera, and heading off. You can tour all or most of the island in a day or more, depending upon your speed and inclination.

We hope that you do more than we had time for: follow Route 368 around the island through the villages of Saint-Jean, Saint-François, and Sainte-Famille, the island's oldest settlement, dating from 1661. After lunching at Le Canard Huppé, we drove north to Saint-Pierre on

A chalouperie—wooden fishing boat made at Saint-Laurent

La Route des Prêtres (Priest's Road), one of only three routes transect-ing the island. This is the road of the legend in which the northern hamlet of Saint-Pierre accused the parishioners of Saint-Laurent of stealing their sacred relic, the preserved arm bone of St. Clement. For thirty years, bickering and strife ensued until, in 1733, the bishop of Québec decreed that the two pastors and their flocks should meet halfway between the villages. At the meeting, the relic was returned and, to commemorate the occasion, a wayside cross was erected. You'll pass it en route, and drive in the footsteps of the humbled parishioners.

Our destination was the *Économusée du tapis (Economuseum of Traditional Weaving)* (751 chemin Royal, Saint-Pierre G0A 4E0; 418-828-2519). This particularly enchanted us because the artist weaver, Madame Noëlla Lévesque, ushered us through her home and down into the basement, where we could try our hands at weaving on one of her looms. Noëlla's clear and simple explanations (in English) of her craft were delivered in a soft, welcoming manner. Later, she led us through drifts of snow to her studio out back. We loved the gay colors and simple designs exhibited in the hooked rugs available. Another traditional craft is the braided, usually oval rug, made from rags or scraps of material—the flooring equivalent of quilting, that time-honored method of recycling. Called *nattes Bigarrées* in French, we saw many tempting sizes and colors as well as woven, handspun table runners, cloths, and napkins.

Continuing our drive back toward the bridge, we stopped at **La Ferme Monna,** another économusée, where you can taste and buy *cassis* (black currant) wine and liqueurs (723 chemin Royal, Saint-Pierre G0A 4E0; 418–828–1057). In 1997 their 2.5 hectares of fruit-bearing currant bushes yielded 6,000 bottles. Enjoy a very short tour followed by the ambrosia of tasting the cassis products. In 1995, they were awarded a gold medal for their wine.

As we drove back across the bridge to Québec City, we reflected that prior to its 1935 erection, the only way the island inhabitants could be connected to the city during wintertime was to cross the ice after freeze-up. We imagined the horse-drawn sleighs crossing the channel, and thought about how truly isolated the islanders would have been. Even today with the bridge, summertime's population of 10,000 dwindles to about 7,000 come wintertime.

The Côte de Beaupré (Beaupré Coast)

ack on the mainland, turn right to proceed east on Highway 138. Immediately find the turnoff left to **Parc de la Chute-Montmorency (Montmorency Falls Park).** (The park is at 2490 avenue Royale, Beauport G1C 1S1; 418–663–3330; fax 418–663–1214; Web site: www.chutemontmorency.qc.ca; e-mail: montmorency@sepaq.com; open year-round. The $7.00 parking fee April 25 through October 25 at the lower park is refundable if you eat at the Manoir; cable car $7.00 return.) Good old Champlain named this falls, after the Duke of Montmorency, Viceroy of New France and Admiral of France and Brittany.

This is the famous falls so often depicted with the frozen "sugar loaf" of ice that forms at its base. In the late 1800s, it was a favorite spot to come in winter. Imagine the scene: horses pulling colorful sleighs, whose occupants were bundled up in gaily colored costumes, kept cozy by glossy bearskins. There were horse races on the ice and, on the sparkling sugar loaf itself, people slid on toboggans. In *A Yankee in Canada* (published in 1850), American author Henry David Thoreau wrote, "In the winter of 1829 the frozen spray of the falls, descending on the ice, made a hill one hundred and twenty-six feet high."

Climb the stairs beside the falls or enjoy a cable car ride up. At the top is **Manoir Montmorency Manor,** a reconstruction of the 1780 English-style manor home built by Governor Handimand that was destroyed by fire in 1993 (2492 avenue Royale, Beauport G1C 1S1; 418–663–2877). Its reconstruction one year later is true to the original. There's an excellent museum inside. Queen Victoria's father, the Duke of Kent, stayed here from 1791 to 1794, after which the house was nicknamed Kent Lodge. But this was no mere country home. The museum explains how in 1885, the falls supplied Québec City with electricity—supposedly the first time electrical energy was carried over a long distance (7 miles). By 1897 energy from the falls powered Québec City's first electric train. In addition, there was a cotton factory and sawmill.

The Manoir Montmorency has a superb dining room that affords great views. We had an amazing lunch here: *cuisse de canard confite à l'orange*—duck thigh in orange sauce—as part of their table d'hôte at about $16. If you do stop for lunch, you might want to return to your car by crossing the bridge over the top of the falls and taking the trail and steps down.

Birds
There are more than 350 bird species in the province, of which only 5 to 7 percent winter over.

Now take the first left turn off Route 138 onto Côte de l'Église, which takes you up to the old road, **Avenue Royale,** the King's Road. Turn right (east). This was the first road built in the area and is particularly interesting because of the many *maisons anciennes* (old homes) built right "on the road." Building homes right on the street's edge is also reminiscent of old British houses; the reason is the same, too. Originally, the road was much narrower. When expansion and pedestrian sidewalks were built, what front garden there may have been was paved. Also, settlers had to do road maintenance themselves, so it would behoove them to be as close to the road (and to the market of passers-by) as possible. Watch for homes whose ground floors are old shop fronts. The actual residence was on what is the second—or main—floor, often with an overhanging, quite ornate front porch.

You can spot many old root cellars tucked away into the hillside on your left. There are also many bake ovens where housewives have baked their specialty breads for centuries. Such a spot is **Chez Marie** (8706 avenue Royale, Château Richer G0A 1N0; 418–824–4347). The 1652 dwelling is typical Québecois style, with curved roofline and red tin roof. The 150-

year-old bread oven where Marie bakes her simply fabulous bread is outside. Get yourself a loaf, and while there, don't miss buying a slice and spreading it with the scrumptious maple butter. A divine taste sensation.

Also as you drive, look south, across the channel of the St. Lawrence called *Chanal de l'Île d'Orléans,* to the island you've just left. You'll see the rise of the land mass and, at the top of the island, the line of dwellings that you passed, reflecting the settlement patterns of the day.

Next stop is the *Atelier Paré Économusée des Légendes (Economuseum of Legends)* (9269 avenue Royale, Sainte-Anne-de-Beaupré, Québec G0A 3C0; 418–827–3992; fax 827–3583). This is a must-see as inside its doorway you step into the imaginative world of Québec's folk tales. Françoise Lavoie is not only charming and bilingual, she also animates the carved legends by spinning the tales just for you. We lingered here, admiring the beautiful carvings, and afterward we discovered a book, *Legends of Québec,* written by one of the économusée owners/artisans, Scott Kingsland. If you want an English-language copy of this province's colorful folk tales, buy it here: We never saw that book again in all our travels.

Winter fun

*W*hen we stayed at the Château Mont Sainte-Anne, we went on a moonlit snowshoe exploration of the forest. We had brought our own torches, but the moon was bright enough to manage without them. The next day, I visited the tiny **Musée de Ski,** which celebrates over a century of skiing in the region. There's old equipment, photos of the area's first skiers, and wonderful replicas of European woodblock prints depicting skiing in the Old World.

I satisfied a life-long goal: to drive a team of sled dogs. I adored it! It was all arranged at Château Mont Sainte-Anne, and after a brief stroll up to the dog kennels, the operator—named Bruno—introduced me to my dogs. The leader was an energetic canine named Jack who even obeyed my (probably irritating) commands to slow down while I got my "mushing legs." With the wind whipping my cheeks to an excited rosy red, I whisked through silent, snow-clad forests with the dogs. Sheer heaven, I can tell you.

Eric bought himself a half-day ski pass and rented the newest gear, just for fun. Although he hadn't been downhill skiing for a few years, his ski legs soon returned and by the end of the morning he was running the black diamond (most difficult) slopes and thrilling to the magnificent view of Québec City from the peak. We'll certainly be back for more. Even if it isn't winter, there's still tons to do: biking, hiking, horseback riding, golfing: Make your own discoveries.—Katharine

Now enter the pilgrim's world of **Basilique Sainte-Anne-de-Beaupré** and **Musée de Sainte Anne** (10018 avenue Royale, Sainte-Anne-de-Beaupré G0A 3C0; 418–827–3781). The colossal cathedral and adjacent museum are surrounded by a sea of cars and worshippers. The cathedral has been a celebrated sanctuary since 1665. In that year Marie de l'Incarnation wrote these words about its miracles, to her son: "The paralytic walk, the blind see, and the sick, whatever their illness, are healed." Nowadays over a million people visit annually.

Rejoin Route 138 Est. The next destination is **Mont Sainte-Anne,** only a few minutes from here. Keep in mind this is a Québec City suburb: It takes only twenty-five minutes or so to drive here from the capital. The view from the top of the mountain, whether you hike up or take the gondola (and ski down, perhaps, in winter) is simply unforgettable. You are rewarded with a bird's-eye view of the territory you've driven through, and by looking east you will see the widening St. Lawrence River plus the Laurentian Mountains you have yet to explore. We stayed at **Château Mont Sainte-Anne** (500 boulevard Beau-Pré, Beaupré G0A 1E0; 888–824–2832 or 418–827–5211; fax 418–827–3421; Web site: www.quebecweb. com/hcmsae-mail: hcmsa@total.net).

> **Moo to you too**
>
> *Québec boasts Canada's largest dairy industry. The main producer is the Holstein, the large black and white cow.*

For summer visits, camping is available only 7.7 kilometers east of the alpine resort. Turn left onto Rang Saint-Julien to find **Mont-Sainte-Anne Camping** (CP 400, Beaupré G0A 1E0; 418–827–4561; fax 827–3121). They have jogging trails, swimming, and cycling paths as well as showers, picnic areas, washers-dryers, and a playground for kids.

The Charlevois Region

Continue east on Route 360 to rejoin Route 138 Est to Baie-Saint-Paul, a half-hour away. You enter the Charlevoix region of Québec. There were lots of moose signs, although we didn't see any moose while driving here in August. What we did find, in great abundance, were wild blueberries for sale. If you hike, just watch for them in early to mid-August. We picked a lot of them.

Be sure to stop at the Tourist Information Center right on the highway at **Baie-Saint-Paul.** The center is located right on the highway, before you descend into the town. It houses an interesting, small **Charlevoix Museum,** which depicts the story of how this region's topography was

The Charlevoix Meteor

*M*uch of Québec north of the St. Lawrence River is ancient Canadian Shield, among the oldest rocks on earth, dating back some 2.5 billion years. The St. Lawrence marks the shield's southern edge, where it abuts the sedimentary Appalachian Mountains. Some 350 million years ago, a 2-kilometer-diameter, 15-billion-ton meteor slammed into the Charlevoix region, carving out a crater 28 kilometers in diameter. Like a drop falling in water, the shattered central part rebounded. Over time, the mountains have been eroded by glaciation and the St. Lawrence River. From the information center, you can clearly see the curve of the crater's valley with the rugged mountains on its perimeter.

shaped by an ancient meteor. It illustrates how Charlevoix sits at the crossroads of three significant geological formations: Canadian Shield, St. Lawrence Lowlands, and Appalachian Mountains. On November 18, 1988, Charlevoix became a UNESCO Biosphere Reserve, joining more than 325 others that exist in over seventy-five countries. We also confirmed that caribou once roamed these parts in giant herds. In fact, 10,000 were reported up to the turn of the twentieth century. By 1925, they had disappeared because of habitat loss and overhunting. That's why we wanted to head north, to the Parc des Grands Jardins—the last spot in this area to spy them. Ask at the museum entrance for the printed English guide. Admission is free. This is also a good spot to pick up detailed maps and current information about the region. Staff members are friendly and speak English.

Baie-Saint-Paul is a gorgeous town. The road sweeps downward into the meteor's crater. The village boasts delightful Québecois-style and Victorian homes as well as cafés, many galleries and bookshops, and inns. The brilliantly hot-pink Second Empire café called *Le Flâneur* on Rue Ambroise-Fafard (just across from the Catholic church) is inviting, its wide veranda full of people relaxing with drinks, laughter cascading to the sidewalk.

Armed with new geological knowledge, we turned north on Route 138 to camp overnight and hike at *Parc de conservation des Grands Jardins* (418–622–4444), only 30 kilometers north of Baie-Saint-Paul. The hills created by the meteor's impact formed a beautiful backdrop to the pastoral farmland we now drove through.

For a local taste treat, cheese-lovers stop at the *Économusée Laiterie Charlevoix* (1151 boulevard Mgr. De Laval, Baie-Saint-Paul G0A 1B0;

418–435–2184). We bought delicious three-pepper spicy cheese curds, as well as a raw milk cheese. A few years ago the Canadian government tried to ban the sale of raw milk cheeses, raising the ire of souls like us who've enjoyed them for years. Another cheese maker, *Maison d'affinage Maurice Dufour* (1339 Highway 138, Baie-Saint-Paul G0A 1B0; 418–435–5692; open June 20 to September 4, daily 10:30 A.M. to 3:30 P.M.; free), famous for its Migneron de Charlevoix cheese, is nearby.

Soon Route 138 veers right; we went north on Route 381 toward Chicoutimi. At Saint-Urbain village, the houses crowd the street. We gained elevation and, on our right, passed the *Musée Renaissance (Renaissance Museum)* (Highway 381, CP 313, Saint-Urbain G0A 4K0; 418–639–2210; daily 9:00 A.M. to 4:00 P.M., $2.00 admission). Suddenly the landscape became extremely rugged, looking like mountains in British Columbia. Devastation from a recent forest fire dramatically emphasizes the rocky starkness.

Pull off the highway at the *Accueil* (ranger station) on the left-hand side of the road after passing through the Pied de Montagnes (Foot of the Mountains) sector of the park. If you have reservations, you can continue on to the camping area, but you might want to stop for a more detailed map or to arrange fishing permits. We pressed on to a second Accueil 8 kilometers farther along a bumpy gravel road, through extraordinary wilderness scenery. We had reserved a campsite at *Lac Arthabaska* (418–846–2057 summer, 418–435–3101 winter; fax 418–435–5297). We selected a choice lakeside spot with a shelter over a picnic table, a firepit, and flat campsite. After pitching our tent, we hiked 1.7 kilometers through taiga to Lac Beaumont. Along the way we passed moose tracks and a "kettle," a deep pit created when a ball of glacial ice melts below the surface.

Laptop constellations

*T*he sky was exceptionally clear the night we camped at Parc des Grand Jardins and the stars were brilliant. I remembered that I had a program on our laptop computer that showed the constellations, so after a late dinner we brought it out. Our view from the picnic table looked south over the lake, and we soon identified the constella-tions. To see the northern sky, we had to walk back behind the trees. We heard some murmuring from nearby campers who must have been wondering why on earth these people were wandering around a near-wilderness campground, their faces illuminated by the glow of a laptop computer.—Eric

At Lac Beaumont are photos of the thirty caribou that the Québec government flew in, blindfolded, in 1966 to replace the decimated herd. Now the herd has grown to 103 animals. Sightings are usually in winter; the park staff gives you a form to fill out, should you see one, to help them monitor these shy beasts. Guided three-hour taiga walks with a naturalist are available in English for $10, and you can stay in a bed here for $16 plus taxes. Cabins are also available, but book ahead. *Centre d'acceuil et d'interpretation (office and interpretation center) Château Beaumont,* (418) 846–2058 summer, (418) 435–3101 winter; fax (418) 435–5297. Unless you decide to follow Highway 381 to Chicoutimi, backtrack 30 kilometers to Baie-Saint-Paul and turn left along the coast on Route 362 toward Les Éboulements.

The Charlevoix Coastal Drive

This is a fabulous drive, sometimes punctuated by exhilaratingly steep grades. The coastal views are extraordinary: lush hayfields, pastures dotted with grazing cattle, picturesque architecture, and the long strips of seigneurial farms slipping down, ribbonlike, to the blue waters of the St. Lawrence. Headily picturesque, you'll want to drive slowly and putz along, exploring as you go.

As you approach *Les Éboulements,* which sits picturesquely on a rise of land on either side of the highway, watch for *Moulin Banal, the Seigneurial Mill of Les Éboulements* on the right (157 rue Principale, Les Éboulements G0A 2M0; 418–635–2239; adults $2, ages 12 and under free). An informative English pamphlet explains the history of the site, which has hardly changed from its construction in 1790. With its white clapboard exterior with jaunty red trim, it is lovely, nestled in the woods beside the falls.

Just past the mill, we temporarily turned off the highway to plunge down a 19 percent grade (test your brakes!) to the pretty coastal village of *Saint-Joseph-de-la-Rive.* Artists studios abound, and you'll find *Économusée du papier (Economuseum of Paper)* (304 rue Félix-Antoine-Savard, Saint-Joseph-de-la-Rive G0A 3Y0; 418–635–2430; fax 418–635–2613), where you can watch paper being made by hand using seventeenth-century techniques. Across from the quaint économusée is the *Exposition Maritime Museum* (305 place de l'Église, Saint-Joseph-de-la-Rive G0A 3Y0; 418–635–1131), where a giant wooden boat was under construction when we stopped at this old shipyard. Nearby the village church has for a baptismal font a giant clam shell from Florida. In the village you can catch a ferry to *l'Île aux Coudres* (Hazelnut Island), a popular island with good B&Bs, excellent cycling, nice beaches, and some interesting museums.

Drive back up the hill to rejoin Route 362 Est into *Les Éboulements. Éboulements* is a French word meaning rock fall. In 1663, this region suffered a gigantic earthquake that caused a huge section of the hillside to slip into the St. Lawrence River. In fact, you'll see large rocks that have rolled off the slopes in the low tide as you drive along this coast. Today the farming community and village itself has taken painstaking care of the heritage buildings. You'll pass by many "photo opportunities," lots of artists studios, and at 304 rue Principale, a display of charming miniature Québecois-style bird houses and feeders (*mangeoires* in French). Made from wood and rocks, they are the handiwork of local craftsman Normand Simard.

In the 1600s, young men of Québec thrilled to the notion of adventure, excitement, and potential riches that the fur trade represented. Typically, they were based in Montréal and ventured deep into the interior, where they traded with the native peoples. The main fur trade years spanned from the mid-1600s to 1760.

Continue eastward, upriver toward Saint-Irénée. What unforgettable vistas greet you. You'll note that many homes have spectacular views over the St. Lawrence—and that it must be blustery, for many have sheltered, glassed-in, protected decks.

On your left, atop a hill, watch for a fieldstone B&B, *Gîte Manoir Hortensia* (320 chemin Les Bains, Saint-Irénée G0T 1V0; 418–452–8180; fax 418–452–3357; Web site: www.cite.net/hortensia; e-mail: hortensia@cite.net). Hosts Alida and Marcel Landry have fashioned a sun-filled lodging here. Some rooms have private balconies overlooking *la mer*, as people here call the St. Lawrence, which truly resembles the sea. It's a prime spot, and when we visited in early August, flowers were in full bloom and right out front the little cherry tree was fruiting. This stretch of coast is truly "B&B land." We'd advise you to arrive early, find a bed-and-breakfast that suits you, and then explore.

You start a long curvaceous descent to St. Irénée. The promoter of the Québec-Charlevoix Railway, Rodolphe Forget, lived here in a superb mansion. Follow the signs in the village to the *Domaine de Forget* (398 chemin Les Bains, Saint-Irénée G0T 1V0; 418–452–8111; fax 418–452–3503; Web site: www.cite.net/~dforget; e-mail: dforget@cite.net). The mansion was bought in 1977 by a nonprofit company that has created a cultural center to promote the performing arts. Every summer, internships are offered here to musicians who come to study with international masters. And from mid-June through late August, you can attend dinner concerts.

Return to the village and Route 362, turn left (east), and all of a sudden the road ascends, affording lovely views of the village and surrounding coves. The highway continues to traverse pretty farmland. Old homes, many with manicured lawns and ornamental pools, line the road. This is renowned tourist country: The fresh salt breeze, magnificent forests, and river have attracted visitors for well over 150 years. Scoot past what was once U.S. President Howard Taft's favorite golf course, then pass the entryway to the splendid *Manoir Richelieu,* a hotel with grandeur akin to that of Québec City's Château Frontenac. Next door to the Charlevoix Casino, the Manoir offers some very affordable packages, especially during the winter. Try a romantic weekend of skiing and snuggling up near the big fireplace. (181 rue Richelieu, Pointe-au-Pic G0T 1M0; 418–665–3703; fax 418–665–3093; Web site: www.quebecweb.com/manoir.richelieu.)

A bit farther along Route 362, you arrive in *Malbaie.* It used to be called Murray Bay, after a former Governor General of Canada, James Murray. At the heart of the pretty bay find the Tourist Information Center on your left and, to your right, the *Quai Casgrain,* a little park stretching out into the water—a good spot to stretch your legs, breathe in some salty air, and look at the historical plaques on the quay. You'll learn about the sandbanks here formed by deposits of the Rivière Mailloux, which have provided sand used in the construction of many buildings, including the Manoir Richelieu.

After crossing the bridge at the end of the bay, the highway starts to rise. Very soon on your right, you'll see the shingled roofs of an old seigneurial home (marked PRIVATE) and, just a few hundred meters farther, you'll find its match, on your left. This is the famous seigneury now owned by Francis H. Cabot, an American living in New York City. *Les jardins du Quatres Vents (Gardens of the Four Winds),* the largest private gardens in Canada, are at this home. They are open to the public by reservation only (418–434–2209), and only four times a year: one day each in June, July, August, and September, so that serious gardeners can watch the evolution of a garden's blossoms throughout summer.

Next is the old resort town *Cap à l'Aigle* on the right, with its unusual 1872 Anglican Church *Saint Peter on the Rock* overlooking the St. Lawrence. Farther on is a wonderful, bright yellow, pottery workshop and boutique, *Poterie de Port-au-Persil* (1001 Route 138, Port-au-Persil G0T 1X0; 418–638–2349; fax 418–452–1019), where you can even sign up for pottery workshops. How lovely it would be to come here for a week of classes in these inspiring surroundings. We lingered as long as we could, delighted with imaginative glazes, forms, and colors we saw nowhere else.

Back on the coastal road, don't just rush past nearby **Saint-Siméon**, for its blond sand beach looks as if it will never end. To get there, follow the ferry sign in the village (the crossing goes to Rivière de Loups on the South Shore). There's a cluster of hotels, restaurants, snack bars—and a municipal campground costing around $15 a tent. The beach can be extremely hot (there's no shade, so be forewarned). There's a volleyball net, and next to the water, just the spot for building sand castles. After sauntering about, absorbing the holiday atmosphere, we took Highway 170 leading northwest to Saguenay Fjord.

We could hardly wait to experience this world-renowned fjord, where beluga whales bask and where the cliffs are up to a thousand feet high. Unless you're going to return to this part of the world soon, instead of simply heading northwest on Highway 170, it's worth continuing for 35 kilometers instead on Route 138 to **Pointe Noire.** (You'll have to backtrack on Route 138 to Route 170: There's no other route up the south shore of the Saguenay.) Pointe Noire has an excellent (and free) boardwalk lookout and marine interpretation center, with a video in English. Bilingual staff set the mood for the Saguenay Fjord through a series of animations, offered during the summer season. While we were there, we stepped out of the info center to gaze at the confluence of the two rivers. Heads swiveled when Eric gasped, "There's a whale!" How thrilling it was to spy a minke whale in this rich estuarine channel.

Marine Etiquette

Everyone wants to see whales. If you choose to progress northeast along the coast, up to Tadoussac and beyond, you'll be overwhelmed by the number of whale-watch tour operators. But can you imagine how disorienting it is for marine creatures like whales to hear the continual drumming underwater noise of these craft? Reputable whale-watching outfitters follow a code of ethical conduct. The Zodiacs rafts or cruisers, as well as kayaks and canoes, must not get too close to the whales. Be sensitive to this, and don't pressure your guides to go too close.

Saguenay Fjord Tour

At Saint-Siméon, you turn your back on the St. Lawrence and head inland. It was early August when we were here, and there were *bluettes* (blueberries) for sale everywhere. Delicious! The road passes outcrops of Canadian Shield, past beautiful Lac Deschênes and the village of Sagard, and then you drive right through the middle of a huge lumber mill. Almost immediately afterward, the valley opens up and you'll see dairy cattle grazing, with several old homesteads nestled along the road, making a welcome change from the poplar and mixed forest. On the left is the *Reserve faunique de la rivière Petite Saguenay:* The entire river is an ecological reserve. Here the valley really opens up, and when we drove through it, giant round bales of hay wrapped in white plastic made the farms look as if they were growing giant marshmallows.

Turn right just before the village of Petit-Saguenay if you want to find lodging at the *Village-Vacances Petit-Saguenay* (99 chemin Saint-Etienne, Petit-Saguenay G0V 1N0; 418–272–3193; fax 418–272–1234; Web site: www.royaume.com/village-vacances; e-mail: village@ royaume.com. Here you can camp or rent a cabin. It is on the Parc du Saguenay trail system, so there are good hiking opportunities to give you views of the fjord. It has a sandy beach, and mountain bikes and kayaks are available for rent.

Roadside Crosses

Often you'll come across roadside crosses on your travels. Although many were raised to the memory of a loved one who perished on the road, others are Catholic "stations of the cross." Perhaps the best example of these are along the Chemin Royal to Sainte-Anne-de-Beaupré, a center for pilgrims that draws thousands to the site just east of Québec City. Still others, as on l'Île d'Orléans, mark a spot where a significant activity took place. We were told that they were also used to remind people to pray—and to go to Mass.

Back on Highway 170, the helpful Tourist Information Center can help you find accommodations. Also, you can find out all you'd ever want to know about the kayaking, hiking, biking, horseback riding, and fishing activities in summer, or the winter dog-sledding, snowmobiling, skiing, or snowshoeing. Pick up a detailed map of the fjord here. The ones with topographic contours and tidal information will be very useful if you plan to hike or kayak.

At *Petit-Saguenay,* the road crosses the salmon river of the same name. Boulder-strewn, it is reminiscent of Scottish rivers, or of the Cascapédia River in Québec's Gaspé region. Just after the bridge, a left-hand turn takes you along the river to the *Club des Messieurs,* a men's hunting and fishing camp. You can camp or rent cabins here (call 418–272–2393 for reservations).

We'd heard about a lovely lookout overlooking the fjord, so we turned right after the bridge at this village on what soon became a winding gravel road hugging the river. If you are tempted by the many designated fishing pools, remember that you must register to fish here. Suddenly we were there at a convenient parking lot, with a quay extending into the river and with a small picnic ground. Swimmers with a taste for chilly water jump in here.

We returned to Route 170 to proceed up the fjord. As we drove, we reflected on the newly created (1998) *Saguenay–St. Lawrence Marine Park*—the first park to be jointly created by the federal government of

Canada and provincial government of Québec. It protects a 1,138-square-kilometer territory that's a combination of land and river. Several nonprofit organizations are coordinating efforts to educate people about protection of habitats and species and to develop sensitive, sustainable tourism. It's an exciting time. We met only a few naysayers who bemoaned the environmentalists, lack of new lumber mills, and increasing environmental regulations. For the most part, people recognize the need to manage our natural resources more responsibly.

Because of its many layers of lighter freshwater at the top and heavier saltwater below, the Saguenay River and Fjord support astonishing and diverse life forms. The late oceanographer Jacques Yves Cousteau was the first to closely explore the biology here, in 1984. Four years later, a dive by teams of zoologists and biologists discovered the same biology as in the Arctic Ocean, with several invertebrates found that were thought to be extinct.

Continue on route 170 to **L'Anse St. Jean,** which distinguishes itself as the only kingdom in Québec. Yes, kingdom! And you, too, might meet His Majesty King Denys I, right in town.

King Denys I

*L**a Royaume de L'Anse Saint-Jean (Kingdom of L'Anse Saint-Jean) was created by right of democratic referendum on January 21, 1997, by a majority of 73.9 percent of the 80 percent of the village population who turned out to vote. King Denys I was crowned at the village church June 24—Québec's national holiday, St.-Jean-Baptiste Day. After his coronation, he addressed Queen Elizabeth, stating that a majority of Québecers want "an independent Québec within a united Canada"—What exactly that statement means is still hotly debated. But it's not simply a political statement: It all started as a way to raise funds for an outdoor art project. The project calls for trees to be planted in a large area on the opposite side of the valley* *to make a gigantic face of St. John the Baptist, with his hand pointing inland. Trees will be selected for their fall colors to enhance the image. And the funds? If you have a few thousand dollars handy, you might want to buy the rights to become a baron or a duke of this kingdom, complete with coat-of-arms. For somewhat less, you can buy parts of the face or hand, although we understand the entire pointing finger is already taken. Parts still available can be seen and reserved at a Web site: saglac.qc.ca/~sequence/stjean.html (in French only so far). The novelty of the approach has drawn visitors from around the world. We thought the townspeople made a good decision with their referendum to create a kingdom—Eric*

You may find King Denys I at the *Musée Royale,* right on Chemin Principal, in the heart of the village, overlooking the cove. Having a village king is an intriguing concept, and he's a very clever fellow—engaging, smart, and extremely proud of his village and region.

As you drive toward King Deny's Musée Royale, watch for the sign and little parking lot marking the lookout to the town's *Pont Couvert* (covered bridge). You can walk up the hillside on a set of stairs nearby for your "photo op" of the 1929 *Pont Fauberg.* Its likeness is one that not many of us see too often: It's the picture on Canada's $1,000 bill.

After visiting the Musée Royale, return to the fork in the road and turn right, to follow the road that wends about the cove, to the Pointe au Boeuf. Watch out for the horses. You can ride horses throughout the many trails that cut through this pastoral region. To try it out, contact *Centre équestre des Plateaux* (31 chemin des Plateaux, L'Anse-Saint-Jean G0V 1J0; 418–272–3231). We were really impressed with the horseback riding trails that criss-crossed the road, wending their way through the woods. We passed by a group watering their mounts opposite one of the old farms. For now, continue past these old farms, including one that bears a plaque identifying it as the *Ferme Nazaire Boudreault,* built by Thomas Boulianne in 1844.

Continue up along the gravel road to a parking lot beneath an astonishing hydro tower, whose cables span the entire 1.6-kilometer breadth of the Saguenay. Phew! It's really a testament to human engineering skills and to the gigantic hydroelectric projects built by Hydro Québec in the northern hinterlands. There is a pretty hiking trail here, part of a network that can require up to a week for the traverse from Rivière Éternité to Tadoussac. As you drive you'll note many walking trails branching off on either side of the road. Get a good map at Rivière Éternité before you set off.

Rejoin the highway and, at the intersection, stop at the microbrewery right on the highway, *Les Brasseurs de L'Anse* (418–272–3234). There is a tour with tastes—including a delicious dark brew called Royale de l'Anse. You guessed it: It's the royal brew of the kingdom—fit for a king. We hear it's one of the most popular microbrewery beers in Montréal these days, and we can understand why.

Continue on to *Rivière Éternité* (what a romantic name). Turn off at the signs to the *Parc de Conservation du Saguenay,* an abrupt right turn after the bridge. Almost immediately you'll be struck by the sight of dramatic, towering cliffs, surely a rock climber's dream. Continue along this curvy paved road to the end. Just as the *Centre d'interprétation du Fjord du Saguenay (Saguenay Fjord Interpretation Center)*

QUÉBEC CITY ENVIRONS

WORTH SEEING IN QUÉBEC CITY ENVIRONS

comes into view, so does a parking lot on your left. Park here and walk down—but first, look up and check out the cliffs soaring above you. In late afternoon sunshine, they glow with a ruddy hue. At the park office, English signs welcome you and direct you to copies of an English-language audiotape.

You can rent kayaks from **Explo-Fjord** nearby (mid-June through mid-October; 800–262–7606 or 418–272–2716; fax 418–674–1044). They also offer tours, with guides who speak English, German, and French.

This is the start of *La grande traversée,* a hiking trail that goes all the way to Tadoussac. The complete route takes anywhere up to a week (though many do it in four days), but you can choose to do shorter segments. You park here and start hiking, and along the way you can either stay in B&Bs or camp. What a perfect way to get to know this area intimately. You must register for this hike, and the fee of about $30 includes being transported across the fjord for the final leg to Tadoussac. (Call 418–272–3008 for information and reservations.) We cannot think of a better way to experience the beauty of the Saguenay Fjord. August or September may be the best time to make the hike to avoid the worst of the black flies. But come prepared with repellent, plus lots of gear for warmth. It is windy on the cliffs, and when we camped in August, we found that while the days were hot, the nights were cool.

Return to Route 170. After 17 kilometers we turned right just before *Saint-Félix-d'Otis,* following the well-marked signs to the *Site de la Nouvelle France.* At this spot, the movie *The Black Robe* was filmed. The site was chosen by the filmmakers because the landscape resembles that of old Québec City. The cliffs across the fjord are like those of Lévis, and the peninsula to the west resembles l'Île d'Orléans. Because you'll have been to both the capital and the island, it will be fun for you to see if you agree. Today the site takes you back to Champlain's Nouvelle France: The set props are still there, depicting an Iroquois village, complete with actors who play the role of Iroquois of the time. Also on display is a replica of Champlain's home. The tours of the site take just over an hour. (For information, write to 455 Principale, C.P. 120, Saint-Félix-d'Otis G0V 1M0; 418–544–8027; fax 418–544–9122; Web site: www.royaume.com/robenoire; e-mail: robenoir@royaume.com.)

Downhill and cross-country skiers shouldn't miss the slopes of **Mont-Sainte-Anne** (2000 Beau Pré, Beaupré G0A 1E0; 800–463–1568 or 418–827–4561; fax 418–827–3121; Web site: www.mont-sainte-anne.com; e-mail: info@mont-sainte-anne.com), only 40 kilometers east of Québec City. Snow is plentiful in the winter and the view from the top of the mountain up and down the mighty St. Lawrence is magnificent. Summer activities include hiking, mountain biking, and paragliding.

Instead of returning to Route 170 we remained on this back road, which quickly regained elevation. It teased us with glimpses of the Saguenay, now from a considerable height: quite a different perspective. Along the way you'll pass a highly recommended restaurant, **Auberge la Maison de la Rivière** (9122 chemin de la Batture, La Baie G7B 3P6; 800–363–2078 or 418–522–2912).

Soon we reconnected with the highway near **La Baie des Ha! Ha!,** which was like a little English seaside town, with houses right on the road, overlooking the water. The scene soon changes as you approach the large aluminum plant, paper mill, and industrial sites of this busy port. It isn't all industry though: La Baie also has the **Passe migratoire de la Rivière-à-Mars** (salmon ladder), where you can watch salmon as they enter the river (3232 chemin Saint-Louis; 418– 697–5093). People still refer to the Saguenay's waters here as *la mer,* or the sea, largely because it's not only still tidal here but salty, too.

Our destination was only twenty minutes farther, on the opposite side of the Saguenay, at **Saint-Fulgence,** so we proceeded from La Baie to Chicoutimi on Route 170, turned onto Route 172 (Boulevard Saint-Paul), crossed the Pont Dubuc Bridge, and immediately turned right onto Route 172 Est (Boulevard de Tadoussac). It was 8 kilometers farther to the pretty lilac-pink sign to **La Maraîchère du Saguenay,** our B&B for the night (97 boulevard Tadoussac, Saint-Fulgence de l'Anse-aux-Foins G0V 1S0; 418–674–9384; fax 418–674–1055).

The cottage at La Maraîchère du Saguenay

What an oasis of old-charm tranquility! We fell in love with it immediately. Owners Adèle Copeman and Rodrigue Langevin have created a haven out of a 140-year-old former house for sawmill workers. Their home is a pretty, shingled cottage tastefully decorated with antiques that Rodrigue has collected over the years. But it is Adèle who has given these treasures a new life: Her tasteful, Victorian-inspired country touch is everywhere, and the mood she inspires is one of understated, Old World luxury. Also on the site is a cottage that she designed and had built from found materials: all recycled.

Learning French

And the food—superb! Breakfast was beautiful, served in antique dishes at the long kitchen table. Homey and honest, it gives the effect of another time, when folks could linger. All we can say is you simply must visit. Both your hosts speak English—Adèle with her Irish ancestry is the most fluent—and Rodrigue is so involved in local tourism initiatives that he'll fill your itinerary with lots and lots of "must-see" attractions.

We then returned to **Chicoutimi** because we wanted to witness the after-effects of the calamitous flood of July 1996 when all hell broke loose. Chicoutimi has become a symbol to Québecers of human courage in the face of calamity and of the will to survive and rebuild. Television news footage of that summer depicted how the rivers rose, breaking some of the upstream dams, and coursed through the heart of the city.

To get to Chicoutimi from Saint Fulgence, follow Route 172 west and, immediately after crossing the Pont Dubuc (Dubuc Bridge), turn right onto Boulevard du Saguenay. You can't miss the sight of the flood damage: Turn left at your first opportunity, onto Chemin Price, and cross the Chicoutimi River on Pont Price. Drive slowly and look right, up the hill toward the **Cathedral Saint-François Xavier.** To the right of it is a little white house that television coverage made famous when it somehow resisted the raging floodwaters surrounding it. To its right is an old stone home, now boarded up. You can imagine the desperate plight of the village residents as they watched floodwaters surging through the top-story windows of their homes.

Canadians from coast to coast responded to the crisis, giving aid generously. But real tribute should be made to the valor and hard work of the Chicoutimi people themselves for what they accomplished. They completely rebuilt their villages, roads, and bridges. To the outsider, both the infrastructure and the landscape appear to be completely restored, a remarkable feat after such devastation.

Drive up past the cathedral on Rue Taché. Turn right on Le Doré and park at **La Pulperie and Le Musée du Saguenay–Lac-Saint-Jean** (300 rue Dubuc, Chicoutimi G7J 4M1; 418–698–3100; fax 418–698–3158), an 1896 industrial complex that was the "world's finest and best" pulp

Doing the research for this book stretched my relatively limited French. My vocabulary has been pretty good for some time, but I've always been shy to speak it. I hit a real breakthrough while we stayed at La Maraîchère du Saguenay. We were chatting with our hosts and some other guests from France when I suddenly found myself responding in French without thinking about it in English first. We both felt that a week in a place like this would be a wonderful way to polish our French and, who knows, you might even meet us there doing just that someday.—Eric and paper mill, according to an English journalist of the day. By 1910 it was the largest producer in Canada, and founder J. E. A. Dubuc is credited with starting the pulp and paper industry of the Saguenay.

The mill houses two other attractions you shouldn't miss. One is film and photographs of the 1996 deluge that show the horrifying reality of the river carrying off people's homes, shattering their lives irreparably. The second is the home of the late artist Arthur Villeneuve, a naïve-style artist whose house is preserved, in fully air-conditioned comfort, inside the old mill. On a brilliantly sunny, sultry day, it can be totally delightful to enter Villeneuve's cool yet vibrantly creative world.

Our next goal was Lac-Saint-Jean, so we connected with Route 170 through Jonquière toward Saint-Gédéon.

Lac-Saint-Jean

The route from Jonquière to Saint-Gédéon is, well, flat. After about 6 kilometers you'll cross the bridge over **Rivière des Sables.** Look left to see the dam shown in the video footage at Le Musée du Saguenay with water overflowing it during the 1996 flood. You can further appreciate the calamity of the deluge as you drive along here. After another 20 kilometers or so you arrive at Saint-Bruno and a T intersection with Highway 169. Follow the Route 170 signs to jog left, then right again, toward Roberval. As we passed by, golden barley rippled in the summer breeze in the fields. You'll catch glimpses of the lake as you approach Saint-Gédéon.

Québec Architecture

Old-style structures in Québec are typically steeply roofed, designed so that snow won't collect and collapse or damage the dwelling. Such roofs are often up to one-third of the elevation of the building and often are punctuated by quaint dormers. The roofline ends at the eaves with a bell-cast curve, which gives the pitch a picturesque finish. A characteristic feature of these traditional structures is the casement window with as many as twelve panes.

Lac-Saint-Jean is obviously a holiday destination: Campgrounds and cottages hug the lakeshore. It is also blueberry country. The closer you get to Lac-Saint-Jean, the more blueberries and blueberry products you'll see. We bought chocolate-covered blueberries made by the Trappist monks in Mistassini. You'll also find blueberry liqueur and blueberry pies—as well as syrup and, in August, the delectable fruit itself. At wayside fruit and vegetable stands around the lake we discovered all sorts of other local delicacies, including a rather odd potato candy filled with what turned out to be peanut butter.

We stopped for a picnic at **Métabetchouan,** meaning "meeting place" in the Montagnais language. It's easy to spot the blond sandy beach, **Le Rigolet:** On your right, watch for a left-hand-turn that crosses the railway tracks. Here is yet another bike trail, soon to surround the entire lake. Good picnic facilities are here, and if you like beach relaxation and sports, this is the spot. It's free, too.

Our next stop, at **Desbiens,** was at the **Centre d'histoire et d'archéologie de la Métabetchouane (Métabetchouan Center of History and Archeology)** (243 rue Hébert, Desbiens Lac-Saint-Jean G0W 1N0; 418–346–5341; fax 418–346–5720). You can ask the very helpful bilingual staff at the desk for the three-ring binder explaining the exhibits in English. Here, the early history of Lac-Saint-Jean comes alive, from the early Montagnais culture through to the years of the Hudson Bay Company fur trading post that was situated here, then moved farther up the lake to Pointe-Bleue, now called by its Montagnais name, Mashteuiatsh. Beside the replica of the Hudson Bay post are laminated copies of an old letter written in English (since the Hudson Bay Company was British), detailing this move at Lake Saint John. The Montréal superintendent for Hudson Bay observed that since the natives came down from the hunting grounds to Pointe-Bleue, that that site would make a more logical spot for the trading post.

Another intriguing exhibit is a cross-section of earth, mounted on the wall, that reveals past events, such as an exceptional flood that occurred sometime in the sixteenth or seventeenth centuries. Rather interesting, considering the deluge of 1996. In the museum's video room, you can watch tapes, with narration in French, depicting the construction of a pioneer bake oven, wool-making, and the making of a birch-bark canoe, among other things. There's also a good gift shop. Upon leaving, look right to the historic *poudrière* (powder house). You'll also find the memorial to the Jesuit Père Jean De Quen. In 1640 he was given authority over the territory from Tadoussac to Lac-Saint-Jean.

About 5 kilometers past Desbiens is a great lookout over the lake. Continue through **Chambord** and watch for the abrupt, albeit well-signed, left-hand turn to our destination, **Village Historique du Val Jalbert (Val Jalbert Heritage Village)** (Route 169, C.P. 307, Chambord G0W 1G0; 888–675–3132 or 418–275–3132; fax 418–275–5875; e-mail: valjal@destination.ca; $9.00 adults, $3.00 for ages 6–13).

Stay overnight if you can. Different kinds of accommodations can be booked through the office at the telephone numbers above. The main hotel is in the old general store, but when we tried to get in for the night, it was full ($61 single, $73 double; there are only six rooms, and you must make reservations). There are also campgrounds ($17.50 unserviced, $23.00 with services) and mini-chalets (from $48 per night). We stayed instead in a renovated house directly opposite the general store. Completely comfortable and modern inside, our two-bedroom unit had a living room, dining room, and full kitchen, so you can stay a while and cook some or all of your own meals ($95 per night for up to four people, and oddly, $500.01 for a week). The general store has an ice cream and beer bar, plus a small restaurant (good breakfasts) and boutique. Try the red-colored blueberry beer.

Churches

The Catholic Church is a dominant feature towering above Québec towns. Early surviving examples are of fieldstone, which was originally plastered to protect the façade from the elements. A good example is Notre-Dame-des-Victoires in Place Royale, Québec City, whose front door is on the short gable-end of the rectilinear structure. Roofs are most often of metal, and the steeples—or clochers (bell towers)—usually pierce the sky over the main doorway.

This "ghost town" was a company town built by Damase Jalbert, a local merchant who founded the Ouiatchouan Pulp Company in 1901. The company built everything: roads, houses, a convent and school, post office, general store—as well as the mill with its generating station powered by a penstock from a dam atop Ouiatchouan Falls. In 1927, it was shut down due to a sudden drop in demand for wood pulp. The town died. Folks drifted away, some unwilling to leave their homes but eventually forced to do so. By 1942, the bankrupt company's assets were transferred to the provincial government and the buildings deteriorated.

Happily in the 1970s some of the homes that had not completely collapsed under the snows of successive winters were restored. The village deserves a full day's exploration. In the summer months, costumed students dressed in period clothes reenact those early days. In the convent a "nun" began lessons to the assembled crowd of tourist kids.

Although there is now a gondola lift, we had a lovely time walking the 785 steps to the top of the falls. There are superb lookouts over the valley and Lac-Saint-Jean, and we were completely alone after the gondola lift had closed for the day—a real benefit of staying at the site. As night fell, the stars emerged and the falls were illuminated: truly awesome! The former generating station at the base of the falls is now a dining room where you eat overlooking the restored interior of the power plant. Perhaps, as dusk falls, you'll see the ghost of Ovide Tardif who died after being caught in the drive belts of the mill.

We recommend using this ghost town as a base. Experience it, then go farther afield to explore more of Lac-Saint-Jean. Follow Highway 169 Ouest to learn about the local Amerindian lifestyle and history at nearby *Mashteuiatsh (Pointe Bleue)*. Visit the *Musée amérindien (Amerindian Museum)* (1787 rue Amishk, Mashteuiatsh G0W 2H0; 888–875–4842 or 418–275–4842; fax 418–275–7494; open mid-May through mid-October daily, 10:00 A.M. to 6:00 P.M.; $5.50 adults, $3.50 students, $13.50 family). The museum depicts the lifestyle of the Pekuakamiulnutsh people (Montagnais from the Lac-Saint-Jean region). Exhibits include stone knives, old photographs, and videos. There's also a museum boutique. The Hudson Bay trading post moved here from Desbiens. You can learn more about how the fur trade influenced the early economy of this region at the new *Centre d'interprétation de la Traite des fourrures (Fur Trade Interpretation Center)* (1645 rue Ouiatchouan, Mashteuiatsh G0W 2H0; 418–275–7770). For some original Montagnais creations, stop by the *Maison René Robertson Fourrures* (1629 rue Ouiatchouan, Mashteuiatsh G0W 2H0; 418–275–0795), an artisan's studio.

To return to Québec City, you could continue on Route 169 to circumnavigate the lake or return through Métabetchouan to Hébertville. After about 75 kilometers on Route 169 South, you'll join Highway 175 to take you through *Parc Jacques Cartier*. The park is within the Réserve faunique des Laurentides (wildlife preserve), with magnificent views of the Jacques Cartier river valley. Only thirty minutes from Québec City, this popular weekend destination has a wide range of activities as well as semi-equipped and wild camping. The visitor center, 8 kilometers off Highway 175; has maps and information as well as exhibits describing the park and its natural habitat (418–848–3169 or 418–644–8844; fax 418–622–3014; open mid-May through mid-October).

If you decide to head west from Lac-Saint-Jean toward Lake Superior, consider taking Highway 167 from Saint-Félicien to Chibougameau and on to Val-d'Or on Highway 113. From there, you can continue west through Rouyn-Noranda and Kirkland Lake in Ontario to connect with Highway 11 to take you to Lake Superior. It isn't much shorter than the more heavily-traveled southern route, but it does offer an interesting alternative. Stop at the information center in Saint-Félicien for current road conditions and services: There are long stretches of wilderness along this route.

PLACES TO STAY IN QUÉBEC CITY ENVIRONS

BAIE-SAINT-PAUL
La Grande Maison,
160 rue Saint-Jean-Baptiste,
Baie-Saint-Paul G0A 1B0;
(800) 361–5575 or
(418) 435–5575

CHICOUTIMI
Hôtel des Gouverneurs,
1303 boulevard Talbot,
Chicoutimi G7H 4C1;
(800) 910–1111 or
(418) 549–6244;
fax (418) 549–5527

POINTE-AU-PIC
La Romance Inn,
129 rue des Falaises,
C.P. 275,
Pointe-au-Pic G0T 1M0;
(418) 665–4865;
fax (418) 665–4954;
Web site: www.quebecweb.
com/laromance/

PLACES TO EAT IN QUÉBEC CITY ENVIRONS

CHICOUTIMI
La Bougresse,
260 rue Riverin,
Chicoutimi G7H 4R4;
(418) 543–3178

LA BAIE
Auberge des 21,
621 rue Mars,
La Baie G7B 4N1;
(800) 363–7298 or
(418) 697–2121

L'ANSE-SAINT-JEAN
La Maringoinfre,
212 rue Saint-Jean-Baptiste,
L'Anse-Saint-Jean G0V 1J0;
(418) 272–2385

SAINT-ANNE-DE-BEAUPRÉ
Auberge la Camarine,
10947 boulevard
Saint-Anne,
Saint-Anne-de-Beaupré
G0A 1E0; (418) 827–5703

Montréal and its Northern Playgrounds

Welcome to cultural diversity here in the island city of Montréal. The 3 million plus people of today's metropolis hail from many countries, a fact that lends this city an exhilarating, cosmopolitan flair. There's the Greek section of town along Avenue du Parc. Haitians tend to live in Montréal-Nord, Portuguese near rue St. Urbain, Jamaicans in Griffintown, Jewish communities in Outrement and Côte des Neiges. Throughout the city, immigrants from all over the world are settling in, making this land of opportunity their home.

Even the original coat of arms of the city, designed by the first mayor, Jacques Viger in 1883, honors early Europeans who carved their niche in the land. The four insignia are the Irish clover, Scottish thistle, English rose, and French fleur-de-lys. The Canadian beaver unites them.

In Montréal you can "time-travel" back to the 1500s to catch a glimpse of what life must have been like back then. French explorer Jacques Cartier sailed up the St. Lawrence River on his second trip to the New Land in 1535. Stopping on the island, he climbed **Mont Royal**, proclaiming its name. But on his 1556 map of Cartier's discoveries, Italian cartographer Giovanni Battista Ramusio unwittingly gave the site its modern name, writing "Mont Real" on the island. It's hard to imagine now, but when Cartier explored Mont Royal, he found an Iroquois village of 1,500 inhabitants, nestled against the protection of the mountain—a village that had evidently disappeared by the time Champlain arrived in 1603.

How can you locate this past? By exploring the cobbled streets of Old Montréal. Down in the crypt of Chapelle-Notre-Dame-de-Bonsecours you can glimpse life in 1642, when Montréal was founded as the

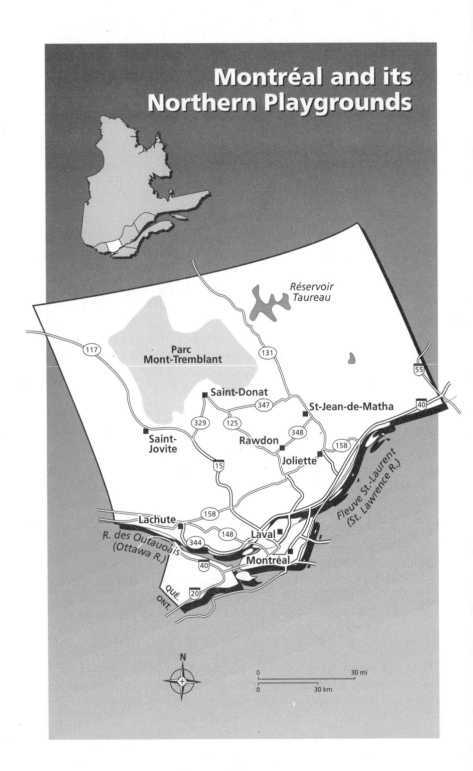

Montréal and its Northern Playgrounds

Réservoir Taureau

117

Parc Mont-Tremblant

131

55

Saint-Donat

347

St-Jean-de-Matha

40

329   125

348

Saint-Jovite

Rawdon

158

15

Joliette

*Fleuve St.-Laurent
(St. Lawrence R.)*

158

Lachute

148

Laval

*R. des Outauoais
(Ottawa R.)*

344

Montréal

40

QUÉ.

ONT.

20

N

| 0 | | 30 mi |
| 0 | | 30 km |

MONTRÉAL AND ITS NORTHERN PLAYGROUNDS

AUTHORS' TOP PICK FOR MONTRÉAL AND ENVIRONS

Chapelle-Notre-Dame-de-Bonsecours

Pierre de Calvet Gîte

Olympic Stadium site with Biodome, Insectorium, and Botanical Gardens

Marché Maisonneuve (market)

McCord Museum of Canadian History

Économusée Fleurineau (Laval)

Musée d'Argenteuil Regional Museum

Le Petit Train du Nord bicycle trail

Parc du Mont-Tremblant

Le Gîte du Catalpa (Rawdon)

French religious colony of Ville Marie. Across from its gilt Virgin is today's Pierre de Calvet B&B, named after the merchant who resided there. Calvet once offered lodging to Benjamin Franklin—which brings us to a story of the bubbling fervor of those times.

One can almost hear the impassioned words as these two men met. Surely they talked long into the night: You can see them springing up from their chairs, shaking their fists, and decrying the British overlords. Democracy was in its infancy. American colonists strained at the British leash while, after the British Conquest of New France in 1759, the seeds of rebellion were stirring here in Montréal. But the British were wise. They may have won the decisive battle on the Plains of Abraham in Québec City, but they knew that the French people's first loyalty was to the Catholic Church. To secure their victory "on the streets," they permitted the French to continue their Roman Catholic faith. Over two hundred years after the Conquest of 1759, French- and English-speaking Québecers continue to dance the dance of negotiation, compromise, and respect.

On the streets of this city, you'll discover that most Montréalers are bilingual. Although French predominates, the reality is that this 350-year-old port is a vibrant mosaic of world culture.

Beyond the city lies the glorious St. Lawrence lowlands with their old seigneurial farms stretching in narrow swathes north from the broad river. Bountiful produce such as delectable strawberries in June are there for the picking. As you drive north you'll find fields of flowers in Laval, then undulating green hills dotted with black-and-white Holstein dairy cows. Suddenly the land steeply rises and you motor through the ancient Laurentian Mountains, once taller than the western Rockies.

This is the playground of Montréalers. Auto routes stream people north to a cluster of luxury resorts offering bicycle paths, lakes, rivers, and golf courses in summertime, skiing in winter: Grey Rocks, and Mont Tremblant. Famous names—and for good reason, for this is spectacular country. Still farther north lies the stunning natural beauty of Mont Tremblant Park, where you can spot a moose from the car or dip your canoe into a lake and paddle off into the sunset. Shall we explore?

Montréal

We'll start our explorations in the heart of Vieux (Old) Montréal. Find Rue Bonsecours and drive down to the *Chapelle-Notre-Dame-de-Bonsecours* (400 rue Saint-Paul Est; 514–845–9991). You can't miss it because it is at the end of Rue Bonsecours at Saint-Paul Est. A gilt Virgin above the front door welcomes worshippers. Look up to see the steeple: This is our eventual destination, as not one but two levels of lookouts offer outstanding perspectives of the old port (*vieux port*) of Montréal.

For now, step inside the cool interior of this 1771 chapel. Modified in 1890, it stands on the site of the original chapel of 1657, when Saint Marguerite-Bourgeoys founded the congregation of Notre-Dame. When we visited the chapel, our guide told us it had just reopened after a two-year restoration of the nave's circa-1888 frescoes, discovered only in

1996. During a short work project, workers had disturbed the stretched canvas ceiling of the nave. The canvas ripped, exposing the hitherto hidden frescoes. Today your upward gaze will be rewarded by paintings that extend themes depicted in the stained glass windows. This chapel is particularly famous for its *ex-votos,* or offerings of thanks. Suspended from the ceiling of the nave are wooden boats carved by sailors who gave them in thanks for their safe passage on stormy seas. English Mass is on Saturdays.

Enter the attached *Musée de Marguerite-Bourgeoys* (400 rue St-Paul Est, Vieux-Montréal H2Y 3C3; 514–845–9991; $2.00 adults; open Tuesday through Sunday year-round, times vary). Climb the stairs to the two steeple lookouts, which we think give you the best perspective of Montréal. Look south to the harbor and time-travel back to 1535 when Cartier sailed upriver. Find *Île Notre Dame,* the artificial island Mayor Drapeau

Angel on the rooftop of Chapelle-Notre-Dame-de-Bonsecours in Old Montréal

had built from 28 million tons of fill. This island was designed for Expo '67. Not only was this a World's Fair, but it was also the celebration of Canada's centenntial anniversary of Confederation. Today the French pavilion houses a casino.

Look north to spy Mont Royal. To the northeast find the white 190-meter "neck" of the 1976 *Olympic Stadium,* often referred to as Drapeau's Folly because to this day, its Kevlar roof still leaks. To date, the always-controversial stadium, designed by Parisian architect Roger Taillibert, has cost Montréalers over $1 billion. Extending below to the west and east are the cobbled streets of Old Montréal. The *Marché Bonsecours* is immediately west and served as the main market of Old Montréal until supermarkets came into fashion in the 1960s.

Before descending, notice how the stone buildings of Old Montréal all have raised gable ends, a required fire-retardant feature in stone homes of the eighteenth century in the city. Below you is a prime example: the 1726 *Pierre de Calvet,* an exceptional gîte with an enclosed, parrot-filled courtyard (405 rue Bonsecours, Vieux-Montréal H2Y 3C3; 514–282–1725; fax 514–282–0456; Web site: www.pierreducalvet.ca; e-mail: calvet@pierreducalvet.ca). Now walk down, down, down to the chapel's crypt to view an exhibit of artifacts dug from the old walls of the city. The original wooden palisade walls have been discovered, and the dig still continues. A maquette in the crypt depicts

The Mother of Montréal

*S*aint Marguerite-Bourgeoys came to New France in the early 1630s. Not only was she founder of the congregation of Notre-Dame, but she also insisted upon erecting the Chapelle-Notre-Dame-de-Bonsecours on the easternmost edge of the parish. In 1653 the French king sent boatloads of young women as wives for the men of the colony, and these girls—some as young as twelve—needed careful guarding and, sometimes, education in household management, sewing, and cooking. Marguerite-Bourgeoys took two boatloads of these filles de roi (daughters of the king) under her direct care.

Today, the doll collection in the Musée de Marguerite-Bourgeoys depicts her life and times. When you exit the main doorway of the chapel, look left to see the marble plaque to her memory, with the obvious addition of the word "Saint"—a sainthood bestowed upon her in 1982. Because of her dedication to Montréal's poor and sick, and to the filles de roi, she is considered the Mother of Montréal. She died in 1770, at almost eighty years old. What a life!

Tip: A Montréal city pass to nineteen museums can be obtained by contacting 800–363–7777.

what archaeologists are revealing even today. Catch an *archaeological tour* if you can (limited to groups of eight).

Return outside to Rue St. Paul Est at Rue Bonsecours. Turn left on Rue du Marché Bonsecours to visit the harbor and perhaps have a picnic on the grass at *Parc du Bassin Bonsecours* (no fees, just a pretty, grassed park beside the river). As you cross Rue de la Commune look right. Beside the broad boardwalk you'll spy gaily decorated *horse-drawn calèches,* which cost $35 for a half-hour ride. In winter, bearskin rugs and the lively tales of the drivers conspire to keep you warm. Then too the frozen surface of the Bassin Bonsecours is shoveled clear of snow so you can join Montréalers skating. In February, Montréal's *Winter Carnival* is held here.

Exploring Old Montréal can be a tad depressing as there are tons of junky souvenir shops. Just ignore them and have fun—for example, by quaffing one of Québec's deservedly renowned microbrewery beers at one of *Place Jacques Cartier's* restaurants. (Try Unibroue's La Fin du Monde—the End of the World—but beware, it's 9 percent alcohol.) Trendy cafés spill out onto the broad expanse of this once open-air marketplace in a lively, jovial atmosphere. Artists, craftspeople, street actors, and jugglers entertain you in summertime, as will the sound of a multitude of languages floating on the evening air. More than anyplace else in Old Montréal, the spirit of convivial *laissez-faire* and *joie de vivre* is infectious here.

At the head of Place Jacques Cartier find the *Colonne Nelson (Nelson Column),* which symbolizes British merchants' desire to publicly express their loyalty to the Crown in 1809. This tribute to Nelson is one of two such columns in the world. The other is in London at Trafalgar Square.

Although the city of Montréal is itself on an island, it includes a number of other interesting islands. At the lower end of Place Jacques Cartier, cross the Rue de la Commune and find the Navettes Maritimes ferry terminus on Jacques-Cartier quay. Admission tickets to the Biosphere include free round-trip passage and bicycle transport aboard the frequent ferry to *l'Île Sainte-Hélène.*

The *Biosphere,* housed in one of the few remaining exposition buildings of Expo '67, is a geodesic dome designed by American Buckminster Fuller ($6.50 adults, $5.00 seniors/students, free ages 7 and under; June 24 through August: daily 10:00 A.M. to 6:00 P.M.; September through June 23: Tuesday through Sunday, 10:00 A.M. to 5:00 P.M.; 514–283–5000).

MONTRÉAL AND ITS NORTHERN PLAYGROUNDS

Enter to explore the habitats of the St. Lawrence River and Great Lakes regions as well as to visit an interpretive center that explains sustainable use of water resources.

In daytime, cross to *l'Île Notre-Dame,* an island created in a mere ten months from fill excavated during construction of the Métro. Unless your visit coincides with the exciting Grand Prix Formula One racing event in mid-June, you can enjoy the peace and beauty of the *Jardin des Floralies,* a 26-hectare expanse of gardens from the 1980 Floralies Internationales. If the weather is suitable, visit the *plage* (the beach)—*Plage de L'Île Notre-Dame.* It makes a fascinating counterpoint to the Biosphere's theme of sustainable use of water resources, as the water you swim in is filtered naturally by an assortment of plants such as bulrushes.

Just north of the Biosphere, you'll find the *Fort de L'Île Sainte Hélène,* which was built in 1825 after the American and British War of 1812 from red stone quarried from the island. Inside is the *Musée David M. Stewart* (514–861–6701; May to Labor Day: daily 10:00 A.M. to 6:00 P.M.; Labor Day through April: Wednesday through Monday 10:00 A.M. to 5:00 P.M.; $5.00 adults). It houses a collection of seventeenth- and eighteenth-century maps and firearms, among other objects, all collected by this Scottish Montréal industrialist.

Even if you don't like rides, you shouldn't miss another legacy of the 1967 World Exhibition, at the north end of l'Île Sainte Hélène: *La Ronde.* This is Québec's largest amusement park, with thirty-four rides, lots of games and, during June and the first half of July, the incomparable *International Fireworks Competition.* Consider walking back to the city across the *Jacques Cartier Bridge,* from whose pedestrian walkways you get a breathtaking view of this island city, especially at night. Cross on the west side for the best view of the city, and the bonus, of course, is that it's both free and you're enjoying an unforgettable stroll in the fresh air.

Top Annual Events in the Montréal Environs

For information on Montréal festivals, contact the **Greater Montreal Convention and Tourism Bureau** *(1555 Peel Street, Suite 600, Montréal H3A 3L8; (800) 363–7777; Web site: www.tourism-Montreal.org)*

June

Festival Interculturel de Laval (Intercultural Festival) June 25 to July 1; (514) 662–4440

Land Insights; aboriginal film & cultural festival; Mid-June; (514) 521–2714

June/July

Festival international de Lanaudiére; classical music, end June to beginning August; (514) 759–7626

Montréal International Fireworks Competition; June through July, weekly; (514) 872–4537

July

Montréal Jazz Festival; first two weeks in July; (514) 871–1881

August

The World Film Festival of Montréal; late August to early September; (514) 848–3883

Former Mayor Drapeau's other significant legacy is the **Métro.** Convenient, inexpensive, and safe, subway stops are identified by circular signs with a white arrow on a blue background. There's a whole "underground happening" here: Musicians play, and some stops have underground markets. Maps are easy to follow, and as in London, Tokyo, and Mexico City, the routes are color-coded. If you decide not to walk across the bridge, the well-marked **Île Sainte Hélène** métro stop will return you to the city.

Madonna of the Bathtub

Roadside Madonnas are a Québec feature. Dressed in blue robes and often with hands outstretched, the religious figurine is mounted in little garden or roadside shrines. Local wags often call such a figurine "the Madonna of the bathtub," since shrines resemble (and often actually are) up-ended, old-fashioned bathtubs.

You mustn't leave Montréal without hopping on the Métro and exploring what is known as the **Underground City**—the largest in the world. More than two thousand shops, cinemas, and services thrive in five different zones, all beneath the city's streets. To get a taste of it, we recommend you descend beneath the train station at **Place des Armes** to enjoy the market flavor there.

A key Métro stop is **Viau,** being central to the **Biodome, Insectorium,** and **Botanical Gardens.** A free shuttle bus takes you from the station to each of these attractions and, if you're tired of walking, there's a free train that drives around the Botanical Gardens, once you pay the admission, that's a lifeline for parents with kids—or even for couples like us who've been "walking forever." We feel so inspired in these gardens. Here you can learn all you want to know about planning your garden, whether from the point of view of color, fragrance, or medicinal qualities of plants.

The **Pie IX** stop is close to the **Olympic Stadium,** is a major landmark and tourist draw. But if you want to check out a section of town that Montréalers love, walk south on Boulevard Pie IX three blocks to Rue Ontario. Turn left to find the lesser-known **Marché Maisonneuve** (market) in the area of town called Hochelaga Maisonneuve. Hochelaga was the name of the Iroquois village Cartier visited on the island of Montréal in October 1535. Populated in the 1870s by mostly French-speaking laborers for nearby factories, this once-industrial sector is now mainly residential. When it was officially incorporated in 1883, Maisonneuve was comparable to the city of Pittsburgh.

In front of the Beaux Arts 1914 market building is an eye-catching fountain. Sculptor Alfred Laliberté's composition includes some puckish-looking boys grasping market animals, such as a calf and a turkey. But the real *pièce de résistance* is the lifelike bronze statue called *"La Fermière."* ("The Farmer's Wife"). Her swinging skirt makes her look as though she's about to stride off the pedestal. Facing her, cross to the market building on the right to find the deli **Première Moison,** where you can buy healthy breads, and a variety of pâtés and patisseries. All are exceptional, including the coarser pâtés called *rillettes.* Most are made from game meats such as deer, rabbit, or bison.

Want a free swim after lounging in the market square? Walk down Morgan Street (opposite the fountain) to 1875 Morgan, the **Piscine Morgan,** a pool that was once one of the city's public

"La Fermiére" fountain in front of the market building, Marché Maisonneuve

baths (872–6657). The front of the building is decorated with another of sculptor Alfred Laliberté's lifelike bronzes.

Our final tip for exploring Montréal is to visit the outstanding **McCord Museum of Canadian History** (corner of Sherbrooke and Victoria, McGill Métro stop). Here, secrets of the city are revealed in the delightful new permanent exhibit entitled "Simply Montréal." It introduces you to the city's social history and has an excellent display on winter. As well, there's a rare photo of working-class Montréal, which contrasts neatly with other displays of fancy balls and the good life.

The McCord houses a superb Amerindian collection and the outstanding William Notman collection of 700,000 photographs of Canada, which the photographer took in the late 1800s. We think this museum's a gem; don't leave town without visiting. (690 rue Sherbrooke Ouest; 514–398–7100; McGill Métro or bus 24; Web site: www. mccord-museum.qc.ca; open daily, times vary by season; $7.00 adults, $5.00 seniors, $4.00 students, children free, entry free on Saturday 10:00 till noon.)

As you leave Montréal, drive north to the mountain **Parc du Mont-Royal,** designed by American Frederick Law Olmstead, creator of

---

WORTH SEEING IN MONTRÉAL

Cirque du Soleil is one of Québec's major attractions. Its 50 meter, blue-and-white big top *(grand chapiteau)* is only visible on Quai Jacques Cartier (Old Port of Montreal) in spring. The rest of the year, this internationally renowned troupe, known for its astonishing acts, travels. Since its creation in 1984, Cirque du Soleil has played to sellout crowds worldwide (514–790–1245 or 800–678–2119; Web site: www.cirquedusoleil.com for performance information).

Fur Trade at Lachine National Historic Site (1255 Blvd Saint-Joseph, Lachine H8S 2M2; 514–637–7433; $2.50 adults; April to mid-October daily 10:00 A.M. to 12:30 P.M.; 1:00 to 6:00 P.M., closed Monday mornings. From mid-October to mid-December open Wednesday to Sunday 9:30 A.M. to 12:30 P.M.; 1:00 to 5:00 P.M., closed mid-December to end March). This interpreted site depicts the mainstay of economic life in Nouvelle France: the fur trade. The Lachine Canal was critical to this trade and it was here that the Hudson Bay Company established its main offices. The company's warehouse was built in 1830. Excellent for kids.

Musee des Beaux-Arts de Montreal (Museum of Fine Arts) (1379 and 1380 rue Sherbrooke Ouest; 514–285–1600; fax 514–844–6042; e-mail: museerp@cam.org; Web site: www.mmfa.qc.ca). A world-class museum; the permanent exhibits are free. Call to find out what the temporary exhibit is when you visit. Adults $10; students $5; half-price on Wednesdays; open Wednesday through Sunday 11:00 A.M. to 6:00 P.M. but Wednesday until 9:00 P.M.

Mont Royal Cemetery is a huge Protestant cemetery that will give you insight into who was who of old and new Montreal. The famous governess popularized in The King and I, Anna Leonowens, is buried here, as are many Molsons of brewing fame. Found on Voie Camillon Houde, it is situated near Montréal's largest cemetery, the *Cimitiére Notre-Dame-des-Neiges*, final resting place for over a million souls. Farther along the road is the *Oratoire Saint-Joseph* (3800 Chemin Queen Mary; 514–733–8211; open daily 10:00 A.M. to 5:00 P.M.; free). Over 2 million pilgrims traverse the 300 stairs annually, sometimes on their knees.

New York City's Central Park. The summer walking paths are good cross-country trails after the snow flies. From its *belvédères* (lookouts), look down over the city. As a nice counterpoint to the beginning of your trip, look east to the Old Port and the Chapelle-Notre-Dame-de-Bonsecours.

North of Montréal

Now we'll start our exploration of the environs to the north of the city. From the park, follow Côte-des-Neiges north to Rue Jean-Talon. At this five-way intersection, turn into the park on Boulevard Laird into the town of Mount Royal—where English-language signs suddenly become evident in a neighborhood of gracious elms and stately homes. Find Highway 15 Nord near where Boulevard Laird meets the Autoroute Métropolitaine.

Laval

The best way to get to the island of Laval is via Highway 15 North. Formerly known as L'Île Jesus because it was granted to the Jesuits in 1636, the island was the cottage country of wealthy Montréalers from 1880 to 1914. Today it is home to a flourishing horticultural industry, and you can drive along pretty backcountry roads (mostly paved) that lead from one fragrant spot to another. A brochure, "La Route des Fleurs," is available at tourist centers and in commercial establishments along the route. Most spots are close to the town of Sainte Dorothée, touted as the flower capital of Québec, and for good reason.

From Highway 15, turn west onto Autoroute Laval which soon becomes Avenue des Bois. At the T-intersection, turn left at Rue Principale and watch for the ***Économusée Fleurineau*** (1270 rue Principale, Sainte-Dorothée; 450–689–8414; Monday through Wednesday 9:00 A.M. to 6:00 P.M., Thursday and Friday 9:00 A.M. to 9:00 P.M., Saturday 9:00 A.M. to 5:00 P.M., Sunday 10:00 A.M. to 5:00 P.M.). Like almost all of Québec's économusées, Fleurineau can be a bit frustrating for English-only speakers. Although the general brochure is bilingual, all interpretive signs are French-only. However, all staff are fluently bilingual, so don't be shy. Ask and you'll get lots of flower info.

In 1994 two brothers started Fleurineau to grow, dry, and arrange dried flowers. At first, they simply thought of growing statice for the local market in Sainte Dorothée, but their business literally grew and now they ship all over the province and into the United States and Ontario. While mum and dad operate the adjacent strawberry patch (great for pick-your-own fruit in June), the brothers manage a fifty-acre operation with twenty-five full-time employees. *Language tip:* The word for "farm" is *ferme* in French; but note that if picking is finished at a fruit farm, a sign with *fermé* will appear. Note the accent on the last letter; it's your clue that the *ferme est fermé* (the farm is closed).

Close by find ***Paradis des orchidées*** (1298 Montée Champagne, Sainte Dorothée; 450–689–2244),

Roadside Springs

Often you'll see little drainpipes gushing water at the roadside. These are roadside springs (called source *in French), and locals flock to them to gather drinking water. You'll find one outside Wakefield Village and another in Quyon, both in the Outaouais. Want some water? You can't do better. Not only is it a good source of tasty, potable water, but it's also a great place to gossip and catch up on news 'n' views.*

Native Blockade

In the hot summer of 1990, members of the Mohawk community at Oka staged a 77-day blockade of the highway after the Oka golf club tried to expand its grounds. In so doing, it infringed on an ancient burial ground. What was perceived as an out-and-out affront to native rights and territory sparked a heated, lengthy standoff.

Eventually the provincial government called in the federal government and Canadian armed forces. The Oka standoff remains a reminder that strong passions can be easily inflamed by insensitivity.

which is open to visitors by appointment only. We couldn't believe our eyes when we entered the greenhouse. As far as the eye could see were wall-to-wall flowering orchids. And it does seem preposterous that such an exotic-looking flower has no fragrance.

From there, rejoin Autoroute Laval to Highway 15 North to the Boulevard Sainte-Rose exit east. You'll soon reach 345 boulevard Sainte-Rose, the **Parc de la rivière des Mille-Îles** (Thousand Islands Park), which is a northerly bayou, a special wetlands ecosystem (open May 11 to September 27: 9:00 A.M. to 6:00 P.M. in May, June, and September, and 9:00 A.M. to 8:00 P.M. in July and August. Interpretation Center open 7:00 A.M. to 9:00 P.M. from June 20 to September 7. Watercraft rentals available. Guided sunset excursion in rabaska canoes Wednesdays from 7:00 until 9:00 P.M. from June 24 to August 26; $10 adults, $6 for ages 12 and under.) The rabaska is a huge Indian canoe, so it's a little piece of history well-worth trying. In winter or in summer, there's much to do here, from a canoe or kayak exploration of the pretty islands to skating and skiing in winter.

Although signs and brochures are in French only, guides are friendly and try their best to explain the flora and fauna of the islands in English. You'll surely see mallard and black ducks and great blue heron and possibly spy beaver, muskrat, bullfrogs, and leopard frogs. Bring your binoculars and camera.

There are boat launches, picnic areas, and hiking trails here, too, though no camping. If you use Highway 15 north of Montréal, you can be here in just twenty minutes. So you could stay in your Montréal lodgings and come for the day. The closest camping facilities are at **Parc du Mont-Laval** (675 boulevard Saint Martin Ouest, Sainte-Dorothée, Laval H7X 1A6; 450–689–1150; $18 to $27).

From Thousand Islands Park, head west on Boulevard Sainte Rose until you reach the junction with Route 148. Turn right (north) and cross the Rivière des Mille Îles on the Pont Arthur Sauvé to **Saint Eustache.** During the last days of the 1837 rebellion, hotly pursued by the British, the patriots fled to **L'Église du Saint Eustache** Church, where bullet holes are still visible in the walls. In late August you can catch the beginning of the Descente des Mille Îles—a 20-kilometer descent of the river by canoes, including rabaskas, which ends in Parc des Milles-Îles.

Now we'll press on to Oka, home of wonderful cheese as well as the site of an Indian reserve and the ferry embarkation point to Hudson, Québec. To get there, turn left (west) on Highway 640 at Saint Eustache. Highway 640 becomes Highway 344 at *Parc d'Oka* (Recreational services du Parc d'Oka, 2020 chemin Oka, P.O. 1200, Oka J0N 1E0; 888–PARC–OKA or 450–479–8337). You could spend several nights camping here. There are over eight hundred camping spots, many miles of walking trails, an observation tower, picnic grounds, sandy beaches, and lovely paved cycling trails. You can ask for reductions in the normal fees if you are camping from Monday through Thursday, excluding St.-Jean-Baptiste Day (June 24) and Canada Day (July 1).

As you swing north beyond Oka, the countryside that hugs the Outaouais (Ottawa) River is incredibly pastoral. You'll pass lots of tiny little huts parked on the river's edge. These are ice-fishing huts, and in winter, they will look jaunty, dotting the surface of the river while fishermen sit inside, hunched over the hole cut in the river, warmed by a little stove.

Now we enter Argenteuil County, a 1682 seigneury (estate) named for a region of France. It is also a good spot to see the evolution of the Canadian seigneurial (or feudal lord) system. Look toward the river to see some homes on the water's edge. These are at the sites of the original houses. At first, seigneurial lots were wider and extended far back from the river bank, as long swathes of perhaps fifty to one hundred acres. However, as the children of the original settlers came along, land was severed to increasingly thin strips of land extending inland. It was important for houses to hug the riverfront, as waterways provided the only means of transportation. Then, as roads were cut parallel to the river, houses "migrated" to border them, for roads superceded river travel in the mid- to late 1800s.

Soon you arrive at *Saint André Est,* the site of Canada's first paper mill (1804) and birthplace of Canada's third—and first Canadian-born—

Steamship Crossing of the Atlantic

The first steamship to travel from west to east across the Atlantic was made in Québec City. The paddle-wheeler Royal William *was built by Black & Campbell in the winter of 1830–31. Because of the 1832 cholera epidemic, the trans-Atlantic crossing was postponed until 1833. But on August 13 of that year, the* Royal William *left from Pictou, Nova Scotia, bound for Cowes, on the Isle of Wight, carrying 324 tons of coal. Samuel Cunard was one of this ship's investors and, although the* Royal William *was sold to the Spanish Navy, this crossing marked the start of Cunard's great steamship line.*

North to James Bay

*F*or something really off the beaten path, consider continuing from Saint-Jovite to the **James Bay hydroelectric power projects** on La Grande River, which flows into James Bay. This is about as far north as you can go by road in Québec. It is a long drive: 1,400 kilometers and twenty-two hours from Montréal. The road is paved all the way, although you should be prepared for rough patches and be on the alert for animals and trucks.

If you (and your vehicle) are up for the drive, continue on Highway 117 from Saint-Jovite for 250 kilometers through La Vérendrye Park to Lac Simon. Turn west on Highway 117 to Val-d'Or, then north on Highway 111 to Amos. From Amos, Highway 109 takes you north to Radisson. You can visit the immense Robert-Bourassa Dam, with its generating station carved 140 meters into the Canadian Shield rock. Farther west, you can also visit the La Grande-1 generating station at Chisasibi near where the La Grande River meets James Bay. (Free tours at 1:00 P.M., daily from June 16 through September 1 and on Wednesday, Friday, and Sunday the rest of the year, or on request. For information and reservations forty-eight hours ahead of time, call 800–291–8486.)

prime minister, Sir John Joseph Abbott. He wasn't exactly enthusiastic about becoming prime minister, ruefully commenting that he was a likely candidate "because I am not particularly obnoxious to anybody."

Continue along Highway 344 for a few kilometers to the ***Musée d'Argenteuil Regional Museum*** (50 rue Principale, Carillon; 450–537–3861; from mid-May to Labor Day, 11:00 A.M. to 5:00 P.M. in early May, September, and October open weekends only; closed Monday; $2.50 adults, $2.00 seniors, $1.50 children, $6.00 family, last Sunday of the month is free for everyone). The museum is located in the historic village of Carillon, where the old portage around the Carillon Rapids on the Ottawa River began. This was the last great rapid before Montréal. Between 1816 and 1843, the 22-kilometer Carillon-to-Grenville Canal was constructed, led by Captain Henry du Vernet, Civil Engineer of the British Royal Staff Corps. Around 1834 he designed the barracks, today's museum.

The barracks played their role in the Rebellion of Lower Canada in 1837. A total of 126 women and children were sheltered from the attacks of the patriots here. It is now owned and operated by Parks Canada. Because this is a federal government department, the extensive exhibits are bilingual. In the museum gift shop, there are many books that explain, in both English and French, this region's rich history.

This not-to-be-missed museum contains not only fascinating reminders of military history and canal-building but also one of Québec's finest regional costume collections. Why? Historian, curator, and museum guide Michelle Landriault told us that this part of Argenteuil was one of the first to be settled by Loyalists and, later, wealthy Scots who helped construct the Carillon Canal. Irish, too, came here to labor on the canals. After its completion, they lingered on, and their wealth permitted them to accumulate fashionable clothing, household items, and fine furniture, much of which was eventually donated to this museum.

An Outdoor Paradise

We'll now head into another exciting region. Start by backtracking to Saint André Est and follow Highway 327 north to **Lachute.** Every Tuesday throughout the year there's a great flea market here (26 Main Street, Lachute; 514–562–2939; Sunday 8:00 A.M. to 6:00 P.M. from mid-April to mid-September). Also at Lachute is *Nouveau Monde River Expeditions* (100 chemin Rivière Rouge, Calumet; 800–361–5033), which offers some exhilarating whitewater rafting.

If you are short on time, you could turn east on Highway 158 to Saint-Jérôme and then north onto the broad autoroute that whisks Mont-réalers north to Mont Tremblant. However, a more interesting route north is on the lesser-used Highway 327. This gives an intriguing glimpse into history as you drive through towns reflecting early British

Cross-country skiing near Mont Tremblant

settlement patterns: Brownsburg, Dalesville, Pine Hill, Lakeview, Arundel—all the way north to **Saint-Jovite.** There's a good tourism center here (305 chemin Brébeuf, J0T 2H0; 819–425–3300), with brochures and seasonal information on Parc du Mont-Tremblant, our destination.

If you're up for a taste of luxury, head north from Saint-Jovite to **Mont Tremblant Village.** Albeit extremely commercial, you may want to drop in just to say you've seen it, or to take advantage of its world-class resort facilities.

The village is home to fabulous hotels like Canadian Pacific's **Château Mont Tremblant** (3045 rue Principale, P.O. Box 180, J0T 1Z0; 819–425–3232; fax 819–681–7097). The only four-star hotel on the mountain, its interior decor features Québecois folk legends, some of which you'll recognize from your microbrewery beer labels. Even if you don't stay here, step inside the foyer to view and read these legends. You'll find a scrumptious buffet here for about $25 per person. You can also rent a fully-equipped apartment in one of the mountain condominiums from **Les Suites Tremblant** (800–461–8711; Web site: www.tremblant.ca/e/index.html). If you stay in these suites, ask about any special add-ons like Jacuzzis. Ours didn't work, and we discovered it was because the owner who rented the unit turns it off. Guests also have the use of a private beach at a lake, but you may not be told about it. So ask what is included and enjoy what you are paying for.

Mont Tremblant Village has lesser-known attractions to offer. If mountain biking is your thing, find out about the astonishing route that hurtles you down the mountain; it's not for the uninitiated. If backcountry

Cycler's Paradise

*T*he 200-kilometer bicycle route called **Le Petit Train du Nord** extends north from Saint-Jérôme through Mont Tremblant to Mont Laurier. Avid cyclists will simply not want to miss this wonderful route. If you do cycle along Le Petit Train, you'll arrive at enchanting little villages such as L'Annonciation (northwest of Mont Tremblant). We recommend you check out the old railway station, which is a Tourist Information Center and local art gallery. This town has several delightful restaurants along the main street, and locals say all the businesses are benefiting from the cyclists in summer and the snowmobilers in winter. We particularly liked the local cheeses and light lunch at **La Cigale** (157 rue Principale, L'Annonciation J0T 1T0; 819–275–3731), where old photos of the town are hung on the walls.

skiing appeals, try the increasingly popular "glade skiing" routes on the back side of the mountain, where you glide through snow-clad evergreens (breathtaking!). If you just like great views, go up in the gondola to take in the spectacular topography of the region. Once you've gained the elevation, you don't need to descend immediately; there are excellent hiking trails and, again, don't forget your binoculars. Of course, if you want to go downhill skiing, this is the place.

Continue on by returning to Saint-Jovite and heading southeast to **Saint-Faustin** on Highway 117. Now turn north to Lac Supérieur toward gorgeous, wild **Parc du Mont-Tremblant**. Lac Supérieur is a pretty little village. Watch carefully, and after 3 kilometers you'll see a left turn to Mont Tremblant Park. On your right, after the turnoff, is a picturesque fieldstone B&B, called **La Marie Champagne** (654 chemin Lac Supérieur J0T 1J0; 819–688–3780). With its powder-blue tin roof, in traditional bell-shaped Québeçois style, it makes a pretty show in the meadows.

After 20 kilometers you enter the gates to Parc du Mont-Tremblant. Now drive a loop that takes you through two of the southernmost sectors of the park and out to St. Donat, a drive of less than 100 kilometers. As you go, you pass many hiking trails, waterfalls, and camping grounds. This park is a treasure. From remote lakes that offer superb wilderness canoeing to little walks just off the roadway, it offers tremendous natural beauty to every level of nature enthusiast. Keep your eyes peeled for wildlife. White-tail deer are common, as are raccoons, beavers, muskrats, red squirrels, and porcupines. Bears are around but less visible.

In the **Sector de Diable (Devil's Sector),** there's a *sentier* (trail) called **Le sentier du Toit-des-Laurentides** (Roof of the Laurentians Trail) whose trailhead is at the bridge called **Pont de la Sablonnière**, a couple of kilometers inside the park gate. A 15-kilometer round-trip hike, it takes six to seven hours and reaches an elevation of 935 meters. It leads to Mont Tremblant and, get this, you can descend the mountain by the gondola lift and explore Mont Tremblant Village this way. If you attempt this, be sure to find out how to deploy your vehicle. You may be able to stay overnight at Mont Tremblant Village, take the gondola back up the mountain, and return to your car the following day. Investigate by calling the park office at (819) 688-2281.

If that trail sounds like too much, drive on. At **Lac Monroe** there are lots of activities, including swimming, mountain biking, hiking, and boating. Lac Monroe also has handicapped access to swimming and there is quite a selection of campsites, both serviced and not. For those

Canada's Constitution Act of 1791 established Lower Canada (now Québec) and Upper Canada (Ontario). Québec City was the capital of Lower Canada.

of you who are driving on but want to quickly see some natural scenery, try the easy 800-meter walk to **Les Chutes du Diable (Devil's Waterfall).** Your reward comes as soon as you hear the rush of water, surely one of the most soothing sounds on earth.

None of the signs or park information pamphlets are in English, but everyone we spoke to was able to deal with our questions. All campsites should be reserved in summer's peak seasons in Parc du Mont-Tremblant, (819–688–2281 from May 11 through October 10 for reservations).

Stay on the main road and before long the **Saint-Donat** park gates appear. This loop through the park took us one hour and twenty minutes, which included the walk to Les Chutes du Diable. The road now becomes Highway 125; in ten minutes you arrive at **Saint-Donat,** where flags from all over the world lined the street when we passed through. This prosperous-looking town is thriving thanks to recreational tourism. (For information on Saint Donat's lodgings and attractions, check with the tourism office at 536 rue Principale; 888-Saint-Donat; it's also a good alternate number for information on Parc du Mont-Tremblant.) Traveling in winter? You can rent snowmobiles at **La Cuillère à Pot Sport** (67 route 329, J0T 2C0; 819–424–4761), where you'll find Québec-made Bombardiers, of course. There is an amazing network of trails in the park.

At Saint-Donat, **Lac Archambault** (819–424–2833) has a wonderful sandy beach, which is great for kids. You can also take a boat tour with

Strongest man in the world

*I*magine the scene on December 10, 1881: More than 10,000 spectators gasped in awe as strongman Louis Cyr dramatically held back a team of four straining workhorses with his bare hands. The stunning feat was only one of many, for he was truly a legend in his own time. A farm boy from Saint-Cyprien, Québec, Louis' strength enabled him to push a railway engine up an incline, lift a platform holding eighteen men whose combined weight was 4,300 pounds, and lift 588 pounds off the ground with one finger. Cyr impressed the world. Before his death at forty-nine in 1912, he thrilled spectators throughout the United States, England, and Europe, earning his title "the Canadian Sampson."

Les Belles Croisières du lac Archambault aboard the *Evelyne* (June through October departures at 10:30 A.M., and 1:30, 3:30, and 7:30 P.M.; call the Manoir des Laurentides, 290 rue Principale, J0T 2C0; 819–424–1710).

Our destination now is **Saint-Côme.** We're heading east again, to avoid the main route south to Montréal. It is 14 kilometers to **Notre-Dame-de-la-Merci.** Here are beautiful glimpses of the **Ouareau Forest** and a suspension bridge over the river that you can explore (for information, call 819–424–2113).

Pass Highway 329 Sud to Montréal and, after approximately ten minutes, watch for the church at Notre-Dame-de-la-Merci. Turn left; it is then 28 kilometers to Saint-Côme. After about 8 kilometers watch for a signed right-hand turn to Saint-Côme. Almost immediately there's a sheer rock cliff on your left. Take care on this winding road. Although spectacularly picturesque, it has soft shoulders and goes from paved to gravel surface a few times. Drive on, past the turnoff to Parc Chute à Bull, toward **Sainte-Émelie-de-l'Énergie.**

At the **Town Hall** (241 rue Coutu, Sainte-Émelie-de-l'Énergie; 450–886–3823), you'll find a rare collection of old photographs on the history of this village, which was nearly destroyed by fire in 1924. Note the surnames: Although many are French, other nationalities are represented through names like Bernhardt and Johnson. Nearby, opposite the park, find the blushing hot-pink **Auberge d'Emilie,** both an inn and restaurant.

Want to go on a pretty nature hike? Head north on Highway 131 until you reach Rang 4 (rural route 4). Turn right and park in the lot. At the **Matawinie Trail** and **Parc Vieux-Moulin** (information from the tourist office at 450–886–0688), you can view the seven waterfalls that cascade along the **Rivière Noire (Black River).**

Return to Highway 347 and after about 13 kilometers turn right onto Highway 131 South, where you'll drive 14 kilometers to **Saint-Jean-de-Matha.** This is the home town of Louis Cyr, known as the world's strongest man. His life and times are honored at the **Musée-halte Louis Cyr** (185 rue Laurent, J0K 2S0; 450–886–2777), directly behind the town hall. There's parking here as well as a tiny, beautiful garden complete with a gazebo where you can sit and admire the statue commemorating the competitive Cyr.

Go on to Rawdon, our destination. Continue south on Highway 131 for Highway 348 toward Sainte-Mélanie, driving through a broad, open valley. The long, low, gray, barn-like sheds are on poultry farms: This region is known for its turkeys. Past Sainte-Mélanie you'll note how

Joliette

Joliette is one of Montréal's "playground" destinations northeast of the metropolis. But there are some notable aspects to this town. First of all, during winter, you can skate for more than 4 kilometers on the Assomption River. Joliette is well-known for its early-July through early-August classical music festival called **Festival international de Lanaudière** *(1500 boulevard Base-de-Roc, Joliette J6E 3Z1; 800-363-1775; Web site: www.lanaudiere. org). Also of special note is the* **Musée d'art de Joliette,** *which houses a superb collection of Québec art (145 rue Wilfred Corbeil, Joliette 6JE 4T4; 450-756-0311; open in summer Tuesday through Sunday 11:00 A.M. to 5:00 P.M. and the rest of the year Wednesday through Sunday from noon to 5:00 P.M.; $4.00 adults, $3.00 seniors, $2.00 students and children).*

the topography has dramatically altered, from the rugged Mont Tremblant Park to beautiful rolling farmland. The land soon becomes almost flat: This is one of Québec's great agricultural regions. The lush pastureland of prosperous dairy farms, complete with lovely old farm houses—some with Second Empire–style mansard roofs—and tidy flower and vegetable gardens now predominate.

At **Rawdon,** a fabulous B&B awaits you, **Le Gîte du Catalpa** (3730 rue Queen, P.O. 1639, J0K 1S0; 450–834–5253; $35 to $50 single, $50 to $65 double, $10 for kids). The catalpa tree is also known as the tree of heaven. Its white and pink blossoms in mid-June are simply gorgeous, resembling chestnut blooms. Here you'll find Micheline (Mimi) Trudel—one of the most enchanting hostesses you could ever meet. Surely she's the queen of antique hunting, for her treasures are integrated everywhere into her 1842 farmhouse. Although it is situated in the midst of the village, the B&B has maintained its old-style charm. With its long and narrow, sheltered back garden, you feel as if you're in the country. If it's apple season, ask Mimi to show you the Montréal Peach apple tree, an old species that gives deliciously juicy yellow-to-apricot-colored fruit. Every room is a treasure. We stayed in the Victorian chamber, as romantic as it is secluded. And, while we're on the topic of delicious treasures, you'll be delighted by Mimi's incredible five-course breakfast, all served to you in antique dishes that she's picked up in her flea-market forays.

Rawdon is intriguing. It was settled by the English in the early 1800s and later, in the 1920s, by Russians fleeing their homeland. Instead of seeing only the predictably immense Roman Catholic Church, there are also Anglican, United, and other denomination edifices. Before leaving town, visit **Parc des Chutes Dorwin (Dorwin Falls Park)** (off Route 337; 450–834–2282; fax: 450–834–3084; $2.00 adults, age 11 and under $2.00, parking $2.00; May through October open daily 9:00 A.M. to 7:00 P.M. The falls take their name from the family who owned the property. Unbelievably, people actually jump for sport from these cliffs, into the boiling waters. Please don't try. The 2.5 kilometers of trails are part of an ecological reserve; a brochure explains thirty woodland species of trees and plants.

For an unforgettable dining experience, go to *Au Parfum de la Nature* (6703 chemin Pontbriand, J0K 1S0; 450–834–4547; fax 450–834–4547; open Tuesday through Friday 5:00 to 10:00 P.M., Saturday and Sunday 11:00 A.M. to 10:00 P.M., closed Monday; groups of 4 to 30). This is an intimate concept, where you actually have your meal in chef Bruno Gagné's home, set in a wooded glade. You must book ahead at least two weeks in advance. Bruno will discuss the menu with you—he features local produce and game like pheasant and guinea-hen—and he buys the ingredients from the local farmers' market. He doesn't have a liquor licence, but as in many Québec restaurants, you can *Apportez votre vin*—bring your own wine. Consult with Bruno to see what he would recommend, and ask about our Québec wines.

Now drive toward Montréal on Highway 337 Sud. You pass many flea markets and market gardens en route through this flat, agriculturally rich countryside. The road becomes Autoroute 25. Pass the exit to Mascouche and watch now for exit 22 east for *Terrebonne*. Terrebonne is a pre-industrial cultural center on *L'Île des Moulins (Island of Mills)*. It is a "village," or collection of nineteenth-century buildings, such as the 1846 flour mill, 1850 seigneurial office, and an 1803 bakery. Wander its streets, and relive pre-industrial French Canadian life (for information, call 450–471–0619).

Return to Highway 25 Sud and scoot back to Montréal.

Calixa Lavalée

Québec musician Calixa Lavalée composed the music for our Canadian National Anthem. Lavalée had just returned to Montréal after serving with the 4th Rhode Island Regiment band during the American Civil War.

PLACES TO STAY IN MONTRÉAL

McGill University residence rooms can be rented; some have great views over Mont Royal and have kitchenettes, refrigerators etc.; 550 Sherbrooke Ouest, West Tower, Suite 490, Montréal H3A 1B9; (514) 398-3770; e-mail: Reserve@Residences.Ian.Mcgill.ca

Les passants du Sans Soucy Auberge B&B, 171 Ouest, rue St-Paul, Vieux-Montreal H2Y 1Z5; (514) 842-2634

Hôtel Auberge Universel Montréal is near Olympic stadium at Viau Métro, cinemas, and malls (good for kids!); 5000 Sherbrooke Est, H1V 1A1; (800) 567-0223 or (514) 253-3365; fax (514) 253-9958; Web site: interresa.ca/hotel/universl

Montréal Oasis B&B; 3000 chemin de Breslay, Montreal H3Y 2G7; (514) 935-2312; fax (514) 875-6270; e-mail: Lena.Foss@quel.hexacom.montreal.qc.ca

Mont Tremblant Village, 3005 chemin Principal, Mont-Tremblant J0T 1Z0; (819) 681-5661 (arrange unusual but fabulous accommodation such as a condo on the mountainside)

PLACES TO EAT IN MONTRÉAL

(All area codes 514)

Schwartz' Montréal Hebrew Delicatessen at 3895 boulevard Saint-Laurent, 842-4813 serves absolutely the best smoked meat. You don't go for the decor; you do go for excellent food. Otherwise, try *The Main* (3864 blvd. St. Laurent; 843-8126), where the meat is marinated and smoked on the premises.

Binerie Mont-Royal serves *fèves au lard* (baked beans), otherwise called "binnes," at 367 avenue Mont-Royal Est, Montréal; 285-9078.

Chez Clo is a typical Montréal neighborhood restaurant with loyal local clientele; try the *tourtière*, a ground meat specialty. 3199 rue Ontario est, Montreal; 514-522-5348; daily 6:00 A.M. to 11:00 P.M.

Globe (3455 blvd. St-Laurent, Montreal; 284-3823) has simply outstanding fare in a trendy restaurant—try the lamb salad!

For an inexpensive Greek meal, try the delicious chicken souvlakis at *Arahova* just east of Avenue du Parc (256 Saint-Viateur West, Montreal; 514-274-7828). The nearby *Psaropoula Restaurant* (5258 avenue du Parc, Montreal; 271-2130) is more expensive but has a wider selection and excellent table d'hôte.

The Eastern Townships

The Eastern Townships lie south of the St. Lawrence River between Montréal and Québec City. We'll explore this region using Montréal as the starting point, heading east through a historic area of Québec known as Montérégie before plunging into the environs known as L'Estrie, or the Eastern Townships.

The Richelieu River flows north from Lake Champlain through the heart of Montérégie. This was a historic water route, its strategic importance underscored by a series of forts such as Fort Chambly, built by the French in 1665 to protect the city of Montréal from their fierce enemies, the Iroquois. Farther south, the star-shaped Fort Lennox was originally French; it too fell to the British, and briefly to the Americans.

This region strongly reflects the passions of patriotism throughout the centuries. After the Americans declared independence in 1776, hundreds of immigrants streamed north to settle in a country still governed by Britain. These were the United Empire Loyalists and, during your explorations of this area, you'll see many houses and buildings reflecting colonial American architecture. As we drive some of the scenic back roads, we'll hug the American border south and east of Frelighsburg.

In the 1800s, another influx of immigrants came to the New Land. After Northern Ireland became part of the United Kingdom, many Irish families crossed the Atlantic to settle here. Twenty years later, another Irish "invasion" occurred—but this time the potato famine spurred their departure from home.

In 1837, French patriotism flared in rebellion against British rule. The Maison nationale des patriotes (Museum of the Patriots) in Saint-Denis honors the memory of French Canadian freedom fighters. By the 1860s, many French Canadians lived in this region because so many of them worked in the lumber, agricultural, and railway industries. As the

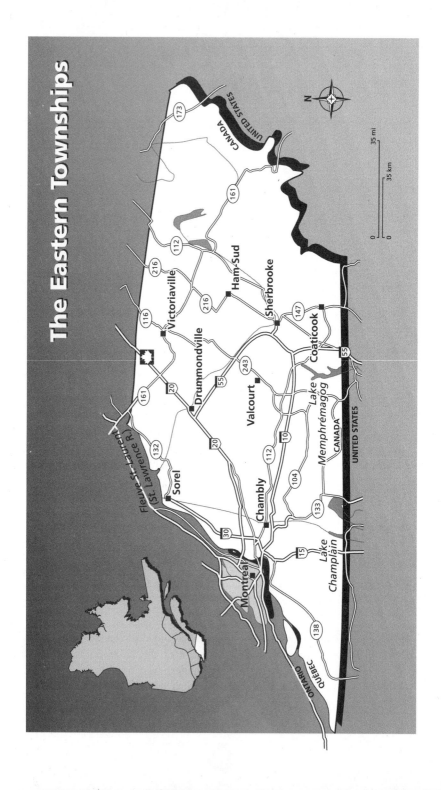

The Eastern Townships

demographics shifted, with a greater proportion of French-speaking inhabitants toward the end of the nineteenth century, the region started to become known as L'Estrie, or the Cantons-de-l'Est, the Eastern Townships).

Traveling through this region today is delightful. An increasingly easy rapport between national and ethnic mixes is discernible here. People of American, French, and British ancestry rub shoulders amicably. And as you discover the pastoral beauty of this area, it is easy to understand why settlers would flock here, for this is a rich agricultural land. Orchards full of blossoms that turn to crisp, tangy apples in fall, ripe for the picking, will surely beckon you. Grand, historic lakes and rivers offer themselves for recreation.

In Montérégie, strange cone-like "mountains" erupt from the otherwise flat valley floor. These mountains are Cretaceous igneous plugs that forced their way into fissures in the limestone that forms the valley floor. When the softer sedimentary limestone eroded, the harder igneous rock remained exposed. At 416 meters, Mont-Saint-Hilaire is the highest of these remarkable formations. Once part of the Gault Estate, a large part of it was designated as a bird sanctuary in 1952 and six years later was bequeathed to McGill University of Montréal (less than an hour away). In 1978 it became an international biosphere reserve.

As you can see, it's a diverse region, so let's not waste any more time. We'll start out from Montréal right now.

The Richelieu River Environs

n Montréal, get on Highway 20 East and drive to **Mont-Saint-Hilaire,** about 24 kilometers, then turn south on Highway 133 toward Otterburn Park. Whether it is winter or summer, **Centre de conservation de la nature du Mont Saint Hilaire (Nature Conservation Center)** beckons with a network of 22 kilometers of hiking or skiing trails on this, the first UNESCO biosphere reserve in Canada. The mountain offers outstanding examples of the vegetation that once covered 90 percent of western Québec but which is now reduced to 17 percent. Biologists have recorded eighty-five species of birds nesting in the mixed deciduous/coniferous woods, so bring your binoculars along. (The center is at 422 chemin des Moulins, Mont-Saint-Hilaire J3G 4S6; (450) 467–1755.)

Proceed now down the *Chemin des Patriotes* on the east side of the Richelieu River. We're going to satisfy our passion for sensational Belgian chocolate now. Are you with us? Once in *Otterburn Park,* turn left on Rue Prince Albert, then left again to find *La Cabosse d'Or Chocolaterie* (973 Ozias Leduc, Otterburn Park J3G 4S6; 450–464–6937; fax 450–464–9933; Web site: www.cabossedor.qc.ca). Before indulging, try the mini-golf course celebrating and explaining the history of chocolate. The Belgian proprietor of this chocolaterie, Martine Crowin, told us that four times a year, she imports five-ton blocks of Belgian chocolate. We can tell you that the chocolate milkshakes are richly and darkly outstanding.

From here, proceed north along Chemin Ozias Leduc and turn right onto Chemin de la Montagne, which hugs the base of the mountain. We're en route to *Cidrerie du Verger Gaston* (1074 chemin de la Montagne, Mont-Sainte-Hilare J3G 4S6; 450–446–2552; fax 450–446–2485). Not only is this a working orchard and cider-making operation, it also is one of Québec's économusées. Like most, there are no written explanations in English. But many of the implements, such as the apple press, are self-explanatory and the helpful staff can answer questions. Don't leave without tasting the cider. There's sparkling juice; then a dry, light cider that is 7.4 percent alcohol; and also a *pommeau,* which is a sweeter, heavier aperitif with 17 percent alcohol content. Buy now and drink later, after you've finished driving. Try some of the other delicious apple products, too. We loved the cider mustard, the apple syrup (divine on pancakes), and apple jelly.

Now that you're full of chocolate and apple delights, continue along the Chemin de la Montagne. You now enter the Rougemont area, noted for its orchards. In 1913 the co-op started, and by 1926 there were twenty-seven orchards here. You'll note that many, like the Cidrerie du Verger Gaston, are organic. Others, termed *ecologique,* do use some chemicals. We traveled these roads in June when we could just see baby apples starting to plump up. We can only imagine the

---

Day Trip Up the Richelieu River

Explore the northern section of the Richelieu River to where it joins the St. Lawrence at Sorel by following Highways 133 and 233 along its banks. Be sure to stop at **Maison nationale des patriotes** *in Saint-Denis (610 chemin des Patriotes, Saint-Denis J0H 1K0; 450–787–3623). This village is the site of the only victory enjoyed by the patriots in the Rebellion of 1837. It is a place of pilgrimage for those who want to learn about the nationalist movement in Québec.*

sight and fragrance here in this gentle valley when trees are blossoming. It's hard to say whether a trip would be best in spring or during autumn's harvest.

You'll turn right briefly on Highway 227 and then make almost an immediate left onto Rue Rougemont. The ice storm of January 1998 was extremely severe here, leaving people without electricity for five to six weeks. You can imagine how devastating six inches of ice buildup on the trees was. All around as we drove here in the summer of 1998, the shattered remains of once-lovely forests and ornamental trees were a sad sight. Because they are pruned to be weight-bearing, many of the orchards were relatively unscathed, however.

Continue to **Rougemont,** named after Sir Étienne Rougemont, who left La Rochelle in France in 1665 on the ship *Justice* to fight the Iroquois here. As you enter this village, you will note many signs of the English, Irish, and Scottish settlers. As in Otterburn Park, many of the street names are English, and St. Thomas Anglican Church dates back to 1840.

Find the Rougemont Tourist Information Center (11 chemin Marieville; 450–469–3600; fax 450–469–0175). Helpful staff here had trouble with

English but, with persistence and good will, lots of information was obtained. Ask for pamphlets in English, including the "Richelieu Valley Tourist Guide" and the day-trip guide called "A Day in the Valley." Cider is not the only product grown and produced here in the Richelieu Valley: The staff will be happy to give you details about the *route des vins* (wine route) too.

Outside the center is a small **demonstration orchard** with a walking circuit where old varieties of apples are being grown. Apples were first brought to Québec in 1617 by Louis Hébert, and the first orchards of any size were managed by monks on Mont Royal in 1650. Some of the old apple varieties are delightful. See if you can find Honey Gold, Lubsk Queen (from Russia), and the Ladi, or Lady, named because its taste was supposedly "just as lovely as the kiss of a beautiful woman."

For something completely different, turn left onto Chemin Petite Caroline to find the *atelier*, or studio, of the intriguing artist **Claude Gagnon** (245 Petite Caroline, Rougemont J0L 1M0; 450–469–1148). Her studio is unmistakable: it's the only brilliant purple barn you'll find on the road. Step inside to discover this amazing woman's allegories, peopled by characters she knows and themes that are universal, such as war and love. This atelier must not be missed. Claude herself will probably be there and is delightfully chatty. Her self-portrait hangs on the central chimney, dressed for renovation work and clutching a chainsaw.

As an interesting contrast to the previous *cidrerie,* continue along Chemin Petite Caroline to **Cidrerie artisanale Michel Jodoin** (1130 Petite Caroline, Rougemont J0L 1M0; 450–469–2676; fax 450–469–1286), where the cider is aged in the old style, in oak casks. We enjoyed a superb tour of the welcoming coolness of the aging cave before sampling the delicious ciders.

Then proceed on this road, doing an abrupt turn at its end to return to Route 112 on Chemin Grande Caroline. For yet another apple product—

The studio of artist Claude Gagnon

THE EASTERN TOWNSHIPS

albeit less appealing to taste—we recommend a stop at *Verger Pierre Gingras*, which makes cider vinegar (1132 Grande Caroline, J0L 1M0; 450–469–4954).

Press on to Chambly. To get to this gorgeous historic town, head west on Highway 112 through Marieville and Richelieu. Cross the bridge at the opening of the river to the Bassin de Chambly (Chambly Basin), which forms a picturesque lake.

Our destination is *Fort Chambly* (2 rue de Richelieu, Chambly J3L 2B9; 450–658–1585; fax 450–658–7216). Operated by the federal Parks Canada, this historic site is bilingually interpreted. Fluent guides will give you a superb tour, and you can get insightful answers to your questions. Don't miss Fort Chambly, and do ask for the English video. You can discover all sorts of things about American and Canadian politics and about the patriot and separatist movements in this province. Whatever the settlers' backgrounds, they were passionate about their roots. Today, we reap the harvest of such sentiments—just as we reap our delicious Québec apples.

Although first constructed of wood by Jacques de Chambly of France in 1665, the fort was rebuilt in stone by the French in 1709 to protect themselves from the British army's cannon artillery. The fort succumbed to British attack on September 1, 1760; in the American invasion of 1775 it fell into U.S. hands, but they lost it again to the British the following year. During the War of 1812, the British increased their fortifications here, but by 1870 they closed it. A local resident, Joseph-Octave Dion, recognized the historical significance of the fort and, after getting federal funding to restore its walls, actually lived inside the fort until he died in 1916. A remarkable historian, he was the fort's first curator.

Is all this history revving up a thirst? Head to the *Unibroue Brewery* (80 Des Carrières, Chambly J3L 2H6; 450–658–7658; fax 450–658–9195; Web site: www.unibroue.com/indexa.htm). Arrange a tour and you'll not be disappointed. This young brewery is making quite a mark in Québec and further afield with its selection of natural beers. Their bottle labels are dramatic, inspired by Québec history and folk tales. You'll recognize an old painting of Fort Chambly on the label of their Blanche de Chambly beer.

You must be ready to sit down and enjoy a French Canadian meal. We heartily recommend dining at *Fourquet Fourchette,* a restaurant and beer interpretation center (1887 rue Bourgogne, Chambly J3L 1Y8;

450–447–6370; fax 450–447–3032). The food is superb. All is prepared with beer and is presented by servers dressed in old-fashioned costumes. Outside is a patio overlooking a garden with hops and herbs used in beer brewing. Beyond the patio is the Richelieu Basin, and in the near distance you'll spy Fort Chambly. Try some of the fresh, ripe cheeses made from raw milk, real local specialties. We also enjoyed heart of bulrush, and we're convinced you will too.

Black Robes

Jesuit priests were called black robes because of their flowing garments. The movie Black Robe *tells a story of the Jesuits. You can see the movie set and animated depictions of Jesuit and native life at the Site de la Nouvelle France (Site of New France) near Saint-Félix-d'Otis.*

We also discovered a B&B, with a great view of the river, called *L'Air du Temps,* operated by the entirely delightful Lucie Chrétien (124 rue Martel, Chambly J3L 1V3; 450–658–1642; fax 450–658–2830; toll-free 888–658–1642; Web site: www.clasalle.qc.ca/airtempf.html). When we arrived, it was a sweltering 30 degrees Celsius. Our only complaint was that there was no air-conditioner that day, but you might be fortunate and not arrive in a heat wave. Lucie is sweetness itself, and the amount of work she completed to create this B&B is remarkable. She and her husband bought the old house May 18, 1998, and opened the B&B on June 29. Wow! Stroll down to the river in the evening to take in the sunset. If you are boating, you can tie up at their dock.

Drive south on Highway 223, where you will see sections of the *Chambly Canal* as you drive along the west bank of the Richelieu. Built between 1831 and 1843 by over five hundred workmen, the canal was constructed to improve trade between Lower Canada and the New England states. Until 1910, barges plied the waters, heading south with Canadian lumber and agricultural products and returning from the States with coal. But by that year, road and rail transportation gained supremacy, and by the 1970s, recreational boating took over.

Along this 19-kilometer canal extending from Chambly to *Saint-Jean-sur-Richelieu,* you'll find a good, paved *bike path*. This southernmost entry to the canal sports a Victorian charm. Cafés, such as *Le Mannekin-Pis* (320 rue Champlain; 450–348–3254), directly opposite the locks, look inviting for a patio pick-me-up. The bike path, which follows the old towpath used by horses when they pulled the barges, is almost flat, so it's a great spot for kids or those who simply want a leisurely tour. Note the "islands" defining the canal channel, which attest to the soil and fill those five hundred men dug with their pickaxes and shovels. You can park your car at the northern end of the canal, at *Parc des Ateliers* (1840 Bourgogne Avenue, Chambly).

Stay south on Highway 223 to the town of Saint-Paul-de-l'Île-aux-Noix, named for the annuity that Pierre Jourdanet had to pay his seigneur: a bag of walnuts. Our destination here is **Fort Lennox** (at No. 1 61st Avenue, J0J 1G0; 450–291–5700), a star-shaped British island fort and one of the four defense posts on the Richelieu. The first fort here was built by the French, who lost it during the siege of Saint-Paul-de-l'Ile-aux-Noix in 1760. During the American occupation of 1775, American General Shulyer used it as his base of operations for his attack on Montréal. A year later the Americans retreated, and the fort became the most southerly defended spot on the Richelieu. The British refortified it and, between 1819 and 1823, did so again. It was at this time they named it Fort Lennox after the Duke of Richmond, Charles Lennox, who died in 1819 after a rabid fox bit him. The British feared an American invasion from Lake Champlain and so decided to construct shipyards here, too, but after many years of peace, they closed the fort in 1834. Concurrent to this was the opening of the Chambly Canal.

Note the huge marinas on a big turnaround cut directly northwest of the fort. People boat upriver from New York, navigating the Hudson River, Lake Champlain, and finally the Richelieu River, following in the footsteps of such settlers as Philemon Wright, the American who founded the Québec town of Hull.

Continue south on Highway 223, passing flat fields full of strawberry farms where you can pick your own in season (June). Stop at the **Blockhouse** at Lacelle, approximately 8 kilometers south of Fort Lennox. It's the only surviving original blockhouse in Québec and houses a particularly excellent hands-on collection of artifacts that will get adults and kids thinking about our military past. Look for the musket-ball holes in the blockhouse wall.

A bit farther south, turn left onto Route 202 toward Noyan. As you cross over the Richelieu River, look down on the tops of trees in the woods devastated by the 1998 ice storm. The resort town of **Venise-en-Québec** is situated on the north end of Lake Champlain, with many campgrounds and wall-to-wall RVs. Some beach campgrounds, like the **Domaine Florent** (272 avenue 23 Est, J0J 2K0; 450–244–5607) have wheelchair access, a pool, and washers and dryers for clothes.

> ## Breweries
>
> *Englishman John Molson came to Montréal in 1782 and founded a family of brewers and bankers. He established his first brewery at St. Mary's Current in the harbor of Montréal. Molson also introduced steam navigation to the St. Lawrence in 1809. Eventually his steamers plied the Ottawa and St. Lawrence Rivers, as well as the Great Lakes.*

Loyalist Country

During the course of the revolution between the British and their American colonists (1775–1783), thousands of British crown Loyalists avoided persecution or worse by fleeing north to the Canadian Colonies, settling primarily along the southern borders of the Southern Ontario, the Gaspé region, and Québec. In 1789 Lord Dorchester, the governor-in-chief of British North America, proclaimed that those who had crossed into Canada during the war should be called United Empire Loyalists (UEL) to honor their support of the crown. This area, close to the current U.S.–Canadian border, is home to many descendents of UEL settlers, living in little tidy towns like Frelighsburg and Stanbridge East.

To get there, continue east along Highway 202 through Pike River and Bedford to **Stanbridge East.** En route you drive through flat farmland filled with corn and poultry barns. Note all the names with Belgian, Swiss, Polish, and Dutch origins on the mailboxes, and the street in Bedford called Rue Dutch. About 5 kilometers east of Bedford, watch for signs to Stanbridge East; you'll turn left (north) to jog up to this town with its beautiful Gothic church.

Musée Missisquoi

In Stanbridge East, be sure to visit **Missisquoi Museum** (2 River Street, Stanbridge East J0J 2H0; 450–248–3153). This is a real treasure with three different buildings. The Cornell Mill is an 1830 brick structure housing the main collection as well as an exhibit that is changed annually. Up the street is the old-time country store operated by the Hodge family for seventy-seven years—still jammed full of original merchandise. Still farther up Main Street is the Annex, where interesting old farm machinery has found a home. Museum staff are English-speaking and extraordinarily helpful. Stay for a picnic and find the old cannon in the mill's park that was hauled out of the Richelieu River. Note that the Missisquoi Historical Society is old for Canada: It was founded in 1898 and is often approached by genealogists searching for family records.

Go southeast to Frelighsburg on Highway 237, which continues to the U.S. border. Stop in *Frelighsburg's General Store:* We defy you to find better maple syrup pies. How we managed to stop at only one tart each remains a mystery. Wander behind the store to eat yours on the bank of the stream. Look left here to spy the old mill built in 1839, now a private home. Beyond the village, hiking trails to nearby Pinnacle Mountain will reward you with good views over the undulating farmland. This area is well-known for its local artisans' work and has an art festival called *Festivart* on Labor Day weekend (first weekend in September).

Just south of the village, turn southeast toward Abercorn on the Richford Road, surely one of the most beautiful country roads you could ever find. Stop at the kiosk-like, sleepy *border station* on Chemin de la frontière (Frontier Road), where the lone customs officer on duty seemed to welcome our brief visit and chat. Ahead of you is the U.S., but turn left here and slowly drive along this lovely border road. Off in the distance, you'll see our peaceful, shared border cut through the wood-clad hills. Especially because of all the wars and skirmishes in our shared past, it's a good time to reflect on our peacefully shared present.

You eventually connect with Highway 101 Nord to Abercorn, getting splendid views to the south of the Appalachian's Green Mountains as you go. At Abercorn, turn east again onto the well-named Chemin Scenic for the 11-kilometers or so to Glen Sutton. The road becomes even prettier—if that's possible—following the broad Rivière Missisquoi on your right. At Glen Sutton you pass the inviting *Auberge Glen Sutton* (1388 Dela Vallee Missisquoi; 450–538–2000). You can eat here, rest up, and head off, invigorated.

Continue to tiny *Dunkin,* settled in 1798 by Colonel Hendrick Ruiter, who came here from New York after the American Revolution due to his loyalty to the British. He was granted 2,400 acres of land and, with the

Divine Diva

Céline Dion is presently one of Canada's greatest singers. The youngest of fourteen children, she was born in Charlemagne, just east of Montréal. At twelve, she composed her first song, "Ce n'était qu'un rêvé" ("It Was Only a Dream") and sent the recording to Rene Angelil, who "discovered" her. He mortgaged his home to underwrite her debut. It started an impressive list of accomplishments including, in 1983, her winning gold-record status in France—the first Canadian to achieve this. In 1994 at Montréal's Notre Dame Basilica, Angelil and Dion were married in what was a "royal-caliber wedding."

help of his large family, set to clearing the bush and building the first grist- and sawmill.

Proceed on Route 243 toward Mansonville in Potton township, just a few miles from the Vermont border. Colonel Ruiter sold this part of his land to John Lewis and Joseph Chandler, who built a sawmill here, then sold it to Robert Manson in 1811.

We've been traveling on beautiful side roads through old hamlets. *Mansonville* is completely different as it caters to the Mont Owl Head ski area just west of Lake Memphremagog. Find the *Mansonville Museum,* operated by the Association du patrimoine de Potton (Potton Heritage Association) in the 1850 *Reilly House.* A multifunctional abode, it houses a local museum, realty office, tea room, and the *Tourist Office of Mansonville* (302 rue Principale, P.O. Box 375, J0E 1X0; 450–292–3109). Brochures on historical facts about this region are available here and staff members are bilingual. If you are interested in biking and hiking, stop here first to get brochures like "Cyclo-Route Potton," about a well-interpreted 28-kilometer bike route.

At the Mansonville Museum you'll find all sorts of intriguing if not perplexing items, including a supposedly ancient, fanciful lion's head (we thought it looked more like a dragon's head) that was reputedly found in the area. Tall tales as well as intriguing archaeological finds and postulations reside here, and they're fun.

White Indians?

*T*he Mansonville Museum is really thought-provoking. Look for the brochure written by Gérard Leduc called *Arkeo Potton: The Fingerprints of a Lost Culture in the Eastern Townships. Leduc claims that petroglyphs (writing on stone), stone cairns with quartz rocks placed at their summit, and many other archaeological finds prove there was a permanent, not nomadic, native culture here. More than this, Leduc conjectures that this group was a caucasoid (white and European-based) group. "What happened to these White* Indians?" *Leduc asks. He postulates: "Native Americans have themselves reportedly told early European settlers that the stone builders were white people and that they had been exterminated by Red Indians."*

Leduc claims that in the woods and meadows surrounding Mansonville, there are several ancient sites built, among other things, to celebrate the solstice. To inquire about how to see the sites that are on private property, contact the Tourist Office of Mansonville.

Visit an Abbey

*A*t Bolton East, take a side trip on Chemin Bolton-Est toward Austin, then follow the signs southeast to the **Abbey Saint-Benoît-du-lac**, operated by Benedictine monks. There is a daily Eucharist where you can hear Gregorian chant at 11:00 A.M. as well as evening Vespers starting at 5:00 P.M., except for Thursdays, when it starts at 7:00 P.M. The Abbey itself is a collection of different architectural styles. Parts were built by the internationally celebrated French Benedictine architect Dom Paul Bellot (1876–1944). Situated near Lake Memphremagog on its west bank, the Abbey commands a splendid view and is a noted landmark. Its gift shop not only sells recordings of the chants but also the cheese and cider made here by the monks. It's open from 9:00–10:45 A.M. and 2:00–4:30 P.M.; closed Sunday.

Want to stay in this most peaceful of surroundings? You can. There's a men's guest-house retreat on site, and women can stay nearby at a home operated by nuns. Men stay for free, women have to pay. Go figure. You must reserve by calling (819) 843–4080.

Now continue up Rue Principale and, opposite the Catholic Church, find the circa 1910 round barn. Folklore dictates that such barns were circular so the devil couldn't hide in the corners. Round barns were first introduced in North America by the Shakers, who built one in 1865 in Hancock, Massachusetts. Shakers considered circles the perfect form. Moreover, four-cornered structures were also supposed to sap energy from living beings, either man or beast. Hence, round barns were considered less stressful.

Proceed up Highway 243 Nord to South Bolton. The road still hugs the Missisquoi River. On your right look for Sugar Loaf Mountain, so named because settlers bought slices of sugar cut from a pressed "sugarloaf." It's astonishing shape and dramatic elevation make it a famous landmark of this area, lying on the west bank of Lac Memphremagog.

This region was known for its copper mines, a railway, cheese factory, and bobbin mills, the last of which closed in 1995. But don't for a minute think it has the look of a stolid, dilapidated major industrial region. **South Bolton** is very pretty. Once known as Rexford's Corner, the village is distinguished by many lovely buildings, including the 1832 schoolhouse. **Bolton Centre**, 5 kilometers north, was settled by Loyalists, and both the 1866 United and 1875 St. Patrick's Anglican Churches are beautiful. Stop and wander around on foot.

Take Highway 243 North from Bolton Centre toward Eastman. As you drive, you'll see the Western side of Mont Orford, one of the major ski centers in this region. Cross the autoroute into Eastman, then turn right on Highway 112. Watch for a left turn onto Chemin Georges-Bonnalie, which goes north to Highway 220, where you turn left, west, to Bonnesecours.

Mordecai Richler

Controversial novelist and columnist Mordecai Richler pokes fun at Canadians with his sardonic wit and oft-berating style. A Montréaler, Richler needles separatists and federalists alike with logic and humor. His book Oh Canada! Oh Québec! Requiem for a Divided Country *is mandatory reading for anyone trying to get an insider's look into "the language question." Meanwhile, his many acclaimed novels, including* The Apprenticeship of Duddy Kravitz, *are part of high-school and university curricula.*

At Bonnesecours turn right on Rue de l'Église to drive 6 kilometers to **Mines Cristal Kébec** (the Crystal Sanctuary) (430 Rang 11, Bonsecours J0E 1H0; 450–535–6550; fax 450–535–6694). Continue on this gravel road past Lawrenceville until the T intersection with Rang (rural route) 11, where you turn right and follow blue signs to these "new age" mines, supposedly the only ones in Canada that produce top-quality quartz crystal. In the gift shop, you can purchase crystals and read about the mines' discovery in 1959 by farmer Gerard Adam, who was curious about the sparkling stones in his fields. Today's operation was started by Gaudry Normand in 1989. His brochure says "Our hope is that, by freeing the crystals from the dark underground, the ancient knowledge of quartz energy may be brought to light." Many believe that crystals transform and focus energies. For $6.00 you can take a 90-minute tour, but call first to confirm timing as it fluctuates seasonally.

Let's proceed now to a different type of power. We're headed to **Valcourt**. Drive east on Rang 11 to reconnect with Highway 243 North, then watch for Rang 4, which is a signed left-hand turn to Valcourt. Follow the blue signs to Valcourt, where winter and sport are celebrated at the museum that honors the inventor of the snowmobile. This is the **J. Armand Bombardier Museum** (1001 J. A. Bombardier Avenue, Valcourt J0E 2L0; 450–532–5300; fax 450–532–2260; Web site: www.ucctech.com/museejab/jabhom_e.htm).

This high-tech museum tells of Bombardier, a Valcourt boy who doggedly pursued his dream of creating a machine that could give ease and comfort to travel during the long Canadian winter. The museum chronicles the development of the original dangerous, but exciting, machines. They had open propellers in the rear, no brakes, and couldn't back up: yikes! Bombardier technology is also credited with the Montréal Métro subway cars and the trains for the Chunnel linking France with England. Attached to the museum is this gentle family man's original workshop, a white- and red-trimmed garage that quaintly defines the man himself. The guides are passionate in their admiration and love of this man, who died in 1964. And no truck is given to any "greenie," or environmentalist, who might murmur that the machines are bad for the environment. After all, Bombardier is the employer of this region and, when environmental issues raised their "ugly" heads, production plummeted and the townsfolk were unimpressed.

Because snowmobiling is banned in most of Europe, many tourists come to Québec for this winter sport. The Eastern Townships have a network of more than 2,000 kilometers of snowmobile trails. For snowmobile rentals, contact *Centre de la motoneige enr* (9060 de la Montagne, Valcourt; 450–532–2262). Want to find out about Québec's entire network of trails? Contact the *Québec Federation of Snowmobiling Clubs* (4545 avenue Pierre-de-Coubertin, P.O. Box 1000, Station M, Montréal H1V 3R2).

Drive east from Valcourt, passing the gigantic Bombardier plant, to rejoin Highway 243. Turn north toward Melbourne for about 20 kilometers to a museum that explains the heritage and geology of nearby slate quarries. As you drive, you'll notice not only roofs of slate but also slate outcrops at the roadside. The museum was recently moved from the pretty village of Kingsbury (many brochures still say it's at this gorgeous little village) to *Melbourne.* To get to the museum, pass Highway 55 to Drummondville, drive to the end of Highway 243, and turn left at Rivière Saint-François onto Chemin de la Rivière. Turn left again on Rue Belmont to find the 1853 church, home of the *Slate Study Center* (5 rue Belmont, Melbourne; 819–826–3313). The roof of this red brick church is slate and, at the rear, is an example of how roofs are constructed of these slate "shingles."

Watch for more slate outcrops as you proceed northeast via Highway 116 Est through dairy farms and cornfields to Danville, where the Victorian architecture is simply breathtaking. Old homes are obviously cherished here. You'll find gaily painted Queen Anne–style houses with whimsical massing and turrets. Of the four Protestant churches, one has been converted into a restaurant that serves regional cuisine. *Le Temps des Cerises,* in an olive-coloured clapboard church, serves Danville lamb as well as caribou (79 rue du Carmel, Danville J0A 1A0; 800–839–2818).

Claude Jutra

Born in Montréal in 1930, Claude Jutra was one of the province's most accomplished and beloved filmmakers. His 1971 movie Mon oncle Antoine, *set in a little Québec town on Christmas Eve, portrays the journey of a youth to manhood. Tragically, this leader of Canadian filmmaking disappeared in November 1986, only to be found drowned five months later in the St. Lawrence River at Cap-Santé.*

Pauline Julien

A singer, actress, and song-writer, Pauline Julien was born in Trois-Rivières in 1928. She studied in Paris in the 1950s and, upon her return to Canada, intro-duced the songs of Berthold Brecht and Kurt Weill to Québecers. Soon she started to sing the songs of Québec songwriters Gilles Vigneault and Raymond Lévesque. An ardent femi-nist, she began writing her own lyrics in 1968.

Take a sidetrip east of Danville on Highway 255 to *Asbestos,* which has one of the world's largest open-pit mines. You can't miss the gigantic 200-ton truck by the side of the road. Its monstrous size becomes dwarfed by the mine, however. From the nearby roadside viewing platform, which lets you peer into the mine, you appreciate how distance, combined with the vastness of the open pit, combine to make these giants look like Dinky toys. Tours of the *Johns Manville Asbestos Mine* are available, but times vary by season, so call ahead (819–839–2911).

Scoot back onto Highway 255 to rejoin Route 116 and head 9 kilometers north to *Kingsey Falls* and *Parc Marie-Victorin* (385 rue Marie-Victorin, Kingsey Falls J0A 1B0; 819–363–2528). Named after a famous botanist, the 22-acre park has bird and medicinal plant gardens. All printed information is in French, but if you are a gardener, it's an interesting place to go to get ideas on landscaping and plants.

Kingsey Falls was founded in 1886 and named after a village in Oxford county, England. Early on, the first settlers built a flour- and sawmill on the banks of the Nicolet River, taking advantage of the waterfalls. Later, a paper mill was built, and today Kingsey Falls is home to its descendant, *Les Industries Cascade Inc.,* the largest paper recycling center in Canada. (In fact, the garden benches at Parc Marie-Victorin are composed of recycled materials.) Find Cascade Inc. beside the gardens. Admission is part of the gardens tour, and a convenient walkway over the Nicolet River takes you to the plant. Also ask at the gardens for information about the 19-kilometer canoe ride down the Nicolet. Admission to the Parc Marie-Victorin, Cascade Inc., the canoe ride, and an evening supper-theater put on by *Théâtre des Grands Chênes* (Theatre of the Great Oaks) varies depending on the package you buy.

Now drive north on Highway 116 through Warwick to *Victoriaville.* Notice how many names here are very English. Although one franco-phone resident of Danville insisted they were of aboriginal derivation, all are British. Don't miss visiting the exceptional *Économusée de cuir (Leather Museum)* (857 boulevard Bois-Francs Sud, Arthabaska, a sub-urb of Victoriaville, G6P 5W1; 819–357–3138). Inside you will find an assortment of intriguing displays, including samples of hide from crea-tures as odd as a frog. The craftspeople inside will explain the difference between real alligator (or ostrich) hide and stamped imitations, and you'll also see *cuir haché*—reconstituted leather made of pieces of hide bonded together. Descend to the basement workshop where you can see the craftspeople at work. Free, and very intriguing.

Before leaving the Arthabaska sector of Victoriaville, stop at the **Musée Laurier** (16 rue Laurier Ouest, Arthabaska G6P 6P3; 819–357–8655). This home was built in 1876 for one of Canada's most famous prime ministers, Sir Wilfred Laurier, for the then-princely sum of $3,000. It is suitably impressive, being graciously set back from the street. Although the downstairs was bilingually interpreted, the upstairs and temporary exhibit had only French explanations.

Now proceed southeast on Highway 161 through gentle hills and rich dairy land along the Nicolet River.

At the junction with Highway 216 Sud, turn right toward Saint-Adrien. Situated on top of a hill, the lofty spires of the village's white clapboard church survey the rolling countryside. Watch for Highway 257 Est and drive southeast to **Saint-Joseph-de-Ham-Sud.** Turn right to proceed to **Mont Ham,** which rises to 710 meters, just north of the next village, Saint-Camille. Mont Ham is one of Estrie's highest mountains. It has a good network of hiking trails, one of which affords a great view of the surrounding countryside from the summit. It's seasonally open, so first

Fly fishing

*C*alling all trout fishermen! If this is your sport, and if you have your own equipment, then we have a spot for you. Turn right (south) of Highway 161 into **Notre-Dame-de-Lourdes-de-Ham,** where you can arrange to fish for brown trout in two sectors of the Nicolet River. The 11-kilometer length of river is open for fishing and has pools and rapids for fly- and spin-fishing. You need to purchase a right of access (adults $23, ages 15 and under $11) at the Reception Center (30 rue Principale, Notre-Dame-de-Ham G0P 1C0; 819–344–5844 in fishing season, 819–357–3388 out of season; Web site: www.mygale.org/07/cgrbf/); e-mail: cgrbf@ivic.qc.ca. The center is open during the fishing season (April 25–September 28).

Only thirty-five people are allowed on the river each day. You must reserve a date, purchase a right of access, get a Québec provincial fishing licence ($52 for the season or $22.75 for three days), and you must return to the Reception Center to register your catch. Fishing is on foot (no boats). Camping is available but it is completely rustic. Opposite the Reception Center is a B&B, **Gîte La Maison de Morphée** (23 rue Principale, Notre-Dame-de-Lourdes-de-Ham; inquire at reception center).

call the **Mont Ham reception center** (103 route 257 West, Ham-Sud; 819–828–3608).

Continue southwest on Route 216 to **Saint-Camille**, one of the Eastern Township's oldest francophone villages, founded in 1848. The hills around the Sainte-Antoine Chapel rise to 400 meters, so you can easily see nearby Mont Ham. In Saint-Camille is **Le P'tit Bonheur de Saint Camille,** which is a delightful rural community interpretation center (162 Miquelon Street; 819–828–2664 to find out what exhibitions are on. Open daily, but Saturdays by reservation only).

Follow Highway 216 southwest into Sherbrooke, a city with a population of about 80,000, and the regional capital of the Eastern Townships. It's really pretty. Orient yourself to Sherbrooke by visiting the **Centre d'interprétation de l'histoire de Sherbrooke,** which has audiotape tours of history for walking and driving (275 Dufferin Street, Sherbrooke J1H 4M5; 819–821–5406). Otherwise, contact the **Tourist Office of the Sherbrooke Region** (48 Dépôt Street, Sherbrooke J1H 5G1; 800–561–8331; fax 819–822–6074).

Les patriotes

Les patriotes was the name given after 1826 to people in the popular movement of mostly French-speaking merchants and liberal professionals who rebelled against British rule. The rebellions of 1837 and 1838 resulted in the torching of patriotes' homes, hangings, and imprisonment. Their demands for the right to self-government were rejected by Britain but laid the seeds for today's call for separation from Canada.

You'll see lots of bicyclists in Sherbrooke. The 53-kilometer cycle loop called **Les Grandes Fourches** (contact Sherbrooke Tourism at 800–561–8331) is a must if you are a cyclist. It takes you around a lake, along rivers, and to the old Capelton copper mine, where shafts extend over a mile underground. Do a mine tour; there are stands to secure your bike. The bike route also goes over one of Québec's classic covered bridges. These bridges were covered to preserve the wood from rot. Or so they say. They're also known as kissing bridges, for their seclusion allowed unchaperoned lovers to steal a kiss. This cycling path is the very best way to check out this area's rich heritage.

Continue south to **Lennoxville** via Highway 143. Because it is home to the Neo-Gothic–style **Bishop's University,** this city is the English language educational and cultural center of the Eastern Townships. St. Mark's Chapel, part of Bishop's, was built in 1855 and is a beautiful replica of thirteenth-century Gothic architecture.

An interesting section of Lennoxville is where Highway 143 becomes **Queen Street.** There are lots of colorful flower markets, all open-air and joyful looking. Around 240 Queen Street find "antiques row," which gives you some shopping opportunities. Along this road you'll find a student area with inexpensive places to eat. *Sebby's* offers all-you-can-eat meals; *Café Cordelia* has trendy espresso and cappuccino. Just before crossing the Rivière Massawippi, you'll see the Les Grandes Fourches biking trail.

Beyond the bridge on Highway 143, Highway 147 veers to the left. Stay on Highway 143 for a few kilometers to turn right onto Highway 108, to find the old *Capelton Mine* (800 route 108, Canton d'Hatley J1M 2A3; 819–346–9545). This is the oldest mine in Canada, and visitors can try their hand at mining copper with a pick and shovel. Call for seasonal openings; cost is $10.95 for adults, kids 5 to 12 $7.95. The property contains 650 acres and offers good hiking, biking and, in winter, dog sledding and skiing. Directly opposite the mine is the covered bridge, originally built in 1842. The ice storm of January 1998 badly damaged the bridge, but it has been restored.

Return the short distance to Highway 143 and turn right (west), and you'll soon see a sign to Waterville. Turn left (south), following the Waterville signs as you jog for a block on Highway 143. The road changes to Chemin de Compton to take you through Waterville and out along the gentle slopes of the west bank of the Coaticook River. Watch for the sign directing you east across the valley to *Compton.* As you cross the river, you'll see the remains of another covered bridge. Compton is the former home of one of Canada's prime ministers, Louis St. Laurent. Stop at the *Louis S. St. Laurent National Historic Site* (6 rue Principale Sud, Compton J0B 1L0; 819–835–5448 or 800–463–6769; fax 819–835–9101; Web site: parcscanada.risq.qc.ca/Saint-laurent/en/frame_useful_infos_.html). Stop in at J.B.M. St. Laurent's General Store—originally Louis St. Laurent's father's store—which is part of the site and displays merchandise of the sort sold in the early 1990s. Compton also has a "heritage circuit" to trace a century of history of local mills, buildings, and bridges.

Farther south on Highway 147, you'll reach *Coaticook,* a name derived from the Indian word *Koatikeku,* meaning "river of the land of pines." Stop for a picnic and explore *Parc de la Gorge de Coaticook* (135

Michaud Street, Coaticook J1A 2T7; 819–849–2331). The gorge, more than 50 meters deep, is not only spectacular in itself but also features the longest suspended footbridge in the world at 169 meters. In the park you'll find the reproduction of a round barn, as well as an 1887 covered bridge.

Don't miss **Beaulne Museum** (96 rue de l'Union, Coaticook J1A 1Y9; 819–849–6560; fax 819–849–9519; Web site: www.cscoaticook.qc.ca/lepont/musee). A wonderful collection of costumes and antique textiles is housed in a whimsical wood and fieldstone Victorian home, complete with turrets and a broad, sturdy veranda entryway. The collector made his fortune by designing and patenting a railway-car jack. Perhaps appropriately, the museum is nestled among old trees just below the railroad.

Head west now on Highway 141. After about 8 kilometers, you reach **Barnston,** a small rural village renowned for its still-operational round dairy barn. To see it, drive through the village. The barn is on the north side of the road on the outskirts of town. Avoid turning around on this fairly narrow road by taking the next right turn, then right again, to reconnect with Highway 141. Turn left (northwest).

Now drive through more dairy country to **Ayer's Cliff,** situated on the banks of Lac Massawipi, a popular recreational boating area. Very English, the lake has a good public beach and boat launch.

Continue on Highway 141 to **Magog,** a major recreational resort on the northern tip of **Lac Memphrémagog**. Not surprisingly, neighboring **Parc du Mont Orford** is another major draw for recreationalists. Its

The round barn at Barnston

two mountains, Orford and Baldface, are 853 and 600 meters high, respectively. In winter, downhill skiers thrill to a vertical drop of more than 540 meters on over 40-plus kilometers at Mont Orford trails (800–567–7315 or 819–843–6548 or 514–878–1411 in Montréal; Web site: www.rsn.com/goski/gsresort). You can rent equipment here, and if you don't want to commit for a full day, you can buy a ski pass in 2- to 3¹/₂-hour blocks. In other words, if you feel like trying it out, there's no excuse not to. For information about skiing or about hiking in summer, contact **Station Touristique du Mont Orford** (P.O. Box 248, Magog-Orford J1X 3W8; 800–361–6548). If exercise isn't particularly your thing, simply take the gondola to the summit of Mont Orford for a perspective on where you've been and a grand view of the topography of this area.

It's time to return to Montréal. Get on Autoroute 10 Ouest (west), and in less than an hour, you can be back in the city.

PLACES TO STAY IN THE
EASTERN TOWNSHIPS

CHAMBLY;
La Maison Ducharme,
10 de Richelieu Street;
514–447–1220;
fax: 514–447–1018.
This old armory was used
to house up to 400 soldiers
in the War of 1812.

EASTMAN
Le Centre de Santé d'
Eastman
(Eastman Health Spa)
895 chemin des Diligences,
J0E 1P0; 800–665–5272.
You can have a wonderful
massage, hydrotherapy, and
stay for $85. This "*forfait*"
or package deal is a com-
bined B&B plus health spa.

LENNOXVILLE
Bishop's University,
(800–567–2792,
extension 2651;
fax: 819–822–9615)
has family accommodation
on campus available sea-
sonally from May through
September, from $38.95.
This includes tennis, sauna,
indoor and outdoor pools
and is a great deal; 438
rooms, 10 apartments.

PLACES TO EAT IN THE
EASTERN TOWNSHIPS

CHAMBLY
La Maison Bleu
"The Blue House,"
2592 Bourgogne avenue;
514–658–6426;
picturesque heritage home
serves regional cuisine.

EASTMAN
La Sucrerie des Normand,
416 chemin George
Bonnalie;
450–297–2659.
Sample maple sugar in
March when the sap is
flowing.
Take a sleigh ride, tube
with inner tubes on the
snow-clad hills, or try the
"*tire sur neige,*" where
maple syrup is poured on
the snow.

TINGWICK
Le Chante Grive
Restaurant,
101 rue Saint-Joseph,
J0A 1L0;
819–359–3090;
just north of Danville;
offers regional cuisine,
including a selection of
wild game.

The Outaouais: Natural Splendor

Pronounced *Ooo-ta-ways,* this spectacular sector of Québec includes the almost-unknown westernmost region called the Pontiac, whose natural beauty beckons at every twist and turn of the road. Rushing rivers allowed fur traders to penetrate the hinterland throughout the Outaouais. The historic Ottawa River, the transportation route from the St. Lawrence to the Great Lakes, here meets its mightiest tributaries. Québec's famous triple play of rivers—the Noire (Black), Dumoine, and Coulonge to the west—as well as the Gatineau, Rouge, and Blanche to the east, all drain into the Ottawa within this region.

Hugging the rivers are thousands of miles of forests punctuated by pristine lakes, wild country where deer, wolves, and bears still roam. You'll find pastoral fields dotted with grazing cattle, corn "as high as an elephant's eye," and prosperous farms. Villages here reflect the pattern of immigration to the New Land. There's Luskville, named for Irish immigrant Joseph Lusk; Shawville, honoring Englishman John Shaw; Fort Coulonge, an early French voyageur trading post; Maniwaki, a village with an Algonquin name; Ladysmith, formerly Schwartz, a German settlement dating from the mid-1800s; and Papineauville, too, for Louis-Joseph Papineau, leader of the Rebellion of Lower Canada in 1837. Indeed, this region of Québec is truly a microcosm of Canada: Poles, Lithuanians, Germans, French, English, Scots, Irish all settled here.

Peppered throughout the Outaouais, alternative communities are part of the ebb and flow. Some are vestiges of circa-1850s communities, such as the area north of Shawville and Otter Lake called the Polish Hills, for the many Polish immigrants who settled in the region. In the sixties, communes were established on inexpensive land in these back of beyond spots. And more recently, tired urbanites have renovated old farms in the Pontiac region, wishing to live in what they consider more natural, self-reliant ways—ways considered by the more technologically prone as alternative. At the Polish Hills Wilderness Farm, for example, a B&B run by Jack and Debbie Gauthier and tucked away on a long unpaved road, they rely on solar energy and wood heat to get by.

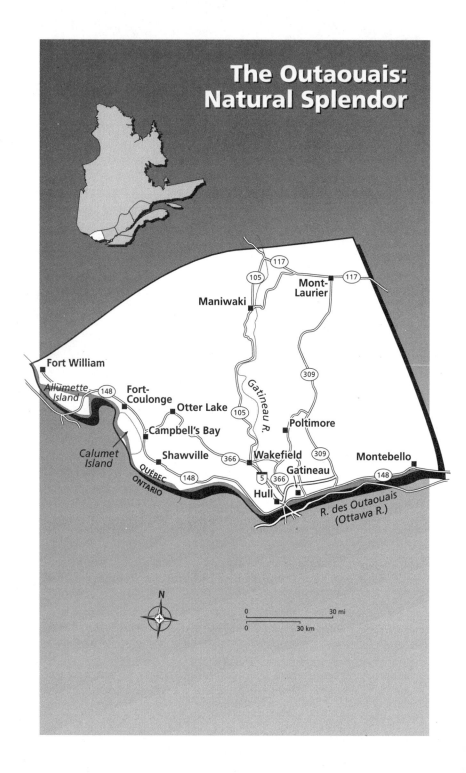

AUTHORS' TOP PICKS IN THE OUTAOUAIS

*Mackenzie King Estate,
Gatineau Park*

Ecomuseum of Hull

Luskville Falls hike

Norway Bay Pier

*Shawville's self-guiding
walking tour*

*Spruceholme Inn in
Fort Coulonge*

Coulonge Chutes

Esprit Rafting

*Polish Hills Wilderness
Farm B&B*

Wakefield

Château Montebello

And there's another aspect to the Outaouais: It's largely federalist. During the referendum of October 1995, well over 90 percent of the population voted an emphatic *non* to the question of Québec separation from Canada. English is spoken freely here. You'll see English in signs and hear it in announcements made at country fairs, sometimes to the exclusion of French. In the Pontiac, people are fiercely proud of their English-speaking background yet united in the many cultured mosaic that is Canada today.

Intimately wedded to the capital of Canada, the south-central section of the Outaouais is part of the National Capital Region that extends south into Ontario. Because of its proximity to Ottawa, the region is a bedroom community for federal government offices employees. Many federal offices are in Hull, an iniative started when Pierre Elliott Trudeau was prime minister in the early 1970s. Because of its great natural beauty, the region is the capital's recreation mecca, providing superb conference and cottage retreats.

We love Québec, but especially the remote, wild countryside in the western Pontiac region of the Outaouais. We moved here in 1989 to our farmhouse snuggled against our beloved Gatineau Park. On a summer's night, with the canopy of stars twinkling overhead, we can sip a glass of wine on our front porch and hear the wolves howl, from one ridge to the next. And if we want to take in a show or meet with a client, we can be in Ottawa–Hull in less than an hour. It's a little corner of heaven. Come on out and get yourself a hearty Outaouais welcome!

Exploring the Outaouais

The Outaouais is best accessed from Montréal or Ottawa–Hull. Generally, the road system in this large territory follows the river systems used by the native people and voyageurs of days gone by. To the west of Hull, the Pontiac region stretches along the Ottawa River, with rolling farmland near it and other wild rivers flowing down from the north. To the north, the Gatineau Valley extends far up into the rugged Canadian Shield of the Laurentian plateau. To the east, the influence of the seigneurial system of land allotment is still visible in the long, thin farms of Papineauville and La Petite Nation.

Fluently bilingual staff at the *Association Touristique de l'Outaouais* (Tourism Association of the Outaouais) will happily answer questions (103 rue Laurier, Hull J8X 3V8; 819–778–2222; fax 819–778–7758; Web site: www.achilles.net/~ato).

If you use the Hull area as a base to explore this vast territory, be sure to spend some time in nearby Gatineau Park.

Gatineau Park

Managed by a crown corporation called the National Capital Commission (NCC), *Gatineau Park* is a jewel of the National Capital Region. Over 200 kilometers of groomed trails welcome skiers, while other trails are open to snowshoers. In summer a shared network of trails welcomes mountain bikers and hikers; others trails are only for hikers. *Lakes Lapêche, Philippe,* and *Meech* offer excellent canoeing, and camping is delightful at Lac Lapêche and Lac Philippe. Ask the Visitor's Centre (819–827–2020) about the overnight accommodations at Brown Cabin. The parks people are continuing to develop hut-to-hut hiking and skiing. The park's National Trail connects to the Trans-Canada Trail.

Also in the park is the *Mackenzie King Estate,* once the residence of our late Prime Minister William Lyon Mackenzie King, who bequeathed his three properties (Moorside, Kingswood Cottage, and The Farm) to the people of Canada in his 1950 will. Today the NCC operate the first two as interpreted historical sites where visitors can learn about the life and times of this prime minister who believed in the spirit world. He held seances to commune and confer not only with his late mother but also with his two Irish terriers—both named Pat.

Other areas in the park, such as the ruins of Thomas "Carbide" Willson's generating station and Canada's first super-phosphate fertilizer plant on Little Meech Lake, have no interpretation signs. The dearth of signage is perhaps due to bare sightings. No, we don't mean "bear sightings." The old mill, as the site of the fertilizer plant is erroneously yet affectionately known by locals, has been adopted by nudists. Signs put up by the NCC assert that nudism is an offense. Well, some signs seem fated to be ignored, and such is the case with these. Nudism is alive and well at this site, so either go in the dead of winter or in the height of bug season if your sensibilities will be offended.

Gatineau Park is accessible by car through five main entrances. To the south, enter via Taché Boulevard in Hull. From the southwest (via the Eardley-Masham road) as well as the northwest, entry is to the Lac

THE OUTAOUAIS: NATURAL SPLENDOR

Lapêche sector. From the north, access Lac Philippe camping via Highway 366 at Sainte-Cécile-de-Masham. To find the park visitor's center or rent a bike or other equipment, head north on Highway 5 from Hull and take exit 12 at **Old Chelsea.**

This little village is a gem, full of great restaurants and shops. Also, Gary Dahl and Dawn Bell-Jack operate **La Maison Dawn House** (253 Old Chelsea Road, Old Chelsea J0X 1N0; 819–827–9162). It was formerly the circa 1870 Dunn Hotel, one of Old Chelsea's four original hotels, which were all operated by Irishmen in the late 1800s. In the cemetery behind the B&B, you'll find the grave of Asa Meech, after whom Meech Lake is named. **Gerry and Isobel's Country Pleasures** (14 chemin Scott, Old Chelsea J0X 1N0; 819–827–4341) sells local artisans' work and books and also delicious teas, soups, and homemade meals. A definite yum, in our opinion. Owner Susan Trudeau and her husband, Peter, know the park intimately and can rent you all sorts of equipment. Don't forget to drop in to the recently redesigned **Gatineau Park Visitor's Centre** (819–827–2020) for trail maps and other literature.

To Hull and Beyond

We'll start our exploration of the Outaouais using Hull as our leaping-off point. Poised as it is on the north side of the Ottawa River across from the nation's capital, the city is unknown to many. To the relief of its city fathers, Hull is now outgrowing its once poor reputation as a "drinking town."

Hull was founded by New Englander Philemon Wright in 1800. Wright and his party of intrepid settlers struggled north using the frozen waterways as their highways. Once established in Wrightsville, as their agricultural settlement was first known, Philemon soon recognized that the very trees they were

---

TOP ANNUAL EVENTS IN THE OUTAOUAIS

Mid-February

Join 2,500 skiers from twenty countries in cross-country ski races in Gatineau Park at the **Keskinada Loppet;** *P.O. Box 554, Station A, Hull J8Y 6P3; (819) 827-4641; fax (819) 827-3337; e-mail: keski@istar.ca*

July 1

Canada Day *celebrations throughout the region*

August

During the first two weeks of August, fireworks from international competitors light the sky at **Les grands feux du Casino** *near Hull's casino; (819) 771-3389 or (888) 429-3389*

Musiqu'en août *(August Music Festival) in Saint-André-Avellin and area; in the streets, churches, and bars; (819) 983-3273*

September

Shawville Agricultural Fair, *September Labor Day weekend; (819) 647-3213*

September/October

Come and see the fall colors during **Coloris automnal** *(Fall Rhapsody) in Chelsea and Gatineau Park in late September and early October; exhibitions, interpreted walks, family activities; (819) 827-2020*

November

Pontiac Old Time Fiddling Jamboree, *first Saturday in November; (819) 647-2805*

They're Off and Running

felling for their farms and villages would be their ticket to prosperity.

In 1806, when Napoleon blockaded the Baltic, Great Britain was cut off from its timber resources. How could the Royal Navy's ships be built? As British eyes cast about for trees, so did Philemon's: In fact, just about all he could see was trees. So he set to work, and in 1807 he and his sons floated their first raft of timber downstream to Québec. This historic trip founded the timber industry that was to make his fortune and which would enshrine the Outaouais and Ottawa Valley regions as Britain's primary source of square timber for its shipbuilding.

And when the days of the square-timber trade waned, the sawn timber industry took over. Huge piles of planks were stockpiled in Ottawa and Hull, products of the sawmills powered by the water of mighty rapids such as the Chaudière. Most of the lumber went to the new market, the United States, whose bustling cities like Boston and Philadelphia had an insatiable appetite for construction materials. Hull was razed by flames in 1900. It started as a chimney fire, but sparks borne by the wind landed on both sides of the Ottawa River. The ensuing conflagration destroyed most of Hull and burned much of the capital, too.

Let's get underway at the *Chaudière Falls,* where Champlain and countless, nameless river traders before him portaged round the rapids known as Asticou, or Boiling Kettle. Native traders hauled their canoes onto the limestone rocks here and paused before paddling upstream. Champlain's journal of 1613 records their tobacco ceremony, practiced on the shore beside the rapids. Native peoples threw offerings of tobacco into the boiling waters to placate the river spirits and to seek safe passage upstream, to the Great Lakes.

You'll find the falls and *Portage Park* on Taché Boulevard in Hull, at the junction of Rue Montcalm, overlooking the Ottawa River. Saunter inside the iron gates of the park and walk to the edge of the ancient waterway. A modern iron sculpture depicting the hull of a boat and a wolf recalls the spirit of portage, and perhaps you can imagine early native traders practicing their tobacco ceremony here.

To your left is the Eddy Mill, named after American entrepreneur Ezra Butler Eddy, who arrived in Hull in 1851 from Bristol, Vermont. Eddy became the "match king" of the British Empire, building mills here that

THE OUTAOUAIS: NATURAL SPLENDOR

WORTH SEEING IN THE OUTAOUAIS

Canadian Museum of Civilization, 100 Laurier Street, P.O. Box 3100, Station B, Hull, Quebec J8X 4H2. A 24-hour information service is available by phoning (800) 555–5621; fax (819) 776–8300; July 1 to September 7: Seven days a week, 9:00 A.M. to 6:00 P.M., Thursday and Friday until 9:00 P.M. The Canadian Children's Museum closes at 6:00 P.M.; September 8 to October 12; seven days a week, 9:00 A.M. to 6:00 P.M.

produced over a million matches a day. A devastating fire in 1875 wiped out his first mills spanning the Chaudière; the new ones were similarly wiped out in 1900. As a measure of his perseverance, he rebuilt after both fires and, when he died in 1906, his mills were in the black.

Continue west along the paved pathway to ***Brewery Creek.*** Yes, there used to be a brewery here, as well as a sawmill and grist mill. In 1947, British High Commissioner Malcolm Macdonald used to paddle over from his official residence at Earnscliffe, in Ottawa, to explore the creek in all seasons. A noted birder, Macdonald's book *The Birds of Brewery Creek* is a classic.

Look upstream and you'll glimpse an island in the midst of Brewery Creek. Here you will find the ***Théâtre de l'Île,*** (theater of the island). Locals luxuriate on its grass in summer, "catching the rays" during our fleeting Canadian summer. You will enjoy the sound of the creek playing background music to the chatter. On a summer's eve, take in the live theater; all performances are entirely in French (1 rue Wellington, Hull J8X 2H3; 819–595–7455).

Come wintertime, skate on Brewery Creek—the oft-overlooked cousin of Ottawa's world-famous Rideau Canal, which is the longest skating "rink" in the world. Hull's version is smaller but delightful. The ice is groomed by the city of Hull, and gaily colored lights illuminate the boardwalks on either side.

A stroll along the creek's boardwalk brings you to the ***L'Écomusée de Hull (Ecomuseum of Hull),*** brainchild of Jerome Giles (170 rue Montcalm, Hull J8X 2M3; 819–595–7790; open daily year-round; $5.00 adults, $3.00 students and children). "Devoted" is not nearly an apt enough description of Giles, the enthusiastic curator-cum-director, who sees boundless potential in every opportunity fortune casts his way. There's always an exhibit "under construction" here, so be forewarned.

Giles is passionate about showcasing the natural and geological history of the Outaouais, so commence your exploration here. There's an excellent collection of rocks, as well as a deliciously creepy insectarium. Check out the bird-feeding area, where you can feed mallards, watch swallows swoop for flies (they consume three times their weight in mosquitoes and black flies daily), and identify creatures using a handy identification board that depicts all the species recorded in *The Birds of Brewery Creek*.

It's now time to leave the city life behind us. Head west on Taché Boulevard, which quickly becomes Route 148 Ouest (West), toward **Aylmer** and ultimately into the Pontiac region.

En route, opposite a Harvey's fast-food restaurant in Hull, you'll find one of the five entryways into Gatineau Park on your right. Look for a large stone surrounded by evergreens, one of the original milestones of the **Old Britannia Road**—the old name of the footpath and wagon road that was precursor to today's Route 148, which connected Hull to Aylmer.

The Britannia Road was once simply a series of portage tracks connecting settlements to one another. The Ottawa River was the main transportation route, but steamboat passengers had to disembark and portage both themselves and their goods around three wild rapids: the Chaudière, Deschênes (Oak), and Petites Deschênes (Little Oak). Soon enterprising folks such as the Klock family operated stagecoaches—but not before landowners whose property fronted the path reluctantly agreed to "road duty" to maintain the road along their boundary. Those tempestuous times are recalled in modern times: In 1997, Route 148 through Aylmer was widened, and local residents lobbied to save the magnificent old trees lining the thoroughfare. In most cases, the grand trees still grace the route.

Continue west on Route 148 until you reach a major intersection with signs pointing left to Ottawa. Get into the left-hand turn lane and descend to the next set of lights. Ahead of you is the Champlain Bridge leading to Ontario and Ottawa. Do not proceed across the bridge; instead turn right onto what is called the Lower Aylmer Road (Chemin Lucerne).

Continue driving and, on your left, just before the first set of traffic lights (intersection with Chemin Vanier), you'll find a long, old limestone wall, with a gap behind which is a parking lot and limestone buildings. One of the buildings is home to a treasure of a restaurant that is only open for dinner: **L'Échelle de Jacob (Jacob's Ladder)** (27 boulevard Lucerne, Aylmer J9H 1M2; 819–684–1040). After parking, turn to look at the cut-limestone buildings; you'll note a grassed gap and walkway between them. Walk up here and turn left to enter the door leading upstairs to the restaurant.

Seigneurial System

The French king gave large tracts of land to seigneurs, who subdivided it to the colonists. Typically, strips of land extended about a mile back from a water frontage of 540 feet, with central parcels set aside for a mill, the seigneurial house, and the church.

Ask for the table d'hôte and always inquire about the specials. The smoked sturgeon we enjoyed here was simply delectable. Owner and chef Peter Bryce will spin tales of the history of the building, which was once the terminus for streetcars that took passengers from Aylmer to Hull. It also served as an ax factory. Peter is fluently bilingual and one of the most gracious hosts you'll ever meet.

Reconnect to Route 148 by proceeding along the Lower Aylmer Road (Chemin Lucerne). Off to the left is the Ottawa River. Eventually the road curves right and connects with the highway. Turn left at the lights at Rue Principale (Main Street); a little fountain and park mark this corner, on your left. For now, continue through the old part of Aylmer until you glimpse the river ahead.

> ### Chief Pontiac
>
> *The Pontiac area of the Outaouais region is named for native Chief Pontiac, who led a rebellion against the British in 1755. He was the chief of the Odawa people from Michigan and died in Illinois. The Odawa gave their name to Ottawa, the capital of Canada, and also to the Outaouais region.*

On your right, at a bend in the road, you'll see what was once the **Symmes Hotel,** a magnificent cut-limestone building with white, double-story front, and back wooden porches. Artist W. H. Bartlett's engraving of this old hostelry was published in London in *Canadian Scenery Illustrated,* in 1842. The picture shows the frozen expanse of a widening in the Ottawa River behind the hotel. The hotel exhibits classic Québecois architectural features, with a bell-shaped, sweeping roofline designed so that snow will fall off instead of accumulating. It was built by Charles Symmes in 1832 as a hotel for the steamboat passengers who needed accommodations prior to pressing on upriver. Now it is a cultural center.

Park your car at the **Aylmer Marina** (1 rue Principale, Aylmer; 819–682–9998). Wander its grounds or, in summer, swim at the sandy beach behind and to the right of the main building. Note the bicycle path, which you can explore equally enjoyably on foot or by bike. It will return you, eventually, to Portage Park in Hull, passing along the waterfront and through pretty woodlands.

In front of the marina (and beside the Symmes Hotel) is the totally delightful **Parc L'Imagier.** Wander this grassy, out-of-the-way area to discover all sorts of unlikely "installations." There's an oversized picnic table painted by local artists, many of whom participate in annual studio tours. Kids will enjoy expending some energy at the small swing-set and slide. Then soak up more culture inside the **Centre d'Exposition L'imagier Art Gallery** (9 Front Street, Aylmer J9H 4W8; 819–684–1445). This gallery is located in a colorful chocolate-brown, board-and-batten house that sports a flirtatious hot-pink trim. It's the creation of owner and art-lover Yvette Debains, who is tremendously supportive of the regional art scene. In fact, it is she who encouraged the city of Aylmer to create this magical park. Don't miss the couple permanently enjoying their bath in the gallery's back garden.

Proceed right on Front Street (past the gallery) to rejoin Route 148 and turn left, west, toward Luskville and Fort Coulonge.

Almost immediately you leave built-up streetscapes behind you. Now you're in the *Pontiac region* of the Outaouais, where spectacular nature is your companion. Look left to the mighty Ottawa River, which flows downstream to Ottawa and Montréal. Imagine this: 5,000 years ago native copper traders would be paddling past; in 1613 Champlain canoed these waters, and two hundred years later, steamers plied the route. On a summer's day now, sailboats dot the river, and in winter you can see the "villages" of ice huts, where hardy types fish through holes in the three-foot-thick ice.

The drive offers incomparable panoramas of farm life. Keep your eyes peeled: Not only will you see beef and dairy cattle but also the old draught horses, such as Belgians, which many farmers here still raise, primarily because they love them. At country fairs, you'll be able to watch up to eight-team hitches of these gentle giants, proudly pulling their gaily colored wagons.

Watch for *St. Augustine Church,* an old stone church perched right beside the highway, atop a hill, about ten minutes out of Aylmer. This is *Ghost Hill,* a local landmark where ghostly sightings, murder, and mayhem abound. (See page 111 for more on its legend). The descent is abrupt and winding: Take care. At the bottom is a marsh where people have

Country Fairs

*T*hroughout Québec are many country fairs, and the Pontiac region is no exception. During the first week of September come to the **Shawville Fair,** largest in the region, where horses are featured. English and western competitions as well as old-fashioned heavy horse pulls are popular events that draw city and country folk alike. You'll find the giant pumpkin competition, and vegetable and flower arrangement contests where platters of eggplant and scarlet tomatoes gleam beside vases of pretty flowers. Earlier in summer, around Canada Day (July 1), visit the Quyon Fair. On Île des Allumettes, at Chapeau, there's a winter fair.

Gatineau River

Nicolas Gatineau dit Duplessis was a Québec-based notary who got bored. Yes, he forsook his office existence, and in the early 1600s became an explorer. In search of the best beaver pelts, he paddled north for adventure. Legend has it he drowned in the river that now bears his name.

occasionally seen the will-o- the-wisp, that bouncing ball of wavering light created by marsh gases, or the ghost of a lost soul. You pass over a small stream, Breckenridge Creek, that once sported a sawmill, grist mill, and general store. Today it's merely a bend in the road.

After Ghost Hill and Breckenridge (and before you get to Luskville's four-lane stretch) look for signs to **Wanaki,** a gîte (B&B) and retreat owned by Ken Fisher (133 avenue des Plages, Luskville J0X 2G0; 819–455–9295). Turn left onto Chemin des Dominicaines and follow the signs through the low-lying farmland to the B&B. This is a particularly good spot to stay, and not only because of its rather spectacular location on a gentle rise overlooking the Ottawa River. Because Ken has been president of the local tourism association, he is well-informed about the attractions, politics, and people of the region. This modern B&B has a beautiful sandy beach as an extra-added attraction. Get Ken going on tales of the region as you sit beside a campfire built near the river.

Returning to Route 148 West, this section of the drive brings geology to life as you traverse the flat Ottawa Valley plain. To your left is the Ottawa River, to the right is the Eardley Escarpment, the ancient roots of the Laurentian Mountains.

Route 148 suddenly and seemingly inexplicably widens to a short four-lane stretch at Luskville—apparently the result of an election promise! The road used to be quite narrow and winding and there had been a couple of fatal accidents. The incumbent promised to improve the road if reelected, but postponed action until just before the next election.

In this four-lane section, watch for the brown National Capital Commission sign pointing right to Gatineau Park and turn right to **Luskville Falls** picnic ground at Chemin Hôtel de Ville Road (just after the Luskville town hall on your right). There's a picnic ground, barbecue pits, and a splendid, heart-healthy hike up the steep **Eardley Escarpment** beside the falls. The return hike takes approximately three hours. There are outstanding lookouts from the ridge over the Ottawa River Valley and several interpretive panels explain the history, geology, and flora. Take binoculars as you may see raptors (birds of prey), such as the red-tailed hawk or turkey vulture, soaring on updrafts of air along the ridge. At the base of the falls, to the right of the picnic grounds, is a stable where you can rent a horse and go trail riding by the hour or even overnight. Call the **Centre d'Equitation** at 819–455–2290.

Once back on Route 148, keep going west. Antiques hunters won't want to miss following the rustic signs to the **Red Barn of Antiques and Collectibles,** which is open only from mid-May through early October. Turn north (right) off Route 148, following the sign at the corner of graveled Hammond Road, near Quyon, to reach this off-the-beaten-path shop, located on Chemin Steele. Operated by Lorne and John McRae, the antiques are housed in their old family homestead's milk barn. The brothers will enchant you with their Ottawa Valley accents. Don't be shy to dicker for a good price for Depression glass or perhaps a broad ax that the loggers used to fell the great white pines.

Continue along Chemin Steele to its terminus at **Chemin Lac des Loup** (watch your speed; before you get there, there's a wicked **S** bend in the road). At the intersection, turn left to reconnect, after about 8 kilometers, with Route 148. At this junction, on your left is **Restaurant, Restaurant, Restaurant** (5032 route 148, Quyon J0X 2V0; 819–458– 2209; daily 6:00 A.M. to 10:00 P.M.). Owners Diane and Ken Stanton have a great sense of humor as well as patriotic (read *federalist*) stubbornness. They named the restaurant to thumb their noses at Québec's "language police," who insist that French must dominate all signage in the province. Because the

How to Find a Brazilian Artist's Studio Really Far From Brazil

*W*ant to head into the back of beyond? From Route 148 at the second exit to Quyon, turn right immediately after Restaurant, Restaurant, Restaurant onto Lac de Loup Road, which is paved. Follow for about 10 kilometers; it will gain elevation and bisect a cornfield. Immediately afterward it turns into a gravel road. Remain on it for about 2 kilometers, then turn left onto another gravel road, Twelfth Line, which forms a T- intersection, marked by a stand of white pine and, immediately to your right, a small white cottage. Descend the Twelfth Line for 1.4 kilometers, cross a little bridge, and immediately turn right into the lane to **Marcio Melo Studio.** This funky farmhouse, picturesquely perched beside Moffat Lake, is full of Marcio's brilliantly colored, whimsically styled watercolors and acrylics. Marcio welcomes visitors and thoroughly enjoys conversing about his art. He also has a wonderful flower and veggie garden thronged with geese, chickens, and ducks. You can also visit Marcio's during the Pontiac Artists Studio Tour, second two weekends in June. Call first (8 Twelfth Line, Quyon J0X 2V0; 819–647–3416; Web site: www.mha-net.org/users/pasta/melo; e-mail: bw575@freenet.carleton.ca).

word "restaurant" is the same in English and French, the irony is especially amusing and reflects the wry Irish humor of the Stantons, whose ancestors settled here in the early 1800s. A local hangout, Stanton's is unmatched for picking up local gossip and tall tales. Stop here for iced tea, nachos, a particularly tasty clubhouse sandwich, and generous portions of chips and gravy.

Largest Log Cabin in the World

The Château Montebello is the largest log cabin in the world—and it took only four months to build in 1930 on the grounds of a 1700 seigneury.

Now cross the highway very carefully to **Quyon** and go straight to the T-intersection with Rue Clarendon. If you want to visit the fairgrounds for the July 1 Canada Day celebrations and fair, turn left and follow the signs to the **Traversier Saissonnier (Seasonal Ferry),** which crosses the Ottawa River to Ontario (a ten-minute ride, April to December 1; $5.00). There are plans afoot to build a marina at Quyon beside the ferry docks. Sailing is increasingly popular, and the Ottawa River Navigable Waterways Project aims to open the entire river to recreational boating from Montréal to Lake Temiscaming. The impact on villages like Quyon will be tremendous when this is accomplished, it is hoped by 2002. **Gavan's Hotel** is a popular local watering hole and "home" of singer and television host Gail Gavan.

Reconnect to Route 148 by continuing west on Rue Clarendon. This used to be the main highway, but now it passes through the center of the village and past some pretty homes and farmhouses. At the junction with Route 148, turn left. After about 10 kilometers watch for a blue highway sign pointing left to **Norway Bay**. This is a tiny resort community where picturesque cottages nestle beside the Ottawa River, beneath towering Norway pines. In summer, the fragrance of pine in the hot sunshine is sheer Canadian cottage memory. Proceed on River Road (note the road signs are English now that you're in this English-speaking stronghold of Québec) through Norway Bay to **Wharf Road** and go left to the **Norway Bay Pier**. There's a lovely little park here that's great for picnics, plus a safe, sandy beach and very shallow water for toddlers. The landscaped pier extends out into the river, complete with park benches and two cordoned-off deep-water swimming "pools." Come wintertime, the frozen bay is groomed and maintained as a **skating circuit.**

Return to River Road and turn left toward **Bristol**. Drive slowly, as the road provides a good surface for leisurely strolls for four-footed and two-footed walkers. Coming up soon is the 1930s family resort and golf course known as **Pine Lodge** (6 Pine Lodge Road, Bristol J0X 1G0; 819–647–2805). It's a must-see as it's one of those charming lodges that still offer yummy home-cooked meals. Try your hand at golf on the nine-hole course while others laze on the beach with a good book.

Pontiac resident Eric Campbell organizes the **Old Time Fiddling Jamboree** the first Saturday in November at Pine Lodge. Your price of admission is a potluck contribution to what's called a "lunch"—a rural Pontiac tradition consisting of a festive meal served at midnight. A contribution could be some fruit juices, a pie, or something else delicious. The jamboree gives you a rare opportunity to enjoy old-time Ottawa Valley music and tap dancing at its finest. Many of the early settlers here were of Irish or French extraction, with some hardy Scots thrown in for good measure. Therefore, the valley's reels are a lively mix of these cultures. You may just find yourself step-dancing along with the locals who have kept this tradition alive for generations.

Now we'll introduce you to **Shawville,** the "shopping center of the Pontiac." Turn right on the Bristol Road and reconnect to Route 148: turn left. Shawville soon appears on your right. Turn right on Centre Street and find parking near the white building labeled **The Equity,** the home of a newspaper of the same name that has been "the voice of the Pontiac" since 1883 (133 Centre Street, 647–2204; open 9:00 A.M. to 5:00 P.M. daily, 9:00 A.M. to noon Saturday, closed Sunday). Publisher Heather Dickson operates this family-run business, which publishes a primarily English-language weekly that originated in 1883. Step inside to discover lots of books for sale on the region written by local authors and get the feel of a community paper. Ask for copies of Shawville's **self-guided walking tour.**

Shawville

With a population of 1,634 Shawville is the only town of its size in Québec that does not have a Roman Catholic Church. The Pontiac may be the biggest county in Québec, but it only has one traffic light—in "downtown" Shawville.

Adjacent to The Equity is a grain elevator, a landmark of the village and still used to store the produce of Pontiac's fields. What's architecturally very unusual about Shawville is its Victorian red-brick houses built for bank managers, wealthy merchants, and doctors in the late 1800s from the production of two brickyards nearby. Also of interest are the **Mill Dam Park** (you can still see the stone foundation of the old mill by the edge of the creek) and the agricultural fairgrounds. There are many events at the fairgrounds, including July 1 Canada Day celebrations, an Antique Machinery Show during the third weekend in August, and the Shawville Fair held Labor Day Weekend (the first full weekend in September).

Return to Route 148 and head west (right). Just west of Shawville on Route 148 you'll come to a flashing yellow light. Turn left to **Portage du**

Fort, which was a significant portage and stopping place in the late 1700s for *coureurs de bois* ("runners of the woods"—independent, unlicensed fur traders). There used to be a North West Company fort here, which transferred to the Hudson Bay Company during their merger in 1821. The village was once the shopping center of the Pontiac until a devastating fire in 1915 wiped out its bustling business area. Shawville then superseded its position in the region, not only because of the fire but also because of the shift from water to rail and then to road transportation. Portage du Fort is well worth a visit, though. Check out the Chenaux Dam, too, and the remarkable rocks below it that you can view (with caution) from the dam's viewpoint. (Take care if you explore the surrounding rocky outcrops as poison ivy is rampant here.)

Return to Route 148 and continue west to Bryson. Turn left to *Île du Grand Calumet Island.* Between the highway and bridge spanning the river is artist Ariann Bouchard's gallery boutique, *La Marchande de la Rivière des Outaouais* (780 rue Wilson, Bryson J0X 1H0; 648–5127; Thursday through Sunday, 9:00 A.M. to 6:00 P.M.), on your left. Her store is full of local artists' and artisans' works, including her own.

Continue across the bridge and veer right. Watch for the restaurant *Au Bouleau Blanc* (30 chemin des Outaouais, Île-du-Grand-Calumet J0X 1J0; 819–648–2377) on your left, where you can get good country fare like hamburger platters and chicken dishes.

Just before you arrive at the village of *Grand Calumet,* you will find a noted Pontiac landmark: a cairn marking the resting place of a French *coureur de bois* named Cadieux. The tragic *Lament de Cadieux* was written here, where he and his band of Algonquin companions were ambushed by a roving band of Iroquois in the 1600s. His friends fled, and when they returned they discovered Cadieux's half-buried body. Legend has it that he erected his own wooden cross, wrote his own eulogy, and half-buried himself before expiring. These are his words:

> *Lament of Cadieux*
> *Little rock of the high mount*
> *I've come here to end my days*
> *O, sweet echoes, hear my sigh*
> *I'm sinking fast and going to die.*

Here you have a choice: to return to Route 148 or to visit artist Dale Shutt at her studio, *Island Design.* A silk watercolor artist, Dale's studio is open only by appointment. You must call her (819–648–2441) not only to arrange a convenient time to visit but also to get directions: It is easy to get lost on the island's gravel back roads. Her remote studio is at the north end of Calumet Island, in an old homestead's original barn. Inspired by fantastical dragons (just ask her about the dragon living beneath the hill) as well as by natural, organic forms, Dale's silk paintings, suncatchers, and candles are gorgeous. She has lived here for over twenty-five years and has interpreted her landscape on silk for as long.

Champlain's Astrolabe

French explorer Samuel de Champlain lost his astrolabe, used to calculate the location of celestial bodies, in 1613. A farmer discovered it in his field, near Cobden, Ontario, and sold it to an American. Today it's back in Canada, and you can see it displayed at the Canadian Museum of Civilization in Hull.

In turn, she can direct you to the campgrounds and picnic spots at *Parc Rocher Fendu Park. Rocher Fendu* means "split rocks," and the rocky islands here rise dramatically from the Ottawa River. This park is one of the few public access vantage points where you can actually get down to the water. But take care, as the water can be swift and high. If you like spectacular scenery, it's worth the drive on gravel roads, especially if you enjoy canoeing, swimming, or rustic picnic and camping spots.

Return to Route 148 at Bryson and turn left to Campbell's Bay. A few miles beyond, the large church at Vinton seems too big for this tiny hamlet, but when it was built in 1896, this village was a thriving Irish settlement with several hotels and schools, a sawmill, and a cheese factory.

Farther west, **Fort Coulonge** soon approaches, originally another trading post along the Ottawa, built to protect the interests of the North West Company. Today this predominantly French village is noted for its three historic stone mansions, all built for his family by George Bryson Sr., a timber baron, first president of the Bank of Ottawa (now the Bank of Nova Scotia), and a representative of Pontiac in the Legislative Assembly in Québec City in the mid-1800s. Another Bryson construction is the lovely **St. Andrew's Anglican Church,** opposite the stone homes on Rue Principale.

To visit, continue on Route 148 until you see the pink—it's supposed to be red—covered bridge (also known as the kissing bridge) on your left. Drive across it. The **Marchand Bridge,** second-longest covered bridge in Québec, was built in a matter of months by Augustus Brown and his teams of horses and men in 1898.

Follow the road as it curves back toward the village of Fort Coulonge to **Spruceholme** on your left. In 1996, Glenn and Marlene Scullion purchased one of the Brysons' cut-limestone residences and commenced a major renovation project. In a phenomenal seven months they opened this stately mansion as **Spruceholme Inn** (204 rue Principale, Fort-

Coulonge J0X 1V0; 819–683–5635; fax 819–683–2139). Here you can enjoy a delicious meal and stay in truly luxurious B&B surroundings that are chock-full of family heirlooms, including a woven woolen wall tapestry from Paisley, Scotland. Marlene did the tasteful period renovations, and we know you'll enjoy talking to her. The Scullions are well-informed about Pontiac tourism events and history. We highly recommend you stay here.

Return across the bridge to the highway and proceed west toward Davidson and Waltham. Immediately on the right you'll see the old *Bryson House,* built by family patriarch George Bryson Sr. as his own home. This building is an architectural anomaly here, being an example of a style far more common in the Eastern Townships of Québec. It once stood on a huge farm that had seven barns. The farm grew crops that would nourish the teams of men laboring in the bush at Bryson's lumber shanties. This unique agricultural complex of home and outbuildings was restored, and the local tourism association hopes to use it for an office soon.

Don't miss a visit to the spectacular 150-foot waterfall on the Coulonge River, *Coulonge Chutes* (100 promenade du parc des Chutes, Fort-Coulonge J0X 1V0; 819–683–2770), about 7 kilometers farther west off Route 148. Follow the signs (it's only open in summer). Turn north on Rue des Bois-Francs Road and venture up the winding gravel roads to the Chute parking lot and visitor's center. In 1835, George Bryson built a 3,000-foot water chute for timber from the top of the falls, extending along the canyon wall. It carried logs and prevented them from being smashed in the raging falls and rocky rapids. The logs descended to the Ottawa River, and floated down to Ottawa and Montréal prior to being shipped to Britain. (The last raft of square-cut timber sent down Ottawa's slide in 1909 was from the Coulonge, and another lumber baron of the day, John Rodolphus Booth, charged admission to watch that historic raft go by.) There is a video at the

The Coulonge Chutes

Mishipashoo: God of River Rapids

*T*he ancient peoples who traded copper and tobacco along the Ottawa River paid homage to the god of rapids, Mishipashoo. In Algonquin, mishi means "big," and pashoo means "cat." Old pictograms drawn on cliffs depict a being with a dragon-like head complete with horns and a writhing, serpentine body.

Mishipashoo controlled the rapids, being respected but feared by navigators who understood that the safety of all on board was dependent not only on their skill, but also on the capricious will of Mishipashoo.

So it was that all who ventured on the river gave Mishipashoo a portion of their treasured possessions. In 1613, when he paddled the Ottawa, Samuel de Champlain and his Algonquin guides gave gifts of tobacco to the Mishipashoo at Chaudière Falls. Gifts of tobacco and copper, the most important trade items in the ancient days, were left on the riverbank. Distracted, Mishipashoo crawled out of the river to claim his due, while the clever river-runners sped past.

visitor's center and a self-guided walk complete with informative bilingual signs and several spectacular viewpoints over the falls. English is spoken here.

Return to Route 148 from the chutes; turn left, then right after about 1 kilometer, toward **Davidson.** Go through this old lumber town and find the lane to **Esprit Rafting** on your left. From April through October, you'll find Jim and Erin Coffey primed and ready to pitch you into the heady world of river adventure. (Call, year-round, 800–596–RAFT for information, or contact Esprit at Thomas Lefebvre Road, Davidson, Québec J0X 1R0; camping is $15; hostel dorm is $20). Whether it's a canoe trip on the Noire (Black), Dumoine, or Coulonge Rivers, whitewater rafting on the Ottawa, a kayaking or swiftwater rescue course—or simply a camping spot or hostel bed—the Coffeys will make absolutely sure you have an unforgettable experience. Jim won't let you forget to take in the sunset from the back deck or the rocky beach. Jim and Erin are the real thing: They have sustainable ecotourism as their honest-to-goodness goal. We've traveled with them down the Ottawa and also on one of their Mexican trips. We recommend them highly.

Back on Route 148 and proceeding west, you'll cross the Black River. Look upstream to see the old Waltham Power Plant. Built in the early 1900s, it was Canada's first commercial power plant.

Past Waltham on Route 148, cross a bridge onto **Île des Allumettes** toward **Chapeau**. For thousands of years, Algonquins summered on its southernmost tip. Champlain visited their settlement in 1613 during his fruitless attempt to discover the Indies with "the boldest liar" he'd ever met, the young adventurer Nicolas Vignau, who had claimed to have traveled to the Indies via this route. Today you can visit **Chapeau** for this little town's fair in summer or carnival in winter.

If you are ready for a plain and hearty meal, head to **Freddie's Hotel** (79 Saint-Jacques, Chapeau J0X 1M0; 819–689–2762), where Freddie Mailleur and family have served tasty roast beef dinners with home-made bread (the beef is local) for heaven knows how long. It's a place you have to try. Basic rooms above the bar rent for $16. Diagonally across from Freddie's find **Karl's Bakery** (100 Saint-Jacques, Chapeau J0X 1M0; 819–689–2259), where you can buy tasty sugar pie (try these!), homemade rolls, bread, and other treats.

A remote B&B in a log homestead is located on an extremely secluded part of the island. At **Place Poupoure** (RR1, Chapeau J0X 1M0; 819–689–5519) you'll find camping facilities as well as swimming, boating, leisurely bike riding, and a dining room, which serves a Sunday brunch.

Backtrack to Route 148 and turn left to pass through Chichester. At the nonsmoking B&B called **Auberge Marie Louise** (Chichester J0X 1M0; 819–689–5500), owner Marie Louise will give you a hearty welcome. Because she's been a member of the Pontiac Tourism Association, she knows what's happening in the area. But do call in advance.

Proceed to the "end of the road," as **Fort William** is known. Come

Katharine on the Edge

*H*eights terrify me. So when I was traveling with Jim Coffey of Esprit Rafting on the Ottawa River and I heard him say, "See that big cliff over there? Who'd like to jump off it?" I was astonished to see my hand shoot up in the air. Who? Me? But I found myself dashing up the cliff with Eric and a herd of twenty-somethings. I was just fine until I paused at the edge of the cliff and looked down, down, to the black rushing water below. I froze. Eternity passed, and I heard Jim quietly say, "You don't have to do this." But I wanted to conquer fear. Reading my frustration, he added, "Katharine, let the others jump and, if you really want, I'll jump with you later." So I waited and later on, he grabbed my hand along with that of another rafter who was fearful, and off the edge we jumped. It was a leap of faith and what a rush I felt, hurtling through space to the water below. Jim's the kind of guy who inspires you to do your personal best.

summer, there's a long sandy beach to welcome you. Truly off the beaten path, the scenery here is spectacular. You'll find basic accommodations and a restaurant/bar at the **Hotel Pontiac** (819–689–2605).

From here, you must retrace your travels east on Route 148 to get to Campbell's Bay. Now turn left onto Highway 301 to **Otter Lake**, home of **Belle Terre Botanic Garden and Arboretum** (Otter Lake J0X 2P0; 819–453–7270). You can stroll footpaths through well-established perennial and herb gardens. You can also stay overnight; contact owners Joyce and Wayne Keller, who has operated the gardens for years.

For a truly unique experience, don't miss Jack and Debbie Gauthier's outstanding hospitality at the *totally* remote **Polish Hills Wilderness Farm** B&B (Polish Hills Road, C.P. 15, RR1, Otter Lake J0X 2P0; 819–453–7351). Way, way, *way* off the beaten path, this original Polish settlement farm is tucked away in the back of beyond. There's no phone on site: When you telephone, leave your name and number with their neighbor, some kilometers away. Debbie will call you back promptly and give you instructions on how to reach them. Oil lamps are used, and solar panels power batteries to operate lights. Debbie prepares your meals on her wood or propane stove. Accommodations are rustic, and you share a bathroom on the ground floor.

Jack also teaches how to make willow chairs, loveseats, and coffee tables. If you have room to strap one to your vehicle somehow, by all means make one. They are beautiful and sturdy and, for $100 for a day's workshop, with all tools and materials included, you can't beat it. Jack is

The Black River

*W*ant to head still farther upstream? About 15 kilometers west of Fort Coulonge and just before Waltham, turn right onto the **Chemin Rivière Noire (Black River Road).** The road almost immediately becomes gravel, winding through very old pastures and clearings. You'll pass by old log cabins, now much-beloved private cottages. A bit farther along and, off to your left, you'll catch glimpses of the old logging river, now popular for its recreational canoeing. Roughly 14 kilometers upriver you'll come to the quaint—read very rustic—**Black River Inn.** Here you can rent a very basic room, play a game of pool, and catch the yarns as the lads spin them out over a few pints of beer. (Watch out: Our brew is way stronger than American beer!) Phone Diane Graveline at 819–683–3150 for information about renting equipment for a guided paddle downriver or for room rates. She operates an outfitting company nearby called **Ecoyote.**

hilarious: He is a born storyteller and tree-hugger—an intriguing combination. He is also an accomplished fly fisherman and can give you friendly pointers on that sport. A bush road on their land connects you to nearby **Big Murray Lake,** where you can boat or fish in solitude. Come winter there are miles of cross-country ski trails, and dog sledding can be easily arranged.

Now head south on Highway 303 to **Ladysmith.** Formerly known as Schwartz, this tiny community was founded by German immigrants. Just as Shawville is predominantly English and Fort Coulonge French, this settlement was home to Eastern Europeans who fled religious persecution in the mid-1800s. The **cemetery** has interesting German headstones.

Turn left (east) onto Highway 366 at the **Silver Maple Hotel and Restaurant** (Ladysmith, Québec, J0X 2Y0; 819–647–3106). Here's a real local bar, complete with the requisite bunny head with antlers gracing the wall. Come fall, it's a hunter's mecca, where local lads compete for the biggest white-tail buck's rack of antlers. During the first weekend of October, Ladysmith rocks to **Oktoberfest** (call Clara Steinke at 819–647–2172), where music, dance competitions, art shows, and good times flow unchecked, accompanied by superb German fare cooked by the loving hands of local residents.

Follow the blue signs east on what soon becomes gravel roads to **Cushing Lodge B&B and Raptor Centre** (Fierobin Road, Ladysmith J0X 2Y0; 819–647–3226) to learn all about birds of prey and their habits from birder Jo-Ellen Cushing and husband, Geoffrey. Their lodge, built by this industrious couple in the early 1990s, is on the banks of a totally secluded private lake, and during summer you may spy the family of otters. Many miles of cross-country ski trails in winter and hiking trails in summer allow you to enjoy this retreat.

Still farther east on Highway 366, the gravel road changes to pavement at **Lac des Loup (Wolf Lake).** Continue to the hamlet of Sainte-Cécile-de-Masham, where there's another entry through a covered bridge into Gatineau Park. Enter here to hike or ski such trails as Kennedy Road or to swim, camp, or hike at Lac Philippe. This is also the access point to **Lusk Cave,** a noted geological feature of the Outaouais. If you explore this cave, be sure to wear old clothes you don't mind getting wet. And don't forget a flashlight: You'll need it. The main park information center is located at Old Chelsea (819–827–2020).

After Sainte-Cécile-de-Masham, you'll see the junction with Highway 105. Turn left to descend into Wakefield Village. At the foot of the hill you'll need to make a choice: Turn left to continue on Highway 105 to

Maniwaki; turn right to explore the village of Wakefield; or go straight across the bridge over the Gatineau River toward Val-des-Monts and the Laflèche Cavern.

The hour-long trip north on Highway 105 to Maniwaki takes you past Kazabazua (where you'll meet the junction with Highway 301 west to Otter Lake), Gracefield, Blue Sea Lake and its cottage country, and through the River Desert Indian Reserve. You hug and then lose sight of the Gatineau River, passing through rugged bush and spectacular cliffs and then through a sandy region of glacial till.

At **Maniwaki** visit a unique forestry museum, **Maison Logue** (8 Comeau, Maniwaki J9E 2R8; 819–449–7999), which highlights not just the logging industry, but also forestry protection techniques and technologies. An online connection to the nearby forest fire monitoring center displays up-to-the-minute information about lightning strikes and fires over a vast area of eastern Canada and northeastern United States. Originally a residence built in 1887 by Irishman Charles Logue, the Second-Empire house is built with locally quarried limestone and was refurbished in 1988. Today it houses the museum, the local library, and an art gallery.

Horseback riding

For another great adventure, call Craig Clost who will take you on hourly or up to three-day horseback riding and tenting adventures at nearby **Captiva Farms** *(RR 2 Box 16, Wakefield J0X 3G0; 819-459-2769; Web site: www3.sympatico.ca/ horseback.riding). e-mail: horseback.riding@ sympatico.ca;*

Maniwaki began as a trading post at the confluence of two of the major Outaouais rivers, the Desert and Gatineau. The town was established in 1851 by Catholic priests from Les Oblats de Marie Immaculée order, and even by that time logging had become its mainstay industry. Today, Maniwaki is the outpost leading to the **Parc de la Vérendrye (La Vérendrye Park)** and to two ZECs (Zone d'exploitation contrôlée, or controlled hunting and fishing zones): the **Pontiac** and **Bras-Coupé Desert.** Maniwaki has many well-qualified outfitters who can help you explore the hinterland by canoe, on foot, or during winter on snowmobile or skis.

To really go into the true "back of beyond," continue north on Highway 105 to Grand Remous and then head northwest on Highway 117 through La Vérendrye Park to the mining town of Val-d'Or. This is a long trip, and you'll either need to return via the same route or continue on through Rouyn-Noranda to Ontario. This region is a canoeist's heaven. The rewards will be many here, such as the sight of a moose and her calf. But be sure your car is in great shape to enjoy this trek.

You can return to Wakefield on Highway 105 South. For a circuit, however, we recommend continuing on Route 107 to Highway 117. Turn east toward Mont Laurier and watch for the right turn onto Route 309. This good paved road takes you beside sandy rivers to Val-des-Bois and Route 307. Follow Route 307 through Poltimore and Saint-Pierre-de-Wakefield, where you can visit Laflèche Cavern or follow Route 366 back to Wakefield.

Wakefield Village

Meanwhile, for those of you who don't choose to head north to Maniwaki, turn south on Highway 105 to *Wakefield* on River Road. It's a pretty little village that once was a major service center to the Irish, English, Scottish, French, and German settlers who homesteaded here. Wakefield is a "secret gem" for people visiting the national capital region. Only twenty minutes from Hull and Ottawa, it makes an excellent base from which you can explore the region.

First you pass the German-style inn *Alpengruss* (Wakefield J0X 3G0; 819–459–2885), which also has an excellent restaurant. If you like German comfort food, then stop here for superb schnitzel, cabbage, and beet dishes.

Just past the inn, turn right across the old railway tracks on Gendron, then right on Sully Road to visit potters *David McKenzie* and *Maureen Marcotte* (26 Sully, Wakefield J0X 3G0; 819–459–3164). This couple creates whimsical plates, mugs, and wall sconces from their home studio. Call for an appointment (don't be shy) to see their artworks and kiln.

Return to River Road. You'll pass by the terminus and turnaround for the *Wakefield Steam Train,* an old Swedish train, complete with dining car. Tours depart from Hull and take half a day, including a two-hour stopover in Wakefield. (165 rue Deveault, Hull J8Z 1S7; 819–778–7246; fax 819–778–5007; Web site: www.ottawa.com/tour/ trains.html; e-mail: train@ottawa.com. Operates mid-May through October; departs 1:30 P.M. Tuesday, Wednesday, Saturday, Sunday, and holidays, and daily in July and August; $23.00 adults, $21.00 seniors, $19.50 students and one-way travelers, ages 12 and under $11.00.)

Wakefield is a good place to enjoy on foot. With the steam train terminus behind you, walk south along River Road. Enter country shops, like Jamboree and the Wakefield General Store. Then a white clapboard Victorian home appears. This charming home is a 1896 doctor's home, now *Les Trois Érables* (*The Three Maples*) B&B, owned by Madeleine and

Les Trois Érables (the Three Maples) B&B

Jacques Mercier (260 chemin River, Wakefield J0X 3G0; 819–459–1118). It's an oasis of tranquility, set on a generous lawn and surrounded by an airy wraparound porch. Madeleine's delightful breakfasts—we enjoyed fresh sliced peaches and strawberries drizzled in maple syrup, followed by poached eggs with mushroom sauce—and the beautifully appointed rooms will make you want to linger.

Farther along River Road, opposite the pretty bay, you will find the popular *Black Sheep Inn* (216 chemin River, Wakefield J0X 3G0; 819–459–3228), whose music-loving owner, Paul Symes, has created *the* spot in the National Capital Region to hear great local bands, from jazz to folk to blues. Call ahead: You may need reservations and, depending upon the band, you may need to purchase tickets.

The inn is on the corner of Mill Street. Turn right and follow Mill Street up the hill to get to the Maclaren heritage buildings.

In 1838, Glaswegian William Fairbairn petitioned Sir John Colbourn, Governor of Upper and Lower Canada, for permission to erect a mill where the Lapêche River tumbled over a falls to the Gatineau River. Permission was granted, and the clever businessman built a prosperous grist mill. Six years later, the Maclaren family, also Scottish, bought the mill and expanded the complex to include a sawmill and woolen mill, general store, brickyard, and lodgings for their laborers. In 1865 or so, the family built *Maclaren House,* a fine Victorian brick home that still overlooks the *Maclaren Mill.* Today these historic landmarks of our pioneer industry languish, abandoned by the National Capital Commission, the government agency whose mandate it is to manage Gatineau Park and these heritage sites. We hope this situation will change. Behind the house, atop the rise, is an old cemetery where the late Canadian prime minister Lester B. Pearson is buried.

If you want to head into Gatineau Park for an exhilarating hike, find the little gravel roadway opposite Maclaren House and walk up it, underneath the overpass beside the Lapêche River. The roadway soon starts to climb into the woods, entering the park trail system. (Katharine's first book, *Historical Walks: The Gatineau Park Story,* is still the only guide to the trails of the park. It's available at shops in Wakefield, and details the network of hiking paths you can enjoy from here.)

Return to River Road and, turning right at the Black Sheep Inn, continue south. Find **Expéditions Radisson** (170 chemin River, Wakefield J0X 3G0; 819– 459–3860), where James Sisstie will rent you a canoe or kayak or take you on any of several one-day or many-day trips down the Gatineau River. You can rent all your gear from James, who will regale you with tales of the river and region. In winter, he organizes dog-sledding trips.

Find the flashing red light. At the corner is a charming, connected series of clapboard buildings known as **Place 1870,** which house a variety of shops. Explore them all: Each has its own charm. Beside Place 1870 is Anne-Marie Bertrand's **Galerie Le Corbeau Bleue (Blue Crow Gallery)** (105 chemin Valley, Wakefield J0X 3G0; 819–459–3640), which sells intriguing, all-local artwork, from fine jewelry to pottery to watercolors. Anne-Marie is a potter and a frequent participant in the annual artist's studio tour, Artists in their Environment, usually held the last two weekends in September. She also exhibits work from the Pontiac Artists Studio Tour, which is held on two weekends in June.

Wakefield's best restaurant is funky **Chez Eric,** named after a fish from the oddball movie *A Fish Called Wanda.* Find it (and Eric, the chubby

Cold? No kidding!

*E*xtreme temperatures are not unusual in the Outaouais. Winter temperatures average well below freezing, but can reach -40 where Celsius and Fahrenheit are the same. Fairly shallow lakes and watersheds fed by precipitation warm up quickly in the spring and are great for swimming by summer when the temperatures can approach 100°F.

When my family moved to this area from mild British Columbia in 1966, we found relief from the summer heat in the lake at our rustic cottage near the Black River. In mid-February of the first winter, we made our way up the road—well-maintained in winter to let the logging trucks through in those days—and stopped at the edge of the frozen lake. After some debate, my parents agreed to let the six of us cross the lake on the ice—but only if we carried long poles in case the ice broke. We headed out in pairs, walking gingerly until my brother Steve and I came across giant fresh tracks: a bulldozer! We flung the poles aside and joined arms to jump up and down, to the consternation of our parents farther back, until they too saw the tracks. The ice was almost three feet thick.—Eric goldfish) just a few doors down in another old frame house. We enjoyed being served on the backyard picnic table. (We don't know if Eric the fish approves of fish entrées, but Eric the co-author did enjoy his grilled salmon sandwich here.) Chez Eric is a popular local hangout, and it's very small. Call ahead to get a reservation (119 chemin Valley, Wakefield J0X 3G0; 819–459–3747).

Farther up this road, you connect with Highway 105. Turn left to Farm Point. You pass a little bakery on the right-hand side of the highway called Au Rouet which makes wonderful European breads (we adore the almond croissants).

Continue and on your right, is a huge sign pointing right to **Carman Trails International Hostel** (RR3, Wakefield J0X 3G0; 819–459–3180; fax 819–459–2113; Web site: www.magma.ca/~carman/maps/map.htm; e-mail: carman@magma.ca). Bordering Gatineau Park, the hostel offers accommodations as well as many things to do, from hiking or skiing in season to guided nature walks. There's also a real Finnish sauna. Manager Robert Grace has a welcoming, easy-going nature and will fill you in on trendy stuff to do in the area. Ask him about shuttle service into Gatineau Park and also about the Adventure Zone, a business he operates with three other outfitters. From here, for example, you can be driven to Esprit Rafting on the Ottawa River, or rent bikes to cycle there yourself.

Another partner in the Adventure Zone, nearby **Great Canadian Bungee,** offers Canada's highest bungee jump. You too can terrify yourself by jumping into the old quarry. Owner Matt Lawrence tells us it's fun, but so far we've not managed to convince ourselves. Perhaps you'd like to try? (Great Canadian Bungee, Wakefield J0X 3G0; 819–459–3714; Web site: infoweb.magi.com/bungee/home.html); e-mail: bungee @magi.com.)

Exploration of Eastern Edge of Outaouais

Return north on Highway 105, through Wakefield to where the bridge crosses the Gatineau River. Turn right and cross the river, following Highway 366 East and then Highway 307 North toward **Saint-Pierre-de-Wakefield.** Your destination now is the 20,000-year-old, geologically fascinating **Laflèche Cavern** (route Principale, St-Pierre-de-Wakefield J0X 3G0; 819–457–4033), the largest known caves in the Canadian Shield rock, discovered in 1865 by a hunter while tracking a bear.

The bruin disappeared into the rock and, investigating, intrepid tracker Joseph Dubois was astounded by his magnificent find. He was actually less intrigued by the amazing stalactites and stalagmites than by the glitter of gold.

He bought the property, visions of wealth dancing in his head. Alas, it was pyrite—fool's gold—and the caves languished until the 1920s, when they became a commercial success. In 1937 Zephyr Laflèche took them over until 1960, when again they were abandoned. Unfortunately, vandals destroyed the most spectacular formations, including columns created when some of the ancient stalactites and stalagmites eventually joined. Reopened in 1995, the caves are well worth exploring. Bilingual tours are available. (As you venture farther east in the Outaouais, English translations are less easy to come by.)

Halloween is a particularly spooky time to go into the caves. Guides dress up and give you the fright of your life. Most of the time, ghouls are

Legend of Ghost Hill

*S*tories of murder, ghostly sightings, and buried treasure mark Ghost Hill, a lonely stretch of highway west of Aylmer, at Breckenridge. Once the village had a store, post office, sawmill, railway station, water tower, and, cluster of homes. Today it's a hill, a bend in the road, and a bridge over Breckenridge Creek. Blink your eye and you've missed the memory.

But once upon a time, what's now Route 148 was a simple dirt track wide enough for a traveler's horse and cart. Trees, marsh, and mist were their companions. One blustery night, as his horse plodded home, one such fellow was aching to get home. Half asleep, roused by a sudden bellowing noise, he recoiled in fear. Dashing straight toward him was the oddest-looking cow he'd ever seen. With fear as his guide, he pointed his rifle and shot. Jumping from the cart, he

inspected the horrible apparition: His best friend lay at his feet, dressed in the skin of a calf.

It's not only the soul of the practical joker that haunts Ghost Hill. It's the ghost of the Armenian peddler, too. The peddler roamed the countryside, as did many folks, buying and selling what he could from his cart. Tall tales of his wealth grew, until one day, he felt sure his life was in danger, so he buried his bag of gold—on Ghost Hill. Sadly, his premonitions proved accurate, and he was brutally murdered. Weaving such legends together over the years are the reported sightings of ghosts at Ghost Hill. Skeptics say it is merely the will o' the wisp, or marsh gas. But on a dark and stormy night, when the skeletal limbs of the trees are a-creaking, who's to deny that anguished souls might cry on Ghost Hill?

not about, so it's safe to go spelunking. For the price of admission you get your own battery-powered miner's light firmly affixed to a hard hat. There are two tours: the 90-minute general tour and one called "wild caving," which promises a three-hour exploration of special galleries. Even in winter the caves are spectacular, with sparkling formations of ice along with hibernating, upside-down bats.

From here, you can return to Hull on the east side of the Gatineau River via either Highway 307 through Cantley or Highway 366 through Val-des-Monts.

East of the National Capital Region lies the easternmost region of the Outaouais, known as *La Petite Nation* ("The Little Nation"), home of the beautiful *Château Montebello* (Montebello J0V 1L0; 819–423–6341). This is one of our favorite places to stay as it's quintessentially Canadian:

Outaouais Geology

*A*t the Chaudière Falls rapids in Hull, you can see the Ottawa River pouring through jutting layers of limestone. This is intriguing to the geologist because this exposed rock is younger than the sinuous ridge of the Eardley Escarpment, which rises just to the north. The ridge is the most ancient rock in the world: Pre-Cambrian rock that formed the weathered roots of a range of mountains once higher than the Rockies. Weathering, glacial action, and faulting conspired to erode them to their present size. The fault line along the base of the ridge is the boundary to Gatineau Park and the northernmost edge of a huge rift valley, extending into the Appalachians of New England.

Successive eras of glaciation covered most of North America, scouring the mountains, depressing the land, carving valleys, and depositing moraine (earth and stone) as the glaciers first grew, then receded. About 20,000

years ago the last ice sheet started to melt and, as it did, the Champlain Sea covered the land. The Eardley Escarpment was its northern boundary. As you stand on the Champlain Lookout in Gatineau Park, your feet firmly atop this ridge, look due south over the flat, Ottawa Valley plain. In the distance the Ottawa River flows past, but 12,000 years ago, if you had stood here, water would have lapped at your feet. Whales, seals, and other marine creatures dwelt here in saline waters. (At Hull's Ecomuseum, you can see fossils from this period.)

Looking out over the plain from the vantage of the Eardley Escarpment is one thing. It's just as intriguing to drive through geological history. As you drive west on Highway 148 from Hull toward Quyon, you will pass several terraces, old beaches formed when the Ottawa River was receding. Keep your eyes peeled for these ancient landmarks.

"My" Gatineau Park

Gatineau Park is "my" park. The wild ways and spaces of this park outside Hull are dear to me, perhaps because it's where Eric and I spent a lot of time when we first began dating. One of our first dates was to McCloskey Trail, which pitches down the back of the ridge to Meech Lake. It was my first time on cross-country skis. You know the drill: The people in the group were close friends, and here I was, new to both the sport and to the group. As soon as we hit the trail, Eric and the rest vaporized in a cloud of snow, leaving me to slip and slide uphill as best I could. I finally took my skis off, turned around, and mur- mured black thoughts. I figured I'd just head back to the car. Suddenly a group of skiers started running uphill toward me. Meanwhile, I had sunk knee-deep in snow. With tears of frustration pouring down my face, I found myself peering into the face of the leader of this athletic group. In disbelief he looked at me, saying, "What are you doing here? If you don't know what you're doing, you'd better get back down." With this, his group dashed off, uphill, leaving me floundering. Some- how I negotiated the descent and, somehow, Eric and I are still together, happily surmounting other chal- lenges.—Katharine

cedar logs with a massive central fireplace, cozy armchairs, an inde-scribably delicious buffet, swimming pool with spa—a little piece of heaven. To get there, follow Route 148 east toward Montréal. Pass through Thurso—with its sometimes smelly pulp and paper mill—to Papineauville and the village of Montebello.

The entrance to the Château Montebello appears on your right, through a grand log gateway. The château qualifies as a national treasure. It's the world's largest log structure, and its grounds were once the home of Québec patriot Louis-Joseph Papineau. Parks Canada now operates his 1846 mansion as the **Papineau Museum** (500 Notre-Dame, C.P. 444, Montebello J0V 1L0; 819–423–6965; fax 819–423–6455). We cannot think of a better eastern bastion of the Outaouais.

North of the Château Montebello on Highway 323, you first pass **Park Omega,** a wildlife park (Route 323, Montebello J0V 1L0; 819–423–5487; open daily year-round, 10:00 A.M. to an hour before sunset; $10.00 adults, $5.00 children). As you drive through the park, you'll spy such animals as bison (buffalo), white-tail deer, and wild pig. In winter, it's beautiful to see the animals in the fresh snow.

Farther north on this road is **Kenauk** (540 Notre Dame, Montebello J0V 1L0; 819–423–5573). This is a little-known seigneurial preserve owned and operated by the Château Montebello. Originally this was all part of Papineau's seigneurial holdings. Today Kenauk offers private cabins on extremely secluded lakes: a pricey but unforgettable Outaouais destination. Just ask about their "blue trout," a mouthwatering delicacy.

A far more reasonably priced stay can be thoroughly enjoyed at a farm B&B called **Les Jardins de Vinoy,** owned by Suzanne Benoit and André Chagnon (497 Mtee Vinoy-Ouest, Cheneville J0V 1E0; 819–428–3774). They speak some English, though their mother tongue is French. Tucked away in a protected little valley, it is a treasure. Suzanne has decorated every room in its own unique style (our favorite has stenciled ivy over its walls), and antiques crowd the hallways. The cuisine is delectable. Vegetables and preserves are homegrown whenever possible; otherwise, local produce is served. You'll be delighted.

Ask them about the nearby goat cheese factory and the **Musée des pionniers (Pioneer Museum)** in Saint-André-Avellin (20 rue Bourgeois, Saint-André-Avellin; 819–983–2624; Web site: w3.franco.ca/petitenation/musee.htm; open daily June 24 through Labor Day weekend from 9:00 A.M. to 5:00 P.M.; $3.00 adults, $1.00 students).

Return via Route 148 to Hull through the city of Gatineau, or else continue east to Montréal. Gatineau is becoming increasingly well-known because of its annual **Gatineau Hot Air Balloon Festival** (800–668–8383 or 819–243–2330; Web site: www.ville.gatineau. qc.ca/c/intro/montgolfiere /e.htm). The festival is held at **Parc La Baie Park** during Labor

Way Off Track

*R*eally and truly off the beaten path are the **Pontiac Artists Studio Tour** in June (contact Dale Shutt at 819–648–2441; Web site: www.mhanet.org/users/pasta), and the **Artists in their Environment Tour** in September (contact Becky Mason at (819) 827–4159). Dale has become a good friend since we moved to the Pontiac. She and I were two of the seven founders of the Pontiac Artists Studio Tour Association, affectionately dubbed PASTA. Since 1989 many artists and writers have joined us, such as whimsical woodworker Richard Blais, Brazilian Marcio Melo, and pen-and-ink artist Michael Neelin. If you like arts and crafts as well as exploring real back roads and country places, consider planning your trip to coincide with a tour. Admission is free, and you will be warmly invited into each creator's private space to view (and, of course, possibly buy) their work.—Katharine

Day weekend in September. It's a fantastic display of brilliantly colored, fancifully shaped balloons depicting everything from a Walt Disney castle to a Holstein cow to a truck.

Whether it's hot air ballooning in Gatineau, running river rapids with Esprit Rafting, or walking the trails in Gatineau Park, the Outaouais offers nature at its best. Enjoy it.

PLACES TO STAY IN THE OUTAOUAIS

AYLMER
Château Cartier,
1170 Aylmer Road, J9H 5E1;
(800) 807-1088 or
(819) 777-1088;
fax (819) 777-7161;
Web site: cchgr.qc.ca/hotel

GATINEAU
Le Manoir de la Montée
Paiement (B&B),
1201 Montée Paiement,
J8T 3K6;
(819) 243-2284;
email: bbguy@cyberus.ca

HULL
Best Western
Jacques Cartier Hôtel,
131 rue Laurier,
J8X 3W3;
(800) 265-8550 or
(819) 770-8550;
fax (819) 770-9705

LUSKVILLE
Au Charme de la Montagne
(B&B),
368 chemin Crégheur,
Pontiac J0X 2G0;
(819) 455-9158;
fax (819) 455-2706;
Web site: www.bbcanada.com/740.html

PLACES TO EAT IN THE OUTAOUAIS

AYLMER
You can bring your own
wine (*Apportez votre vin*)
to Casa Grecque,
2000 rue Principale J9H 6J4;
(819) 685-0600;
fax (819) 685-0175

CHELSEA
L'Orée du Bois,
15 chemin Kingsmere,
J0X 1N0;
(819) 827-0332

CHELSEA
Les Fougères,
783 route 105,
J0X 1N0;
(819) 827-8942;
fax (819) 827-2388

HULL
Café Henry Burger,
69 rue Laurier,
J8X 3V7;
(819) 777-5646;
fax (819) 777-0832

MASSON-ANGERS
Seafood and nightclub
show at
La Ferme Rouge,
1957 route 148,
J8M 1P3;
(819) 986-7013

Exploring the Coastal Region

Our proposed circuit—to explore the coasts of Québec—mixes mountains and rivers, oceans and saltwater breezes. Starting from near Matapédia, we'll take you east on the coast to New Richmond. Then, instead of following the coast to Percé Rock like most people do, we'll head north on an inexplicably underutilized road hugging the Cascapédia River. It's lovely: The road eventually gains substantial elevation as it climbs through the Chic-Choc and McGerrigle Ranges, extensions of the Appalachians that are now part of the Parc de la Gaspésie. The highest elevation is Mont Jacques Cartier at 1,268 meters. We'll take you to an agate mine hidden among its ancient hills and, if you hike or ski the Chic-Chocs, you could even find some caribou.

Quite apart from water and mountains, this coastal drive introduces you to a part of Québec settled by the Acadians, Loyalists, Basque, French, English (many from the United Kingdom's southern isles of Guernsey and Jersey), and Scottish peoples.

Jacques Cartier is far too often credited with "discovering" this land in 1534, but historical and archaeological evidence indicates otherwise. In the early sixteenth century, Portuguese, Basque, and French came to fish the great schools of cod on the Grand Banks, but it would be another hundred years before any attempt at permanent settlement was made. Conditions were just too harsh. It was far easier for fisherman to erect temporary shelters, fish all summer, then return with their catch stowed in their holds, ready for the European market.

But for over 8,000 years, native peoples dwelt here. During the time of Cartier, Montaignais were living a good life, following the herds of caribou and hunting the prolific deer and moose. Around the 1500s these people were driven north, to the north shore of the St. Lawrence (which we'll explore on this drive), by the Micmacs, a name given to the tribe by the French, possibly meaning "allies."

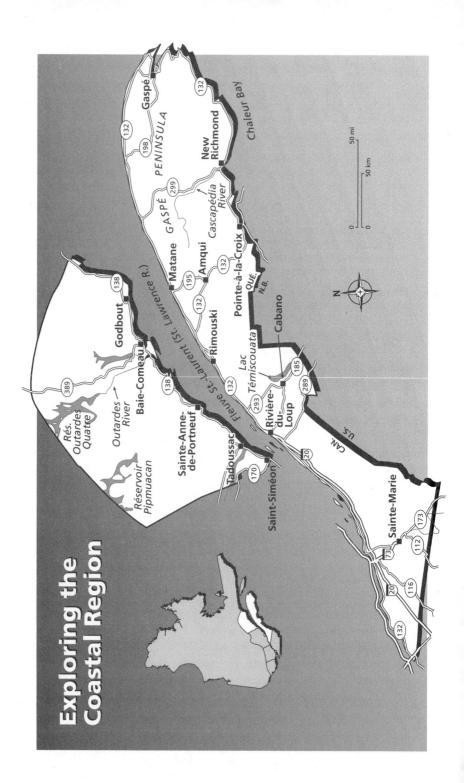

EXPLORING THE COASTAL REGION

The Gaspé Peninsula region is rich with the history of its settlers. There are some excellent museums here, including one called La Bataille de la Ristigouche parc historique national. It depicts the Battle of the Restigouche—another classic battle between French and English, but this time a naval, not land-based, battle. If you want to learn the heritage of British settlement in the Gaspé, don't miss the heritage village and museum in New Richmond, a superbly interpreted village where you can also stay overnight, with advance reservations.

Yet another museum, in Bonaventure, explains the impact of the tragic Acadian Deportation of 1755, the year before the commencement of England and France's Seven Year's War. Because these hardy, successful pioneers refused to give an oath of allegiance to the British Crown, 14,000 Acadians were forcibly moved from their farms. Their homes were burned. Where did they flee? To the *Thirteen Colonies,* primarily—and some made it as far as Louisiana. Upon their return after the Treaty of Versailles in 1763, they discovered Loyalists had taken over their homes and businesses. Then where did they go? They cleared land and established new settlements, such as the one at Carleton, across Cascapédia Bay from New Richmond.

The late 1700s and early 1800s saw waves of arriving Scots and Irish. These were the times of the Scottish Clearances when landlords evicted poor tenants from their crofts in northern Scotland. The crofts were burned to make more grazing land for sheep. It was also the time of the Irish potato famines. The years between 1846 and 1855 witnessed the largest mass migration of these peoples to Canada. Names such as the Scottish Cuthburt, the Irish Duthie, the Acadian Leblanc, and the Loyalist Pritchard have mixed and matched over the years to create the rich cultural heritage that you will enjoy today.

Today's Gaspé region is a blend of all these peoples, though French is by far the majority language here. If you are interested in the Loyalist, Acadian, and English-speaking people's history and genealogy in the Gaspé, visit New Richmond's Centre de l'héritage britannique de la Gaspésie (Center of British Heritage of the Gaspé).

We propose a "water route" as you explore this region of Québec. You'll visit the seaside towns hugging coastlines along the St. Lawrence River

AUTHORS' TOP PICKS IN THE COASTAL REGION
Battle of the Restigouche National Historic Site
Domaine Stanley
British Heritage Center of the Gaspé
Cascapédia River
Mont Lyall Agate Mine
Salmon ladder at the Mathier-D'Amours Dam in Matane
Pointe-aux-Outardes (near Baie-Comeau)
Camping Bon Désir
Fort Ingall and the Témiscouata Rose Gardens

and Gulf of St. Lawrence. And, as we explore inland, we will traverse the banks of two classic salmon fishing rivers, the Matapédia and Cascapédia. Finally, we suggest you really "get wet" by crossing the St. Lawrence to descend its north shore. Several ferries ply its waters. Pack your binoculars because you'll likely see whales. When we made the crossing in early August, we thrilled to the sight of pods of belugas—those smiling white whales—from the ferry crossing between Saint-Siméon and Rivière-du-Loup. And if you are really up to something rugged, Eric has a truly wild 'n' woolly suggestion that will take a bit of planning on your part. You see, after crossing the St. Lawrence, you could head east and end up on a ferry to Newfoundland, then back to the Gaspé via Nova Scotia.

Since this route involves catching ferries, you must make reservations. This inevitably means that you'll need to plan your trip carefully, giving yourself enough time to reach ferry docks a full hour or more in advance. This may mean setting yourself a schedule and booking accommodations at or near the ferry.

We start this trip at Pointe à la Croix, near the New Brunswick border town of Campbellton. Have a good look at a route map to orient yourself: You could make a variety of circuits here. You can also custom design your trip to head north to Rivière-du-Loup and then, after crossing north to Saint-Siméon by ferry, continue west to Québec City.

The Gaspé Peninsula

The first town we propose visiting is ***Pointe à la Croix (Point of the Cross),*** situated on the Québec side of the interprovincial bridge spanning the Baie des Chaleurs, across from Campbellton, New Brunswick, via Highway 11. The "Point of the Cross" refers to a cross the Micmacs once erected to denote the boundaries of their territory.

As soon as you cross to Pointe à la Croix, proceed along the Boulevard Interprovincial and, for now, turn left on Route 132 Ouest (West). On your left you'll see a federally operated museum, ***La Bataille de la Ristigouche parc historique national,*** (***Battle of the Restigouche National Historic Site***) (Route 132, C.P. 359, Pointe-à-la-Croix G0C 1L0; 800–463–6769 or 418–788–5676; fax 418–788–5895; open daily June through mid-October 9:00 A.M. to 5:00 P.M.; $3.50 adults). It is fully interpreted in English and definitely should not be missed as it sets the context for the history of the Gaspé region.

EXPLORING THE COASTAL REGION

This battle was one of the "last hurrahs" for New France. The facts are well-explained at the museum in a series of fascinating exhibits and in an English-language video. British forces numbering 1,700 well-disciplined soldiers and sailors routed the 400 French equivalents with their allies the Micmacs and some 1,000 Acadians. This was a dramatic naval battle that saw French Admiral Giraudais, in his frigate the *Machault,* as well as two other French ships, the *Bienfaisant* and *Marquis de Malauze,* defeated by the British frigates, *Repulse* and *Scarborough,* plus an armed schooner, on July 8, 1760. The French had drawn the British farther and farther into the Baie des Chaleurs, taunting them with glimpses of the *Machault.* Giraudais had attempted to secure his position by sinking several ships in the bay. But the hoped-for blockade of sunken hulks proved no defense against the skilled British navigators, and the needed French reinforcements never came.

This museum provides insight into our current politics as well as that battle of so long ago. Step outside the museum entrance to look out over the Baie des Chaleurs, where the *Machault* sank. Then, inside the museum, find actual pieces of the boat that have been brought from the depths, restored, and displayed.

Now return, eastward, along the coast toward **Pointe-à-la-Croix.** Need a spot to stay? You simply can't miss the red-turreted **L'Auberge du Château Bahia** just south of Route 132. Built as a wooden castle, it has twenty-two rooms and even a banquet hall. There are trails for hiking or biking, and you can swim here, too. English, German, and French is spoken. (Point-à-la-Garde G0C 2M0; 418–788–2048; B&B from $39.00 for two, nearby dorms from $15.)

Continue about 20 kilometers east on the highway to another museum of a completely different kind. Turn right onto Route Miguasha Ouest and follow the signs to the **Parc de Miguasha** (270 route Miguasha Ouest, C.P. 183, Nouvelle G0C 2E0; 418–794–2475; fax 418–794–2033; e-mail: miguasha@quebectel.com). This spot is internationally renowned

Top Annual Events in the Coastal Region

February

Snowmobile drag racing in early February in Rivière-du-Loup with competitors from Canada and the United States; 418–867–3480

June

Matane Shrimp Festival; third weekend in June; 418–562–0404; fax 418–562–8406

July

Annual Montagnais native pow-wow in Essipit during the last week of July; shows, fireworks, bonfires; 418–233–2509

Matane Country Western Festival; folk music, shows and dances, kids activities, last week of July/early August; 418–562–6821; fax 418–562–0325

August

Country music at the Blue Whale Festival in Bergeronnes during the first weekend of August; 418–232–6326

International Jazz Festival in Rimouski at the end of August in theaters, bars, and on the streets; 418–232–7844

for its rich fossil deposits. Dicovered by Dr. Abraham Gesner in 1842, it didn't really gain scientific interest until 1879. During the next seventy-five years, archaeologists and paleontologists discovered twenty-three fish species, four invertebrate species, nine plant species, and sixty-six varieties of spores.

Not only can you wander through 370 million years of natural history here but you can also walk through the museum's grassy lawns to descend a sturdy staircase to the beach. Do wander along the coastal cliffs with their concentration of fossils. Remember that *no* fossils may be removed. If you find any, please let the front desk at the museum know. When you've completed your beachcombing, or perhaps an oceanside picnic, return up a second, more easterly set of stairs, where you'll discover the 1.9-kilometer "Evolution of Life" cliff-top walk. The park museum has a snack bar and, when we were there, a local singer was offering both French and English folk songs. There's also quite a nice gift shop here.

Gaspé

The name of the Gaspé Peninsula comes from a Micmac word meaning "land's end."

You can either return to Route 132 by following the road across the Miguasha Peninsula to Nouvelle or, if you'd like to stop for the day, follow the coastal road to *Camping L'Érabliere* (28 route Miguasha Ouest, Nouvelle G0C 2E0; 418–794– 2913) near the tip of the peninsula. This pretty site has chalets and camping sites overlooking the bay.

We pushed on to the 1756 Acadian settlement of Carleton, hoping to set up our tent at *Camping de Carleton* (418–364–3992) on the spit of land called Banc de Larocque on the east side of town. Famed for its nearby bird sanctuary, we were eager to see tern and heron. However, we were thwarted. The place was full to overflowing, and we joined many travelers who were given special permission (for $4) to camp at the municipal park. Be smarter than we were. Reservations do have their merits.

The night we were in Carleton was the start of *Maximum Blues,* an annual five-day international blues festival held in early August. With thirteen different sites, the place was hopping with large and happy crowds (418–364–6008; fax 418–364–7314). And when we awoke, we saw more than a dozen blue herons in the bay just in front of our tent.

Besides excellent bird-watching, there are several hikes around Carleton. As you approach the town, you'll see a sign pointing left at Route de l'Éperlan (the French word éperlan refers to a small, smelt-like fish) to walking paths on 613-meter-high *Mont Carleton,* called Sentiers

EXPLORING THE COASTAL REGION

WORTH SEEING IN THE COASTAL REGION

Percé Rock,
Percé (on eastern tip on Gaspé Peninsula)

Forillon National Park, on eastern tip on Gaspé Peninsula, is the end of the Appalachian Mountain chain

pédestres de l'Éperlan. In town, just past the quay, find Rue de la Montagne, leading to *Mont Saint-Joseph* (555 meters), for more hiking. Get details at the Tourist Information Center, on your right just east of the turnoff to Mont Saint-Joseph. The fluently bilingual staff is extremely helpful, and there's a little exhibit on the bird life you'll see on the coast. If hiking or lookouts interest you, ask for the brochure and map called "Carleton-Maria: Réseau de sentiers de randonnée pédestre," which gives a detailed description of the trails, which also hook up to Maria, the next town to the east. You can get some great views of the ocean from the summits of these mountains.

If you are camping, there's a very good fish store in town, *La Poisson-nerie de la Gare* at the corner of Route 132 and Rue de la Gare, where you can purchase then cook a local catch. There are many places to stay here—but reserve ahead or get there early if you happen to coincide with the Blues Festival like we did.

At 211 rue du Quai in Carleton, you'll come across an old boat, the *BaBar,* hauled up on the beach. We were told that owner Pierre Landry purchased it for $1.00 in Québec City and floated it here. But apparently it took over 150 men and a bulldozer to haul it up onto the beach. Now it's a very trendy bar where each Wednesday night it's two beers for the price of one. You can imagine how packed it gets. Beer is stored belowdecks decks, where it is kept chilled by the insulating sand.

On the far side of the BaBar, find *Café L'Indépendant'e,* where you can eat the catch of the day or, if you don't care for fish, dine on other specialties of the house (215 rue du Quai, Carleton G0C 1G0; 418–364–7602). For family dining, try *Le Heron* overlooking the ocean atop the rise of land in the middle of town (561 boulevard Perron, Carleton G0C 1G0; 418–364–3881).

In the parking lot just beyond the restaurant, your attention will be riveted by two immense, colorful statues of Monsieur Penouil and Miss Gaspésie, leftovers from parade floats for Carleton's Salmon Festival. Monsieur Penouil is a folk character representing the Basque sailors who came here to fish in the early 1500s, and who made permanent settlements here two and a half centuries later. The Penouil figure is the local doll you'll see in stores throughout the Gaspé. The doll is typically formed from a crab's body, with crab claws as his hands and feet, though the parade statue gives him a human face. His clothing is also

Taiga

The vegetation known as taiga makes up the transition between arctic tundra and the boreal forest, covering hundreds of square kilometers between the 52nd and 56th parallels. Spruce and fir, along with dwarf shrubs and trees, represent the flora here. But it is the rich lichen growth that provides sustenance to herds of caribou in Québec's taiga regions. Taiga is also found in Les Grands Jardins and Gaspé Parks, both of which also support rare herds of caribou.

derived from the fishing industry: a jacket made from old sails and waterproofed with linseed oil.

His beloved partner Miss Gaspésie wears a typical Acadian skirt. Here she sports a skirt that is green for the forests and blue for the ocean, representing the two major resources of Carleton. Her black bolero jacket recalls old French costumes, while her cap is of English origin, being typical of the island of Jersey, from whence so many early Gaspé settlers came.

The couple represent the intermingling and intermarriage between the cultures here in Québec. Love has its way of conquering politics, after all's said and done. On a sign explaining the statue, it is written: "With a little luck, Miss Gaspésie will become as many of the children call her: Mrs. Penouil!"

After leaving Carleton, the next town you come to is *Maria,* appropriately named after Lady Maria Effingham, the wife of Sir Guy Carleton. If you want a hike, watch for Rang (rural route) 3 just west of town, and turn up this road to discover the start of the *sentier* (trail) that leads to pretty *Chute Grand Sault Falls.*

All along this coast we were intrigued with the bird life, especially with the cormorants whose characteristic stance—wings extended as they perch with their breasts facing the sunshine and wind—makes a wonderful silhouette against the ocean backdrop. Cormorants pose like this to dry their feathers.

Pause in Maria to stretch your legs at *Plage Goéland (Gull Beach),* typically rock-strewn, with the village's homes thronging the street. On the eastern outskirts of Maria, you'll pass through Gesgapegiag, a Micmac reserve whose church is built in the form of a giant white tepee.

Immediately after the bridge over the Cascapédia River, you'll meet the end of Highway 299 Nord. We'll follow this route north soon, but for now follow the sign pointing right to New Richmond, and watch for the signs directing you to Domaine Stanley. We insist (not merely recommend) that you stay here if you possibly can. We'll go a step further: Plan to stay one night at Domaine Stanley and a second at the British Heritage Center of the Gaspésie. That way, you will get both sides of the coin: a fancy overnight stay in Governor General Lord

Stanley's former salmon retreat-cum-mansion, and a taste of a more ordinary English home at the British Heritage Center.

Follow the signs and turn right into **Domaine Stanley** (371 boulevard Perron Ouest, New Richmond G0C 2B0; 418–392–5560; fax 418–392–5592). Its long driveway curves through meadows and woods. Then you'll gasp: In front of you, on a landscaped lawn, stands a charming old clapboard estate with the American, Canadian, and Québec flags snapping in the ocean breeze. Step inside, and you'll know you have made a real discovery: handsome tongue-and-groove wood paneling greets you amid a cool atmosphere of calm and repose.

The home was built in 1888 as the retreat for Frederic Arthur Stanley, Lord of Preston, sixteenth Earl of Derby, who was Canada's Governor General from 1888 to 1893. It is he, too, who inaugurated the prized Stanley Cup hockey trophy, in 1893. Two other Governors—General Lord Aberdeen and the Earl of Minto—used it as a summer retreat. It has had various owners, including former Philadelphia mayor John Reyburn. The Canada Council for the Arts operated it as a heavily subsidized artists' retreat from 1972 through 1984, until it became economically and politically untenable. The present owners, the LeBlanc family, have painstakingly restored it.

Madame Lucille LeBlanc is the cook, and she also designed and, in many cases, painted and sewed to create the unique look of each bedroom. What a lovely job she's done! There are eleven bedrooms of various sizes, some with an in-suite bathroom, some with shared facilities. Quite apart from the peaceful interior ambiance, the grounds beckoned us. Situated on twenty-five acres of lovely lawn, woods, and cropped fields, this is a treasure of a place to walk or to curl up with a good book and enjoy yourself. There's a pretty descent to the wind-tossed 1,500 feet of private beach, where you can sit in the sun on picturesque pieces of driftwood logs, watching the gulls on the breeze and the statuesque herons fishing. Across the bay is Carleton.

Almost next door is the historic village of New Richmond's **Centre d'Héritage Britannique de la Gaspésie (British Heritage Center of the Gaspe)** (351 boulevard Perron Ouest, C.P. 395, New Richmond G0C 2B0; 418–392–4487; open daily June 7 through beginning of September, 9:00 A.M. to 6:00 P.M.; $5.00 adults, $4.00 seniors, $3.50 students, $12.00 family). This living museum is a collection of homes once lived in by British settlers to this region. Don't make the mistake of assuming that everyone who's British is specifically English. Here there are Irish, Scots, Jersey, and Guernsey folk—as well as English.

The museum was the brainchild of a group of concerned citizens who wished to celebrate the bicentennial of the Loyalists' arrival here. In 1984, they formed the Cascapédia Bay Loyalist Village Corporation, with the express purpose of preserving their British heritage in this region of Québec. Fourteen buildings were selected and moved to this site, to re-create a village ambiance in the British style. It works well. Volunteers dressed in period costume abound, mending a horse carriage here, animating the plight of the Loyalists there. The entire museum stretches over many acres of woods and meadows. You can take a shuttle carriage or walk.

You pass through time, going from the 1700s to early 1900s, visiting such dwellings as the George Harvey home, built circa 1890 after the American Colonial style. There's also the **Willet House,** now sometimes operated as a B&B (but absolutely only on prior reservation). Loyalist William Willet came to the Gaspé after his father was killed in the American Revolution. Behind J. A. Gendron's General Store (the first village structure), don't miss the Village Store, which is full of local homemade items such as quilts and even samples of rarely made tatted doilies, an old craft that some of the women here still practice. If you are like us, you'll be itching to find some books written in English that tell of the legends and history of Québec and the Gaspé. We found several here, as well as the amusing *Grandma's Kitchen Favourites,* a local recipe book. Some recipes, such as the Queen of Puddings, dates to the 1600s. The book also includes all sorts of colorful anecdotes about life here "in the good old days."

British Heritage Center of the Gaspé

Allow yourselves a good three or four hours to explore these heritage buildings. Genealogists will surely want to spend time here, for the center is renowned for its Loyalist records, the most extensive in the Gaspé. If you call, ask to speak to Joan Gow, who has worked here as a volunteer since the center's creation in 1984, or Frances Cochrane, secretary of the nonprofit association that runs this restored village. Both women are articulate and inspiring.

You may want to proceed through New Richmond about 40 kilometers to Bonaventure, where you'll discover the *Musée acadien du Québec (Acadian Museum of Québec)*. Another bilingual museum, it explains the history of the Acadians, the dreadful deportation years, and their proud resettlement of this region (95 avenue Port-Royal, Bonaventure G0C 1E0; 418–534–4000; fax 418–534–4105; open daily year-round with differing opening hours; $3.50 adults, $2.50 seniors and students, $7.50 family).

To continue our basic circuit, from New Richmond retrace your route for the few kilometers west to head north on Highway 299. This pretty road skirts the Cascapédia River, past some beautiful old farms, farmhouses, and villages such as *Grande Cascapédia.* We noted St. Andrews United Church, established 1899, and realized that all the names on post boxes and even streets were of British derivation. Canadian flags flew in the breeze.

As you leave the settled land of Grande Cascapédia, you drive north into what becomes a stunningly beautiful section of countryside. The *Cascapédia River* tumbles over boulders on your left, and all along the riverbank are pulloffs for salmon fishing, all of them named. We stopped at Number 27, Big Jack, which had a picnic table, like many of the others that we saw. After preparing a picnic sandwich, we took the little rocky trail to the water's edge and sat down to eat lunch. Canoeists paddled past, and the river invited us to take a dip. Brisk, though, that water!

You absolutely *must* have a fishing license prior to fishing here. What's more, fishing holes such as Big Jack are designated to particular fishermen, reserved when a fisherman registers. You'll see signs advising you, *Pêche avec réservation seulement* (meaning that fishing is permitted only by reservation). While we were enjoying lunch, a river warden stopped by to ensure we were not fishing. Respecting these rules helps preserve our Atlantic salmon and other fish.

As we traveled north, we wondered about the many fishing holes along the river with such names as "Maple" or "Lower Joe Martin." Who were the people named? We also reflected on the days of old when the river was the private stomping grounds of the Governors-General like Lord Stanley, whose retreat we just saw. How peculiar and absurd it must have seemed to the natives to think of one person "owning" such a river territory.

Continuing north on route 299, we arrived at a gas station called *Le Relais de la Cache,* where you can get fishing licences and where you must report your catch.

Past it, on the right, are some horrid examples of clearcutting, a rare sight in the Gaspé region, and on the left you'll see towering mountains. Suddenly the road becomes steep, and road signs advise caution. The elevation is 533 meters here, and the road twists and turns around the bedrock, which glints with mica.

Watch for a sign pointing to your right to the agate mine and to Murdochville. Five kilometers down this gravel road, look for the right-hand turnoff onto Chemin des Tresoirs and proceed up a very bumpy road to the *Mine d'agates du Mont Lyall (Agate Mine)* (41 Village-de-l'Anse, Cap-Chat Est, G0J 1G0; 418–786–2439; fax 786–2240). Here, for $20, you get a pair of safety goggles, a geologist's hammer, and a big bucket and off you go, up the side of the mountain, to prospect for geodes and agates for three hours.

We had a ball. No one, we feel sure, could come away without finding

Grandma Says

*H*ere are some quotes from Grandma's Kitchen Favourites, *an old recipe book from New Richmond that's loaded with far more than just recipes.* "The first Jewish mayor of a municipality in Québec was Mr. Isaac Hyman who was mayor of the municipality of Cap des Rosiers for about forty years. He was the son of William Hyman who founded a fish farm in Grand Grève in 1844."

"When the Loyalists arrived on the coast they were without equipment and provisions. The Gov't however, offered assistance: Each family received an axe, hammer, saw, hoe, spade, seeds, a quantity of nails, a pair of door hinges. Each group of 5 families received a shipsaw for making planks and a gun for hunting. They were also to be supplied with some foods for three years."

"One of the first pre-fabs in Canada was Lorne Cottage on the Cascapedia River. All the lumber was pre cut to size and was floated down from Ottawa. It was to be the summer home of Princess Louise (daughter of Queen Victoria) and her husband the Marquis of Lorne. It was at this cottage that the hymn "Unto the Hills" was written by the marquis of Lorne in 1877."

The Phantom Ship

Joan Gow has seen it. Twice. The first time was when she was fourteen. The second time, she called her husband to her side, and he too saw the Phantom Ship of Chaleur Bay.

You see, once upon a time there was a pirate ship that was running hard against the wind, pursued by a man-of-war with all guns a-blazing. While desperately trying to evade capture, the renegade burst into flames and all hands were lost.

The phantom, seen over the years by hundreds of people, appears suddenly, out of nowhere. Some describe the sea as boiling when the apparition strikes. Most, like Joan, say you can clearly see the sailors running to and fro, up and down the rigging, while the captain stands on the foredeck, with a woman in white.

Say what you will, many people in this area believe this tale, and the North-ern Lights newspaper of nearby Bathurst, New Brunswick, even has photos of it.

some sort of treasure. The day we were there, the sun was beating down on the white rocks of which this part of the mountain is formed. Crowds of people were working the mountainside. Kids were excitedly jumping up and down, shouting "I've found one," while adults—also far from calm—were making their finds.

Owner and geologist Val Côté is extremely approachable, sitting on the front deck of his "office" and gift shop, with a twinkle in his eye. He speaks only French, but he has printed explanations of the site and its geology in English. Besides, you don't need language to express your delight at discovery. The gift shop reveals Val's winter pastimes: Polished agates are mounted in necklaces and miniature wire trees. Agate and geode book ends, agate night lights, and crystal necklaces wink and glow in the light. It seems his world is comprised of rock.

Return to the paved Route 299 Nord and turn right, into the **Parc de la Gaspésie**. The countryside becomes increasingly mountainous and, after 15 kilometers, on your right you'll see a campground: **Camping Mont-Albert**. This is a good spot to stop if you intend to stay overnight and do a hike or two. Just past the campground, you can't miss **Le Gîte du Mont-Albert** (C.P. 1150, Sainte-Anne-des-Monts G0E 2G0; 888–270–4483 or 418–762–2288; fax 418–763–7803; e-mail: gitmtalb@ quebectel.com; open year-round). This white clapboard, black-roofed inn has forty-eight rooms and several cabins in the woods. Pick your spot, dine on fine cuisine, and swim in the sunshine. Don't be fooled by the modest *gîte* in the name; this is a first-class hotel with a pool and an

Paper products

In the late 1800s, major North American newspapers were producing dailies. The industry created an insatiable demand for newsprint, and the Chicago Tribune established a plant in Baie Comeau. In 1907, the Bromption (Québec) Pulp & Paper Company of East Angus was the first to produce kraft paper. From the German word meaning "strong," this is the sturdy paper used for cardboard boxes. Because it could be made from a variety of woods, it was an important discovery for the Canadian forestry industry.

excellent restaurant. The campground is also operated by Le Gîte du Mont-Albert, so call them for reservations for either the *gîte* or camping.

About 1.5 kilometers away is the ***Centre d'interprétation de la Parc de la Gaspésie*** (***Gaspésie Park Interpretation Center***) on your right (418–763–7811; open daily from June through September). By this time you will have passed the start of at least one hiking trail—***Sentier du Diable (Devil's Trail)***—but we suggest you procure a copy of the Parc de la Gaspésie map before starting a hike.

There are some outstanding hikes here, including one that is a full day trip that takes you up the north face of Mont Albert. This is a strenuous hike, climbing over 800 meters and crossing the mountain's open, plateau-like summit, where you will find arctic-alpine vegetation such as red alpine campion. Prepare in advance for what can be extreme conditions of wind, sun, heat, and cold here. For instance, you'll need a backpack (at minimum a day pack) so you can carry enough clothing for layering appropriately. Pack not only extra clothing, but also a wide-brimmed sun hat, plenty of water, sunscreen and, throughout the summer, bug repellent. If bugs really like you, you might use a repellent containing DEET.

Many people come to the Chic-Choc Mountains in the hopes of spotting the elusive caribou. Once this area's herd of indigenous creatures was 1,600 strong. Now the herd is reduced to 250, and their status is stated as "menaced." They feed on "old man's beard," a lichen that grows only in old-growth forest and is their winter staple. Ask the park interpretation staff about them. The staff here is fluently bilingual. Also ask for the binders containing English-language information when you explore the interpretation center's exhibits on geology, flora, and fauna; there's also a slide show in English.

In addition to trails for hiking in summer, there are fourteen lakes for trout fishing. Salmon fishing (with a permit) is popular, too, in park rivers, either from canoe or by wade-fishing in their watery pools. There's mountain biking on Mount Logan, guided sightseeing tours of moose in their habitat, as well as guided plant and geology walks, just to mention a few of the many activities. Come winter, try snowshoeing and cross country, telemark, and alpine skiing, as well as snowboarding. There also are some great remote hikes where you can really and truly be off the beaten path. Consider your abilities, check out the options—and go for it!

After exploring the park, we drove north to the south shore of the St. Lawrence, to Sainte-Anne-des-Monts, where we soon turned west, rejoining Highway 132, which circumnavigates the entire Gaspé Peninsula. The descent to this village is spectacular, with the wide mouth of the river directly in front of you, its vastness pierced by the steeple of the inevitable Catholic Church. Continue our "water theme" here by crossing the junction of Route 132 and proceeding "on top of the water" onto the fishing pier.

It's so pretty here—and a completely different landscape from the mountainous terrain we've just been enjoying. Gaily colored fishing boats bob on the tidal swell while local residents fish for *capelin* (a small fish). Pick up the friendly banter, the lilting accents, and try your French. Your generous smile and a "*Bonjour!*" will reap its rewards. While you're there, look back at your route, up at the Chic-Chocs; then turn around 180 degrees to look at the North Shore, then west to the next destination, Cap-Chat.

Start driving through a dramatically different and immensely appealing "maritime" landscape. At times it seems as if the tides will lap into your car, you're just that close to *la mer* ("the sea," as the Gulf of St. Lawrence is called here). Meanwhile, on your left, cheerful cottages hug the road, including a pink clapboard home with an emerald green roof and trim: astonishingly pretty. What a spectacular view these homes enjoy in summer—and what blustery exposure come winter.

In fact, "bluster" is a running theme for this coast, for the wind blows steadily here. As you drive west, almost immediately you'll note an apparition in the distance, atop a hill. It's the "giant eggbeater"—the Éolienne de Cap-Chat (Cap-Chat Wind Turbine). Cap-Chat is enchantingly pretty, situated on a sweeping beach on a protected cove. Route 132 is briefly elevated here, so you can look down on a typical man-made harbor of rocks, with a clutch of boats bobbing on the water.

If you want to stay right on the coast, you can camp at **Camping au Bord de la mer** (Route 132, Cap-Chat G0C 1G0; 418–786–2251; sixty-four sites, $13, showers available). Or on the western outskirts of town, stay at the **Auberge au Crépuscule** ("twilight"), with proprietors Jean Ouellet and Monette Dion (239 Notre Dame Ouest, Cap-Chat G0J 1E0; 418–786–5751).

As you ascend the hill at the the far side of town, watch for the right-hand turn off the highway to *Le Tryton Centre d'interpretation du vent et de la mer (Tryton Wind and Sea Interpretation Center)* (9 route du Phare, Cap-Chat G0J 1E0; 418–786–5507; fax 418–786–2070; open daily from June 1 to mid-October, 8:30 A.M. to sunset; $6.00 adults, $5.00 students and seniors, $4.00 children, $15.00 family). A multimedia show depicts the legend of Cap-Chat, of an Indian maiden and her lover, and of the "crouching cat" formation in the rocks that supposedly gives the village its name. (We couldn't see the resemblance at all.) You'll learn about the early settlers, many of whom were seafaring Scots and Irish, who along with the French made wooden boats to fish these once-rich waters. You will also hear of the 1976 fire that devastated the town. Now people are "farming the sea" with fish-culture ventures along this coast. Ask for headphones to hear the English translation of this multimedia show.

> **Gilles Vigneault**
>
> Chansonneur *(singer)* Gilles Vigneault, (born in Natashquan, Québec, in 1928), stirred the pride of Québecois when he penned and sang "Mon Pays" ("My Country") in 1964.

Afterward, walk down to the 1871 lighthouse that is now the *Germain-Lemieux Museum* and wander along *Le Jardin des Brumes (The Garden of Mist)* hugging the sea cliffs. There is also a little café overlooking *la mer*. At the museum we were told that "everyone here used to be pirates." The museum guide spun the tale of how, in days gone by, locals would light fires along the rocky coast, luring vessels to shore. Once close to the rocks, the ships were destroyed, their goods cast upon the waves in kegs and trunks. A famous pirate here was Frenchman Charles Le Moyne d'Iberville, who plied the coast, plundering booty as he could.

From days of old and swashbuckling images of pirates, look to what may become the way of the future: wind technology. Much hope and great aspirations gave birth to the *Éolienne de Cap-Chat (Cap-Chat Wind Turbine)* (Route 132, Cap-Chat G0J 1E0; 418–786–5719; fax 418–786–2528; bilingual tours daily from June 24 through early September or by reservation). Watch for a well-signed left-hand turn just west of the interpretation center off Highway 132. Unfortunately the astonishing Éolienne (named after the goddess of the wind, Éole) had been damaged by an excessive wind and has not yet been repaired. Plans were also afoot to build seventy-five conventional horizontal windmills, projected to create fifty-seven megawatts of energy. Here on the hill overlooking Cap-Chat, there's usually a steady breeze that can be relied upon for power whatever the season. It's an intriguing spot to visit, one that presents thought-provoking natural alternatives to building dams.

Return to Route 132 and drive west toward Matane, where you can book car passage on the ferry to the north coast. En route, you'll pass an astonishing private residence called Castel des Galets, a turreted and brilliantly colored fantasy to the left of the road.

As you enter *Matane,* drive over the bridge spanning the Matane River. We were checking in at *Auberge la Seigneurie* (621 avenue Saint-Jérôme, Matane G4W 3M9; 877–783–4466 or 418–562–0021; fax 418–562–4455). We immediately turned left after the bridge onto Rue Saint-Jérôme, and then the *auberge* is just on the right. Our hosts Guy Fortin and his wife, Raymonde, installed us in "Anne's Room." Although the *auberge* itself is lovely, we don't recommend this particular room as it is noisy because of its location near the shared bath and shower rooms. But the breakfasts are generous and delicious. Abandon caution and enjoy the homemade jams, jellies, and strawberry butter (*beurre aux fraises*), which is divine spread on croissants.

Matane is a fun spot to spend some time. We first went to the Tourist Information Center, which is located right on Route 132, in the old lighthouse immediately west of town. The center has a tiny nautical exhibit (plus, rather inexplicably, a stuffed beaver). Fluent English is spoken here. In the parking lot, we found a giant shrimp: *Pincette,* the town mascot, is a female crustacean mounted on a wagon, ready for her appearance in the annual shrimp festival in mid-June. We were told that

The lighthouse and information center at Matane

a festival favorite is the equivalent of shrimp *poutine*: fried shrimp with cheese curds and sauce. Ask to see the current copy of *Guide vacances Matane et région (Matane and Region Vacation Guide),* which is full of other attractions.

No one should visit Matane without seeing the **salmon ladder** at the **Mathier-D'Amours Dam**. Return to Rue Saint-Jérôme and drive about a kilometer to the dam. Park and explore the river's edge with its lovely walkway, the *Promenade des Capitaines (Captain's Walk).* At the west edge of the dam, find the salmon ladder (418–562–7006; open daily June 1 through September 30, 7:00 A.M. to 9:00 P.M.; $2.00 adults, ages 12 and under free). Salmon are measured and counted as they pass by two large glass windows in the fish ladder observation post on their way upstream to spawn. Friendly and bilingual museum guide Sylvain Benoit told us that because of the day's heat, he'd seen only four Atlantic salmon (versus the two hundred he sees on some days)—but these were three feet long.

There are many places to dine in Matane. Sylvain recommended two spots: *Le Vieux Rafiot, (The Old Shipwreck)* on Highway 132 near the ferry docks (1415 Du Phare Ouest, Matane G4W 3M6; 418–562–8080), and the *Hôtel Belle Plage,* famous for its smoked salmon made on-site in their own smokehouses (1310 Matane-sur-Mer, Matane G4W 3M6; 418–562–2323). We stopped to examine the smokehouses (and salivated over the enticing smells), but chose a local spot called *Les Delices de la Mer (Delicacies of the Sea),* on the east side of the dam over the Rivière Matane (50 rue d'Amours, Matane G4W 2X4; 418–562–2939). They serve a wonderful *saumon au lard salé* (salmon with salt pork). Try it to discover this unique, salty taste.

For a short side-trip from Matane, here's something you might try. Folks at the Tourist Information Center told us about a wild 'n' wacky house *drôlement colorée* (whimsically colored) in *Saint-Ulric,* about 10 kilometers west of Matane. Owners Léonace Durette and Colette Michaud welcome visitors to their extraordinary home, a one-and-a-half-story affair covered with brightly-colored "found objects." (51 Ulric-Tessier, Saint-Ulric; 418–737–4762.)

Salmon Fishing School

*T*he Société de Gestion de la Rivière Matane (Matane River Management Association) operates a salmon fishing school on the Matane River. Three courses are offered, from beginner to intermediate levels: basic techniques for salmon fishing, wet fly fishing, and dry fly fishing. Book ahead and spend some days learning how to cast—or fine-tune your current skills. There are three sanctuaries for salmon on the river, but also there are eighty unrestricted pools for fishing. As in all waterways of Québec, you must have your Québec fishing licensce. (The fishing school is at 235 avenue Saint-Jérôme, No. 101, Matane G4W 3A7; 418–562–7560; e-mail: sogerm@quebectel.com.)

It was difficult leaving Matane. Some places really make you want to linger, and this is one. But we had to make our 8:00 A.M. ferry reservation for the 2½-hour crossing to Godbout. After Raymonde Fortin's delicious breakfast, served to ferry passengers at a prompt 6:15 A.M., we made the eight-minute trip to the tetrapod docks. (Tetrapods aren't beings from outer space. They are man-made, four-legged concrete "stabilizing rocks" used to build secure water-based structures such as docks and quays.)

Société des traversiers du Québec operates daily ferries to Godbout and Baie-Comeau from Matane year-round. (Vehicles or passenger group reservations call 418–562–2500; fax 418–560–8013; Web site: www.traversiers.gouv.qc.ca/matane/indexa.htm; one-way fares: $10.90 for ages 12–64, $9.80 for age 65 and older, $7.60 for ages 5–11, age 4 and under free, $26.50 for each car.)

As you cross, watch for whales, and compare the difference between the populated coastline you leave behind and the rock cliffs of the Canadian Shield ahead.

The North Shore

The scenery is completely different on the North Shore of the St. Lawrence. It is rugged here, without the quaint seaside towns that make the Gaspé coast so picturesque. Here it's a tough, wild world of forested cliffs plunging down to the water, of settlements scraped from unforgiving Canadian Shield rock.

Our drive takes us through Baie Comeau, a large industrial town with a colossal pulp and paper mill as well as an aluminum plant, and to Tadoussac, famous for whale watching. From there, we cross the Saguenay River on a little ferry to Pointe Noire, where there's an excellent (and free) marine interpretation center. From here we continue south to Saint-Siméon, returning to the South Shore on the ferry to Rivière-du-Loup.

The Matane ferry docks at *Godbout,* a small fishing village and one of Canada's oldest trading posts. For a couple of dollars, drop into the old *Magasin Génerale,* home to an exhibit on the life of Napoléon Alexandre Comeau (1848–1923), a trapper, naturalist, and geologist who is a legendary figure of Québec's North Coast (150 Pascal-Comeau, Godbout G0H 1G0; 418–568–7512; early June through Labor Day; free). A bit farther east along rue Pascal-Comeau, the *Musée Amérindien et Inuit (Amerindian and Inuit Museum)* has an interesting collection of items related to native life on this rugged coast, including a traditional bread oven (134 Pascal-Comeau, Godbout G0H 1G0; 418–568–7724; open daily June 1 through October 20, 9:00 A.M. to 10:00 P.M.; $2.50 adult, $2.00 students, 75 cents for ages 5–15).

If you want to linger here, there is a place to stay near the ferry. The **Gîte aux Berges** offers cabins for just over $55 per night for two (180 Pascal Comeau, Godbout G0H 1G0; 418–568–7748). The seasonal tourism office (117 route 138, Godbout G0H 1G0; 418–568–7795) can provide information about salmon fishing, sea kayaking, snowmobiling, hunting, and fishing in the Godbout area.

Our coastal route turns west here, but there is a lot to see farther east, too. For an unusual route to Newfoundland, read the description of a tour of the lower north shore beginning on page 150.

Otherwise, turn west on Highway 138 for the 58-kilometer drive to Baie Comeau. The road is beautiful. Recently paved, it undulates up and down the cliffs grasping the shoreline. You'll thrill to spectacularly rugged coastal scenery with rock-strewn, narrow beaches. We've now utterly left behind the more gentle southern shore with its picturesque farms and villages. The sedimentary rock of the Appalachian Range is suddenly absent. You now drive through the granitic Canadian Shield, the most ancient rock on Earth, with spruce-ringed peat bogs in the hollows. You really expect to see moose, and in season (early August) bring your blueberry pails, pull off the road, and gorge.

After about 25 kilometers you'll see the town of **Franquelin** (formerly spelled Frankelin, after the man who mapped the St. Lawrence River). Here you'll find the **Village Forestier d'Antan** (27 Des Erables, Franquelin G0H 1E0; 418–296–3203; open daily May through October, 9:00 A.M. to 6:00 P.M.; $5.00 adults, $4.00 students, $3.00 children), a small museum exhibiting the life of woodcutters in bygone days. As you can imagine, forestry is one of the natural resource industries that opened up the North Shore to economic development. They offer guided tours and "bush camp meals."

Past Franquelin you pass the Rivière Mistassini. We stopped and immediately heard the rattling call of a belted kingfisher, enjoying seeing its slim form skimming the surface of Lac Low. Then our attention was caught by more movement: A large, cheeky Canada Jay (also known as the whiskeyjack) swooped down to investigate us, saucily hoping for a handout.

We continued through this rugged lake-and-spruce-strewn countryside, marveling at its grandeur. Suddenly, the stacks of the Reynolds Aluminum plant announced we'd reached **Baie Comeau.** If you've been hankering to see a hydroelectric generating station, head 25 kilometers north on Route 389 to visit the **Manic-2** site on the Manicouagan River. Camping is available at nearby **Camping Manic-2** (Route 389, Baie-Comeau G4Z 2G8; 418–296–9009; May 20 through October 20; 54 sites, $14).

After passing Route 389 Nord, cross the Rivière Amédée and turn left (south) on Boulevard Blanche to **Parc de la Falaise (Cliff Park),** which provides an excellent lookout on the confluence of the St. Lawrence and Manicouagan Rivers. Proceeding farther west on Route 138, find the Tourist Information Office just before the bridge over the Manicouagan.

Our next stop, **Pointe-aux-Outardes,** was gorgeous. Watch for a left-hand turn and a 14-kilometer drive south on a peninsula of land, past a quaint, wind-tossed pioneer cemetery, to **Parc régional de Pointe-aux-Outardes** (4 rue Labrie, C.P. 118, Pointe-aux-Outardes G0H 1M0; 418–567–4226; open daily June 1 through September 30, 9:00 A.M. to 6:00 P.M.; $4.00 adults, $3.00 students and seniors). Extensive white sand dunes, marshlands, spectacular boardwalks, and bird-watching towers conspire to make you want to linger. The park staff here only spoke French, but an English-language tour is offered if you book ahead. If your French is not fluent enough to interpret common names

On the Road to Labrador

*H*ere's something that will impress the folks back home: a drive to Labrador! In fact, with a suitable vehicle, you can use this as a unique way to get to the island of Newfoundland. The road is very rough in places, and four-wheel-drive is recommended. Stop at the Tourist Information Center in Baie-Comeau to pick up current information about road conditions and services. Expect to drive for eighteen hours to cover the 1,100 kilometers from Baie-Comeau to the ferry terminus at Goose Bay—and reserve the ferry accordingly.

Highway 389 Nord takes you along the Manicouagan River, past the Manic-2 and Manic-5 hydroelectric generating stations (free 90-minute tours daily from June 24 through Labor Day; 418–294–3923). The road follows the eastern shores of the 8,000-square-kilometer Manicouagan Reservoir—the remnants of a huge meteor crater now filled with water held back by the **Daniel Johnson dam** at Manic-5—to Labrador City across the still-disputed border between Québec and Labrador. From there, it is all gravel to Goose Bay, and the section from Churchill Falls is recommended for four-wheel-drive only.

From Goose Bay, the 35-hour, twice-weekly **Sir Robert Borden ferry** (Marine Atlantic Reservations Bureau; 800–341–7981 from continental U.S. or 902– 794–5700) will take you to Lewisporte, Newfoundland.

for birds, find a French-English bird list, which will help immensely at this park. To keep the language from becoming a barrier, arm yourself with as much information as your interests dictate.

The wind-swept boardwalk hike is well-balanced by a woods walk through stunted trees. The boardwalk is sturdy and, though there are a few steps here and there, most will be able to enjoy this easy stroll. Signs are all in French, but with perseverance, someone who isn't fluent in French can still interpret some information, such as the pioneer genealogy panel overlooking the bay. Here you learn that the first settlers on the point, in 1850, were English-speaking. Names like Robinson, Marsh, McCormick, Miller, and Ross intermingled with the second wave of French settlers. On further examination of the geneological list, you see the reality of the present and the hope of the future: For example, in 1850, Samuel Miller married Ephémie L'Italien; in 1891, David Malouin married Victoria Ross. Love, romance, and intermarriage: surely the global solution to our differences.

> ## Log shanties
>
> *Menfolk in the early 1800s went to work in the bush from winter freeze-up at the end of November through to the great melt in early April. They lived in shanties, and cut and hauled logs from dawn till dusk.*

The dates and their significance roll on: In 1918 the first school was built at Pointe-aux-Outardes; 1925 the quay constructed; 1930 the first parish; 1931 the first sawmill (*scierie*); 1934 shrubs—the sand rose—imported from France; 1948 electricity replaced oil lamps; 1965 the potato research station; 1993 the creation of this park.

Now retrace your route back to Highway 138 and go west to Raguenneau. Here, from a rocky point, you can look across the bay to the dunes of Pointe-aux-Outardes. This is a totally off-the-wall spot, with life-size dinosaurs and a giant obelisk. When the "tourist information officer" (lounging nearby with her boyfriend) was asked by a Parisian visitor about the significance of all this, she was merely told "it's the symbol of our village." Hmm . . .

A few kilometers beyond is the new Montagnais cultural center of **Papinachois,** a good place to investigate if native life and lore interest you. Call ahead so they can help you custom-fit your experience. You can learn about the Montagnais language, culture, and legends, and how to make traditional foods, moccasins, tents, snowshoes, and canoes. (18 Messek, Betsiamites G0H 1B0; 888–246–5834 or 418–567–8863; fax 418–567–8868.)

Early August is blueberry season, and little huts sell freshly picked baskets of these delicious berries all along this part of the highway. Not to be missed!

Continue the drive, through Forestville (where you can catch another *ferry* to the south shore to Rimouski). We paused at a fish shop *(Pécheries Manicouagan,* 428 route 138 G0T 1P0; 418–238–2132) on the north side of the road at the eastern outskirts of *Sainte-Anne-de-Portneuf.* Here we bought some of the most delicious shrimp we've ever eaten. Half a pound was $5.72, and such tender, tasty shrimp you may never find. Watch for the pretty *La Maison Fleurie (House of Flowers)* (193 route 138, Sainte-Anne-de-Portneuf G0T 1P0; 418–238–2153). Over the past hundred years or so it has seen duty as a grocery store, theater, and post office, and it is now a comfortable B&B where host Germina Fournier can recommend local offerings such as bike rentals, sailboat rentals, or quiet beach walks.

The coast becomes an almost continuous set of salt marshes. Everywhere to your left you'll see pull-over parking spaces and little signs indicating spots to observe birds or see whales (*baleines*). In both spring and fall, this coastline is alive with birds on the move, stopping for food in the rich marshes before the next leg of their migration. The same rich food supplies bring the whales. As you draw closer to the hub of whale watching at the mouth of the Saguenay Fjord, you'll see how this popular activity is shaping tourism along this coast.

As you approach Sault-au-Mouton, you can't miss *L'Auberge de la Rivière Sault-au-Mouton* on Route 138. It stands on a rise of land at the confluence of the Sault-au-Mouton and St. Lawrence Rivers. Its accommodations offer *forfait,* package deals: Phone ahead to arrange whale watching or sea kayaking, for instance. This was a clean and friendly place—but more like a hostel than a real *auberge.* The $75 for bed and breakfast in the fairly basic rooms at the inn may seem pricey unless you plan to take full advantage of the activities and trails on the property (85 rue Principale, Sault-au-Mouton G0T 1Z0; 418–231–2214; fax 418–231–2604).

Even if you don't stay at the *auberge,* do stop at the little park on the Rivière Sault-au-Mouton just down the hill. The well-built lookout beside the falls is a good place to watch for whales in the St. Lawrence below, and there are utterly gorgeous swimming holes in the nearby rounded, exposed Canadian Shield rock. Like many of the rivers flowing south, the water is tea-colored from the peat. One perhaps unexpected benefit is that the water is often warmer than you might think. Below, on the west side of the Rivière Sault-au-Mouton, you'll spy the ruined foundations of a series of mills.

Farther along the coast, you'll descend into *Les Escoumins,* a pretty village in a sheltered cove where river pilots board ocean freighters to guide them through the narrowing St. Lawrence. It is also a mecca for scuba divers: You'll see the red flag with the white diagonal bar at many of the motels and on signs along the road near here. Diving is a terrific way to explore the river's rich marine life.

Right on the riverfront, *Auberge de la Baie* (267 route 138, Les Escoumins G0T 1K0; 418–233–2010; fax 418–233–3378; 12 rooms, $45–$75) is a pretty, white-framed building with scarlet trim, with lots and lots of flower baskets lending a charming effect.

Ardent divers will like *L'Auberge de la Plongée de Les Escoumins* (118 Saint-Marcellin, Les Escoumins G0T 1K0; 800–375–3465 or 418–233–3289; fax 418–233–2765; email: cpaquette@mail.fjord-best.com). Lodging is basic—bring your own sleeping bag—but their dive packages are a great bargain, starting from a one-day package at $49.95 with lodging and breakfast, two meals, as many airfills as you can use, and access to their private dive site. Bring your own gear, or rent equipment here. Drop off your air tank before lunch, and it will be ready for your next dive afterward. They have experienced guides, and they welcome "one-day travelers and groups."

The *L'Héritage I ferry* makes a daily crossing from Les Escoumins to Trois Pistoles between May 15 and October 15. (For information and reservations, contact La Compagnie de Navigation des Basques, 11 rue du Parc, C.P. 490, Trois-Pistoles G0L 4K0; 418–851–4676, or 233–4676 from Les Escoumins; fax 418–851–4750; Web site: icrdl.net/~basques/ traverse/index.htm; $9.85 adults, $6.55 children and seniors, $25.25 for a car.)

As you continue west, you enter the area of the Saguenay–St. Lawrence Marine Park. Watch for the left-hand turn off Highway 138 to the *Centre d'interprétation et d'observation Cap-de-Bon-Desir* (166 route 138, Grandes-Bergeronnes G0T 1G0; 418–235–4703; fax 418–235–4686; open daily June 16 through October 13; $5.00 adults, $4.00 seniors, $3.00 students, $2.00 children, $10.00 family*)*. From its rocky promontory you may be lucky and see whales such as finback, minke, beluga, or even the blue whale—the largest mammal alive. There are guided interpretive walks along the shoreline and lots of information about marine mammals and regional history. Don't miss this spot. As a part of the Canadian federal park system, it is fully bilingual.

Immediately before the gates to the center you'll find a little driveway leading to Philippe Faucher and Marie-Alice Lapointe's *Gîte du Phare,* a funky B&B fashioned partly from a mobile home perched oceanside with a giant lighthouse sticking out of it. Philippe is a talkative, friendly character who has personally carved eleven walking trails in the salt marsh leading to the beach, all named for members of his family. What can we say? Accommodations are compact but very clean, and if you want an unusual experience, we feel sure Philippe's tales and Marie's cooking will please (12 chemin du Cap-d-Bon-Désir, Bergeronnes G0T 1G0; 418–232–1020; fax 418–233–2270; $30 for one person, $45 for two, breakfast included).

Returning to Route 138 West, we soon arrived at *Camping Bon Désir,* on the left side of the highway (198 route 138, Bergeronnes G0T 1G0; 418–232–6297; fax 418–232–6414). Our tent spot cost $18.40, taxes included. Make reservations. It's popular all summer, especially during the weekend of the local *Festival de la Beleine Bleue (Blue Whale Festival)* in early August. Just about the best sites are No. 53, on a secluded spot on a pond, and Nos. 91–99, with good views of the water. Even with all 200 campsites occupied, you may be amazed at the tranquility as well as the courtesy of your fellow campers. Visitors are respectful of peace and quiet, as well as of nature. After pitching our tent we strolled down to the beach and, the next morning, reveled in hot showers (25 cents for five minutes). Great whale watching here—we used our binoculars and spied one in the bay.

> ## Cap-des-Rosiers
>
> *The Cape of Roses on the eastern tip of the Gaspé Peninsula was named for the wild roses that once grew there. In 1759, a French officer there spied General Wolfe's fleet approaching. Immediately a messenger was sent to warn Québec City. Now the gateway to Forillon National Park, its 37-meter lighthouse, built in 1858, is the tallest in Canada.*

Another good choice in the area is a *gîte* between Cap Bon Desir and Tadoussac called *Gîte la Petite Baleine* (50 rue Principale, Bergeronnes G0T 1E0; 418–232–6756; fax 418–232–6653). It's in an old home with wonderful ambiance. It has a little arts and crafts boutique featuring local artisans and products.

Continue west, watching for the left-hand turn on Rue de la Mer to the *Centre d'interprétation Archéotopo* (498 rue de la Mer, Bergerrones G0T 1G0; 418–232–6286; daily, 9:00 A.M. to 6:00 P.M. May 15 through October 15; $4.75 adults, $3.75 seniors, and $2.50 children) located at the base of a quay extending into the St. Lawrence. This center exhibits the archaeology and prehistory of the immediate North Coast region and gives a peek into pre-European native life.

Heading back to Route 138, you can now investigate an intriguingly different whale-watching experience. *Les Ailes du Nord (Wings of the North)* offers flights of the Saguenay Fjord (432 rue de la Mer, Grandes-Bergeronnes G0T 1G0; 418–232–6764; fax 418–232–6770; $72 plus tax per person for a forty-minute flight for either two or three passengers). Pilot Paul Kanaan explains the flight path and how to spot whales. All passengers wear headsets, so his interesting bilingual explanations can be heard by everyone. To protect the whales, he never descends lower than 1,500 feet.

At the rear of the hanger is a selection of old photos, including one that showed English Union Jacks flapping in the breeze as Bergeronnes townsfolk celebrated an anniversary of the community's founding in 1844. Paul said he knew of no native speakers of English in the town today. When we told him about the early English settlers we'd read about at Pointe-aux-Outardes, he was astonished; apparently this wasn't part of the history he'd been taught.

Back on the highway, pass Highway 172 heading right, along the north shore of the Saguenay Fjord. Almost immediately, drive down to *Tadoussac,* surely Québec's whale-watching capital. Tadoussac is very pretty despite its commercialization. Turn left onto Rue des Pionniers and then right onto Rue Morin to find the *Restaurant la Bolée* in the upper level of a trendy pumpkin-and-green colored wood frame building (164 rue Morin G0T 2A0; 418–235–4750). Downstairs is a deli and bakery where you can buy homemade sweet temptations like *gâteau macarons,* a gooey, delicious sensation made of coconuts at $1.50 for a generous square—or pay the same price for a loaf of homemade bread.

Tadoussac is a popular destination with a wide range of accommodations. The well-informed, bilingual staff at the excellent Tourist Information Office at 197 Rue des Pionniers can help you find a place to stay or current information about things to see and do.

Do visit Canada's first trading post, built in 1600 by Pierre de Chauvin: the *Poste de Traite Chauvin* (157 rue du Bord-de-l'Eau, Tadoussac G0T 2A0; 418–235–4657; open daily May through October; $2.75 adults, $2.00 seniors, $1.50 students and children). Here you'll learn about the Montagnais native life and the history of the fur trade in Canada. Jacques Cartier landed here in what the Montaignais called *Tatoushak* ("nipple") in 1534. Chauvin arrived in the winter of 1579 with sixteen men. Unprepared, eleven died of cold and scurvy that brutal winter. From 1600 to 1859, the post Chauvin built was one of the most active on the St. Lawrence. In 1603, Champlain himself came here on the first of several visits.

Also visit Tadoussac's salmon hatchery. At the ferry, there is a little wooden office near the top of the hill on the left. You can get a ten-minute tour of the Atlantic salmon fish hatchery, **Faites le Saut,** while you wait for the ferry or, if you park elsewhere, take the time to enjoy the full forty-five-minute tour (115 du Battu-Passeur, Tadoussac G0T 2A0; 418–235–4569; fax 418–236–9350; e-mail: arsm@fjord-best.com).

The smolt (baby salmon) from the hatchery are transported to L'Anse Pleureuse in the Gaspé to be released in the salmon rivers. Unlike Pacific salmon, which die after laying their eggs (spawning), Atlantic salmon don't die then. Instead, they return many times to the river where they were born. How do salmon know where to return? The memory of their birthplace is retained by the smell and taste of the river water where they were born—or at least where they lived during their early development. They smell and taste the water as it swirls through their mouth. Therefore, it's important to release them while they are very young, else they would return here, to Tadoussac.

As you cross the Saguenay River on the free ten-minute ferry ride, get out on deck to scan for whales and marvel at the magnificent fjord's cliffs. The confluence of this rich estuarine delta is an important feeding ground for marine species such as the beluga. Don't miss stopping at **Pointe Noire** at the top of the hill on the west side. This excellent (and free) marine interpretation center has a boardwalk lookout with a superb view of the estuary and an informative video in English.

Immediately after Pointe Noire, the road toward **Saint Siméon** can become highly congested because there's not enough parking for whale watchers and others.

At Saint-Siméon, take the ferry across the St. Lawrence to Rivière-du-Loup. As you descend toward town, you'll see the sandy beach and the ferry docks. Follow the signs to the ferry parking. Bilingual attendants help direct vehicles to the appropriate lanes. Boarding is first come, first served, and they recommend that you be there ninety minutes before departure during the summer (other times, thirty minutes). During the summer peak season, there were five crossings daily, with 25 percent fare reductions for the earliest and latest crossings. Full fares: $10 adults, $9.00 seniors, $6.65 for ages 5–11, $25.35 for a car. (For current fare and schedule information, contact **Traverse Rivière-du-Loup Saint-Siméon Ferry,** 199 rue Hayward, C.P. 172, Rivière-du-Loup G5R 3Y8; 418–638–2856; fax 418–862–9545; Web site: www.travrdlstsim.com; e-mail: travrdlstsim@icdrdl.net.)

After you park, lock up your car and wander along the beach or stop in at the snack bars and ice cream stands. If you want to stay overnight here, there's a **Municipal Campground** on the beach (120 rue du Festival, Saint-Siméon G0T 1X0; 418–638–5253; tent sites $10, no dogs, no alcohol permitted on the beach). **Auberge sur Mer** (109 rue duQuai, Saint-Siméon G0T 1X0; 418–638–2674) offers motel-like bedrooms and, across the parking lot, is its seafood restaurant.

This ferry crossing takes a couple of hours. You must get out of your car, but there's lots to do on the ferry, from reading the bilingual information panels on the estuarine life to scanning for pods of belugas. We were thrilled to spy a pod of eight feeding, just off the lighthouse at Île-aux-Lièvre. This is only one of **Les Îles-du-Bas-Saint-Laurent (Lower St. Lawrence Islands).** It's possible to stay on some of these islands. A nonprofit conservation society manages them and offers limited access to unique activities and accommodations on them. For example, you can try the overnight escape at a lighthouse on Pot à l'Eau-de-Vie, rent a chalet or camp on Île-aux-Lièvre, or simply take a guided tour of the islands. All transportation starts from Rivière-du-Loup. (For a bilingual pamphlet, contact La Société Duvetnor at 200 rue Hayward, C.P. 305, Rivière-du-Loup G5R 3Y9; 418–867–1660; fax 418–867–3639.)

From Rivière-du-Loup, you could follow the tourist route east toward Rimouski on Highway 132. Or you could take the longer route and follow our side trip along the South Shore. Note that if time is tight and you need to head south, our route will take you toward Edmundston, New Brunswick.

The South Shore

We love gardening, history, and the romantic tale of Grey Owl. So we drove south from Rivière-du-Loup to **Cabano** on **Lake Temiscouata,** on Route 185 Sud (south). During the 45-minute drive through undulating countryside, we saw many peat bogs being harvested by giant vacuum cleaners!

Our main destination was **Fort Ingall,** the largest of several British forts constructed in 1839 to defend the critical Portage Trail, threatened by American forces. After only three years, the border dispute was settled and Fort Ingall was abandoned without having fired a shot. Built of wood, the original fort did not survive. However, the community of Cabano rallied and after ten years of research, put their town—and fort—back on the map by reconstructing it, using the original plans (81 chemin Caldwell, Cabano G0L 1E0; 418–854–2375; open daily June through September, and in May and October by reservation; $6.00 adults, $5.00 students and seniors, $3.00 for age 12 and under, $145 family; admission includes access to rose gardens).

Inside, there is a permanent exhibit about **Grey Owl**, the enigmatic Englishman whose given name was Archibald Belaney. Born in 1888 in Hastings, England, he came to Canada in 1906, traveling to Temiscaming in Northern Ontario, where he became intrigued with the old native ways of life and livelihood, such as trapping. From 1906 to 1910 he lived among the Ojibway and, after seeing military action in World War I, he returned to Temiscaming in 1925. Then he "went native," adopting the name Grey Owl and, in 1928, coming to Cabano with a native woman named Anahareo. A year later he published his first article in an English magazine, *Country Life*, under his new name and delivered his first public lecture at the town of Métis-sur-Mer. The subject? Beavers. Perhaps you've read his books, such as *Pilgrims of the Wild* or *Sajo and the Beaver People*.

Grey Owl's story is an impossibly romantic legend that we both remembered from our childhood. We read his books and believed—as everyone did—he was an Ojibway. His tale is all the more appealing because he fooled so many people for decades. With his long black hair and hawk nose, he was every white person's caricature image of an Indian. His talk of conservation challenged all Canada—and the world—to take care of Mother Earth long before our modern-day environmental movement. Actor Pierce Brosnan came to Québec in 1998 to star in the movie *Grey Owl*.

A companion project that literally surrounds Fort Ingall in flowers is **La Roseraie du Témiscouata (Rose Gardens)**. Here you'll see over 250 varieties of hardy roses: shrubs, climbing roses, and "ground cover" varieties, all of which can withstand the rigors of the weather here. There's a French formal garden and an English country garden; a garden of hybrids, and another of the explorer series developed at Ottawa's Experimental Farm. See which you prefer—and don't hesitate to stick your nose into the fragrant blossoms. Some species are for sale.

If you are leaving Québec at this point, follow Highway 185 South along the lake (and the strikingly beautiful farmland around Notre-Dame-du-Lac) into New Brunswick.

However, to return to the south shore and Route 132, turn northeast on Route 232, then north on Route 293 to **Saint-Jean-de-Dieu**. Watch for the sign pointing right toward **Saint-Mathieu** after you pass the Route 296 turnoff to **Sainte-Françoise**. Turn right on this unnumbered sideroad toward Saint-Mathieu and **Saint-Fabien** where you'll rejoin Highway 132 Est.

This might seem like a zigzag, but is it ever worth it! These villages and roads are too picturesque for words. Clean and tidy towns, all teasing you to stay, with countless little B&Bs dotted here and there. The countryside is folded gently here and the little back road ambles along, transecting one of the valley floors. The farms exhibit the long, thin seigneurial lots that course down to the St. Lawrence. You'll enjoy the old homesteads that cluster together along the road, their old, mature pasture and croplands trailing after them in green and gold ribbons.

At Highway 132, turn east to **Parc conservation du Bic.** Parc Bic is very pretty: A sudden upheaval of knobby hills projects out into the St. Lawrence, with great biking trails, and bird and marine life to observe. The park's campground, however, is squished by the highway, and is totally flat and devoid of positive attributes. Instead you might try **Gîte aux Cormorans** (213 chemin du Golf, C.P. 627, Bic G0L 1B0; 418–736–8113; fax 418–736–4216), a B&B with a large, welcoming veranda. It's just east of the campground, off Route 132, to your right, near the Thêatre de Bic.

Next stop is **Rimouski,** a very pretty city with cafés, bistros, and tons of sights to take in. Look for the cathedral and turn right onto Rue de l'Eglise, then right again a few blocks down, onto Rue de l'Évêché Ouest. Almost immediately, at No. 31 on your left, is **Central Café**. Park in the rear and enter to enjoy the boisterous ambiance and generous servings. We were in the mood for nachos and pasta—delicious! While you're at it, enjoy one of Québec's delicious microbrewery beers.

After dining, we drove south on Route 232 to Rang 3 Ouest. Turn right and proceed 1.5-kilometers to the **Gîte Domaine du Perchoir** (*perchoir* means "roost"), where hosts Marize Bélanger and Gilles Pelletier have created rooms of enchantment. Birds shelter in nests amid branches built out from the walls—both whimsies being the creation of one of several artist friends who have left their personal marks on this delightful B&B. If you can, ask to see all the rooms. English, Spanish, German, as well as French are spoken here, and the breakfast is scrumptious. Organic bread, heavenly thin crêpes, and homemade preserves conspire to make you want to linger. And be sure to ask Gilles, an architectural technician, about his ten-year plan to build treehouses (205 chemin du 3e rang Ouest, Sainte-Odile-sur-Rimouski G5L 7B5; 418–725–5611; Web site: perchoir.cjb.net/; e-mail: perchoir@globetrotter.qc.ca).

Return to Rimouski to follow Route 132 Est. Everyone calls the St.

Lawrence *la mer* here, and it's easy to see why. It is tidal, saline, and expansive. There are *les phares* (lighthouses), seafood restaurants and, near the picturesque "seaside" village of **Pointe-au-Père,** a museum that adds to our water theme: **Le Musée de la Mer.** Just follow the signs to the lighthouse, part of the museum site. You can even climb up the 125 steep steps of the lighthouse's circular stairway to enjoy the view and see the mechanism.

Off the coast near here on May 29, 1914, the luxury ship *Empress of Ireland* was struck by a Norwegian collier and sank in fifteen minutes, taking 1,012 passengers and crew to their deaths. Only the sinking of the *Titanic,* two years

Gîte Domaine du Perchoir windmill

earlier, had resulted in a greater loss of life. The museum is a monument to the *Empress* tragedy and details the discovery of the wreck's precise location in 1964. Successive teams of international divers scoured the bottom, including the late French oceanographer and biologist Jacques Yves Cousteau.

You will thrill to the section of the museum that emulates an actual dive, complete with video footage. The sometimes indistinct images and the sound of the diver's breathing and bubbles eerily evoke the inner exploration of the wreck. Suddenly the camera focuses on . . . a human skull! The museum is operated by Parks Canada and is interpreted bilingually. Well worth a visit (1034 rue du Phare, Pointe-au-Père G5M 1L8; 418–724–6214; fax 418–721–0815; open daily June 1 through October 13; $5.50 adults, $5.00 students and seniors, $3.00 for ages 6–12, $13.50 family).

Right beside the museum is **Le Gîte de la Pointe** (1046 avenue du Phare Ouest, Pointe-au-Père G5M 1L8; 418–724–6614), operated by André Gamache, who has outfitted his new, spanking-clean home as a B&B. An English teacher, he'll be able to help you with your itinerary and can recommend diving outfitters, should you want to explore the wreck of the *Empress* yourself.

The narrow strip of coast boasts a line of restaurants, homes, inns, and campgrounds. To your right are farms with their fields stretching as far as you can see. It's touristy here, and you can see why: It's lovely. Beaches are rocky but beg for exploration, picnicking, and wildlife observation.

You can taste bee products like mead (honey wine) and *la gelée royale* (royal jelly) in the museum section of the **Vieux Moulin** near Sainte-Flavie; inexpensive tours and free tastes of mead. This old mill is also a B&B; call ahead for reservations as there are only three rooms (141 route de la Mer, Sainte-Flavie G0J 2L0; 418–775–8383).

Just inside the village limits of Sainte-Flavie, stop at the Tourism Information Center on your right before leaving the south shore of the St. Lawrence. Find out about the **Centre d'Art Marcel Gagnon** (564 route de la Mer, Sainte-Flavie G0J 2L0; 418–775–2829; fax 418–775–9548; open daily year-round, free), where over eighty life-size statues and several boats are exhibited on the St. Lawrence shores—perhaps a fitting goodbye to the coast? A bit farther along, the aquariums, video presentation, and a humorous "play" at the **Centre d'interprétation du Saumon atlantique (Atlantic Salmon Interpretation Center)** will impress upon you the importance of protecting this resource. During the July/August spawning season, a minibus will take you to view the salmon jumping upstream (900 route de la Mer, Sainte-Flavie G0J 2L0; 418–775–2969; fax 418–775–9466; daily May 20 through mid-October, 9:00 A.M. to 5:00 P.M.; $6.00 adults, $5.50 seniors, $4.00 students, $2.00 children, $16.00 family).

Wave good-bye to the coast as you ascend Route 132 Sud through **Mt. Joli.** It's 155 kilometers to our eventual destination, Matapédia, on the Baie de Chaleurs.

Now we enter rural hinterland punctuated by pretty parishes. After 35 kilometers, for instance, you pass by the village of **Saint-Moïse**. In August 1998, the whole community celebrated its 125th anniversary. We took a short diversion off the highway to drive through the village. People had decorated their homes and front lawns with statues and scenes of pioneer days. It was a grand example of how a community can display its pride.

At nearby **Ferme d'Élevage Cerfs Roux de L'Est (Red Deer Farm),** hosts Marcel Bérubé and Ginette Gendron allow you to observe their herd of New Zealand red deer, explore nature walks, and relax with the superb country views. Accommodation is possible but here you must reserve ahead (503 route 132 Ouest, Saint-Moïse G0J 2Z0; 418–776–2908; nature walks are $3.00 adults, $2.00 children, $7.00 family).

Four kilometers beyond Saint-Moïse, on the left side of the highway, your attention will be riveted by an abandoned slate mine that reveals ox-blood red and gray slate, as well as some intriguing conglomerate. It reminded us of our trip to the slate museum at Melbourne in the Eastern Townships.

As you drive, there are pick-your-own farms where you can harvest luscious *fraises* (strawberries) in June, *framboises* (raspberries) in mid-July, and *pommes* (apples) starting in late August. Look for the signs: FRAMBOISES AUTO-CEUILLÉERE, for example, means "pick-your-own raspberries."

Continue south through large, prosperous-looking dairy farms. This is the start of the famous Matapédia Valley, renowned for its picturesque, tranquil scenery. Continue through Sayabec to Val Brilliant, where there's an excellent lakeside lookout and picnic ground. Lac Matapédia is the headwaters of the famous salmon river of the same name. Amqui, the commercial heart of the valley, is at the south end of the lake.

Farther south on Route 132 at **Causapscal,** just beyond the bridge spanning the Causcapal River, is the **Site Historique Matamajaw.** In 1870 Lord Mount Stephen discovered this superb salmon fishing site and immediately purchased tracts of land beside the confluence of the two rivers, Causcapal and Matapédia. During the early 1900s, wealthy Americans and Canadians purchased his estate, founding the elite Matamajaw Fishing Club. Today the club still stands; part of it is a gift shop. Wander down to the river, and in July and August you will probably see fly fishermen casting here. A tranquil setting for a tremendous sport. There's a little suspension bridge over the river and also a pool with glass windows where you can view salmon (53 rue Saint-Jacques Sud, C.P. 460, Causapscal G0J 1J0; 418–756–5999; open daily all summer).

Continue south toward Matapédia, passing through the Reserve faunique Matapédia, the game preserve that protects the river. Lovely views of the tumbling waters draw you to the coast. Turn left to follow Route 132 Est as it curves towards Restigouche and the start of this trip, Pointe-à-la-Croix.

On your left opposite the bridge to Matapédia, you'll see a sign leading to a *belvédère,* or lookout, that's 210 meters up the hill. It affords a good prospect of the confluence of the Matapédia and Restigouche Rivers and the Baie des Chaleurs—and lets you stretch your legs one last time on this route.

On the Road to Newfoundland

Most people turn west after crossing the St. Lawrence by ferry from Matane. However, there is lots to see to the east—and not many people know it is possible to get to Newfoundland from here. In fact, you can circumnavigate the Gulf of St. Lawrence and see Canada's Maritime provinces without having to retrace your route. (In May 1998, Eric had the opportunity to travel on a supply ship servicing the coastal villages of the lower north shore region from Sept-Îles to Blanc-Sablon on the Labrador border. Although we had to push through pack ice in places, it was fascinating: small isolated villages eking a living out of what few resources are available from the barren land and cold waters.)

Follow Highway 138 Est to Sept-Îles, Québec's largest deepwater port, named for the seven islands around the mouth of its large circular bay. Plan to spend at least a day at the *Mingan Archipelago National Park Reserve,* about 175 kilometers farther along the coast near Havre-Saint-Pierre. This federal park has well-organized water transportation to take visitors to many of its nearly forty limestone islands. Hiking and camping is available on some islands. Particularly impressive are the facilities on Quarry Island. Each very private site is well separated from the others, but all are within a short walk of a centrally located shelter with a wood stove. Sites 1 and 2 are the nicest. There are a total of only forty sites in ten locations on six of the islands, and you must make reservations (1303 de la Digue Street, P.O. Box 1180, Havre-Saint-Pierre G0G 1P0; 800–463–6769 or 418–538–3285 June 8 to September 13, or 418–538–3331 off-season; fax 418–538–3595; Web site: parcscanada.risq.qc.ca/mingan-archi-pelago; e-mail: archipel_de_mingan@ pch.gc.ca).

You can arrange to catch the coastal boat at Havre-Saint-Pierre or continue east on Highway 138 along the coast. The road ends at Natashquan, birthplace of beloved Québec singer Gilles Vigneault. After getting off the boat here, you can enjoy a hearty breakfast at *Auberge La Cache* (183 chemin d'en Haut, Natashquan G0G 2E0; 418–726–3347; rooms from $65.00 double). Ask to see the restored shipwreck table.

You'll need to have arranged passage on the *MV Nordik Express* to continue east from here. Your car will be loaded into a container, and you can enjoy the comfortable but fairly frugal accommodations aboard ship. There are sixteen cabins, with sixty berths, but you can also sleep in the aircraft-like seats in the lounges. The food is surprisingly good, but because some of the staff needs to help during dockings, the restaurant sticks zealously to its posted schedule. (For fare information and reservations, contact Relais Nordik Inc., 205 rue Léonidas, Rimouski, Québec G5L 2T5; 800–692–8002 or 418–723–8787; fax 418–722–9307.) The company requests a 50 percent deposit thirty days in advance. Fares for vehicles depend on the weight: A typical car is about $200 from Natashquan to Blanc-Sablon on the Labrador border. We'd suggest booking passage only from Natashquan to Vieux-Fort; you can drive the last 50 kilometers to Blanc-Sablon.

The coastal villages are all quite different, although most depend on fishing. A favorite is Harrington Harbour where sturdy wooden sidewalks link buildings together. For a stay between ferries to explore the many nearby islands, a great choice is *Amy's Boarding House* (Harrington Harbour G0G 1N0; 418–795–3376), a delightful B&B with a sunny, plant-filled dining area and comfortable rooms.

In 1534, the present site of Vieux-Fort (Old Fort) was known as Brest and was the "capital" of the New World. Then, it was a busy fishing harbor where Basque fishermen prepared salt cod to be sent back to Europe. Now home to only a few hundred people, it is the westernmost end of the road that can take you to Blanc-Sablon and into Labrador. The road is good, and you'll get a chance to see what is behind the rugged shore you've been seeing.

From Blanc-Sablon, *Northern Cruiser Ltd.* operates the daily two-hour crossing across the Straits of Belle-Isle to Sainte-Barbe, Newfoundland. (Call 709–931–2309 for reservations by 3:00 P.M. the day before; $9.00 adults, $4.75 for ages 5–12, $7.50 seniors, $18.50 for a car.)

PLACES TO STAY IN THE COASTAL REGION

BAIE COMEAU
Hôtel le Manoir,
8 Cabot;
418–296–3391

CARLETON
Hôtel-Motel Baie Bleue,
482 boulevard Perron,
G0C 1J0;
800–463–9099 or
418–364–3355
fax 418–364–6165

MATANE
Hôtel-Motel Belle Plage,
1310 rue Matane-sur-Mer,
G4W 3M6;
888–244–2323 or
418–562–2323;
fax 418–562–2562

NEW RICHMOND:
Willett House at the British
Heritage Center of Gaspé;
limited availability, so call
well in advance;
418–562–2562

PLACES TO EAT IN THE COASTAL REGION

BAIE COMEAU
Les Trois Barils
(The Three Barrels),
200 rue la Salle;
418–296–3681

MATANE
La Maison sous le Vent,
1014 du Phare Ouest,
G4W 3M6;
418–562–7611

RIMOUSKI
La Marina,
556 rue Saint-Germain Est,
G5L 1E9;
800–463–0871 or
418–723–1616

TADOUSSAC
Restaurant le Bâteau,
246 rue des Forgerons
G0T 2A0;
418–235–4850

152

French–English Glossary

Here is a short list of French words and their English meaning that might be useful. If your car has a cassette or CD player, consider buying an audio course that you can listen to as you drive.

Accommodations

Auberge—Country inn

Gîte du passant—
Bed and Breakfast (usually reduced to *gîte*)

Hôtel/Motel—Hotel/motel

Où sont les toilettes?—Where is the bathroom (toilets)?

Toilette—Bathroom/toilet

Courtesy

À bientôt—See you soon.

Au revoir—Good-bye. See you soon.

Avec plaisir—With pleasure

Bonjour—Hello (literally, good day)

Bonne journée—Have a nice day

Bonsoir—Good evening

Excusez-moi—Pardon me

Salut!—Hi, or good-bye

Dates and time

Aujourd'hui—Today

Demain—Tomorrow

L'année dernière—Last year

La semaine dernière—Last week

La semaine prochaine—Next week

Le mois prochain—Next month

Janvier—January

Février—February

Mars—March

Avril—April

Mai—May

Juin—June

Juillet—July

Août—August

Septembre—September

Octobre—October

Novembre—November

Décembre—December

Printemps—Spring

Été—Summer

Automne—Autumn

Hiver—Winter

Dimanche—Sunday

Lundi—Monday

Mardi—Tuesday

Mercredi—Wednesday

Jeudi—Thursday

Vendredi—Friday

Samedi—Saturday

À quelle heure?—At what time?

Quelle heure est-il?—
What time is it?

Food and restaurants

À la carte—From the regular
menu of a restaurant

Apéritif—A pre-dinner drink

Bière—Beer

Boisson—Drink

Café au lait—
Coffee with frothed milk

Déjeuner—Breakfast

Dîner—Lunch

Entrée—An appetizer (not the
main part of a meal)

Frites—French fries

L'eau—Water

Menu du jour—
Daily specials menu

Potage—Soup

Quelle est votre spécialité?—
What is your specialty?

Repas—A meal

Salle à manger—Dining room

Souper—Dinner

Table d'hôte—Daily specials;
usually a fixed price for a
complete meal

Veuillez m'apporter la facteur?—
Please bring me the bill

Vin—Wine

*Est-ce qu'il y a un bon restaurant
près d'ici?*—Is there a good
restaurant near here?

General

Allumettes—Matches

Centre d'achats—
Shopping center

Dépanneur—
Convenience store

Je ne comprends pas—
I don't understand

Librairie—A bookstore
(not a library)

Magasin—Store

Mécanicien—A motor or
car mechanic

Météo—Weather report

Parlez lentement, s'il-vous-plaît—
Speak slowly please

Pâte dentifrice—Toothpaste

Québec—the largest province of
Canada (pronounced "kay-bek")

Québécois—From Québec
(pronounced "kay-bay-KWAW")

Quels sont vos prix?—What is the
price (or rate)?

Quincaillerie—Hardware store

Timbre—Postage stamp

Landforms

Île—Island

Lac—Lake

Mont or Montagne—Mountain

Municipalité—Municipality

Parc—Park

Pont—Bridge

Réserve faunique—
Wildlife reserve

Rivière—River (the St. Lawrence is sometimes referred to as a *fleuve*, a large river)

Ruisseau—Stream, creek

Driving and road signs

À quelle distance sommes-nous de . . .?—
How far are we from . . .?

Arrêt—Stop

Autobus—Bus

Autoroute—
Major highway, expressway

Chemin—Road

Cul de sac—Dead end

Droit—Right

En bas—Down

En haut—Up

Entrer—Enter

Est—East

Estationnement—Parking

Fin—End

Gare—A ferry dock (or train station)

Gauche—Left

Impair—Odd

Nord—North

Où conduit cette route?—
Where does this road go?

Ouest—West

Pair—Even

Plein—Full

Routes principales—
Main highways

Routes secondaires—
Secondary highways

Rue—Street

Sortie—Exit

Sud—South

Traversier—A ferry (a seasonal ferry is *traversier saisonnier*)

Vérifier l'huile, s'il-vous-plaît—
Check the oil please

Virage à droit—Right turn

Virage à gauche—Left turn

General Index

Entries for Accommodations and Restaurants appear in the special indexes on pages 163–64.

INDEX

INDEX

Places to Eat

Places to Stay

About the Authors

Katharine and Eric Fletcher are freelance writers, editors, and publishers who telecommute from their "electronic cottage" north of Quyon, Québec.

Sharing a keen love of adventure, the outdoors, and travel, they continue to explore Canada. A travel highpoint was a 14-month backpacking trip through Japan, India, Nepal, Burma, Indonesia, Australia, New Zealand, and China returning via the Trans-Siberian Express, Scandinavia, and Britain.

They have written newspaper and magazine articles and authored several books, including Katharine's first self-published book, *Historical Walks: The Gatineau Park Story*. Katharine offers self-publishing workshops across Canada and her popular *Publish Yourself!* course runs three times a year in Ottawa. She also leads custom hikes, bus tours, and slide shows about Gatineau Park, Ottawa, and the National Capital Region.

Eric is a computer guru who specializes in electronic publishing and document management. His popular course, *The Electronic Cottage,* covers how to work without commuting.

Books: *Promenades historiques dans le parc de la Gatineau* (first edition in French, 1998); *Historical Walks: The Gatineau Park Story* (second edition, 1997, Chesley House Publications); *The Canadian Writer's Guide* (Fitzhenry and Whiteside, 1997); *Back Roads and Getaway Places in Canada* (Reader's Digest Canada, 1994); *Capital Walks: Walking Tours of Ottawa* (McClelland & Stewart, 1993). **Newspapers:** *The Ottawa Citizen, Calgary Herald, The Equity, The Montreal Gazette, Today's Seniors* ("Down the Road" column). **Magazines:** *Scouting, Canadian Living, Ottawa Life Magazine* (travel column), *Explore, Travelling, This Country Canada.*

Comments? We love hearing from our readers. Send us e-mail at chesley@netcom.ca.